Walking Tours of New England

WALKING TOURS OF NEW ENGLAND

By Kenneth Winchester and
David Dunbar

DOLPHIN BOOKS
DOUBLEDAY & COMPANY, INC.
GARDEN CITY, NEW YORK
1980

Library of Congress Cataloging in Publication Data

Winchester, Kenneth J. 1952–
Walking tours of New England.

1. New England—Description and travel—1951–
—Tours. 2. New England—History, Local. I. Dunbar,
David, joint author. II. Title.
F2.3.W56 917.4′0443
ISBN: 0-385-15296-5
Library of Congress Catalog Card Number 79–7884

For Barbara, Betty Ann, and Jimmy

Acknowledgments

Our thanks to our families and friends and to sympathetic Yankees who showed us that you can get there from here. A partial list includes:

SANDO BOLOGNA, Waterbury *Republican-American*
JANET HOUGHTON, Woodstock Historical Society
PRUDENCE LIBBY, *Down East*
BEATRICE OEHL
BARBARA PECK
GEORGE PECK
HOWARD REED, Fairbanks Museum of Natural Science
RISË SEGALL
BOB SULLIVAN, *New Hampshire Profiles*
JAMES H. WINCHESTER

Contents

NEW HAMPSHIRE

MAINE

INTRODUCTION
New England's Timeless Pleasures

Say "New England" and vivid, enduring images come to mind: white towns surrounding an elm-shaded green; mellowed brick and graying stone; narrow cobbled streets along a tangy waterfront; a rumpled patchwork of hills and river valleys.

These variegated landscapes of the mind conjure up impressions of the Yankee—laconic, droll, pragmatic, ironic, and fiercely proud of his special corner of America.

But not all Bostonians like beans and some "taciturn" Vermonters can outchatter an angry squirrel. Yankees only seem consistent when they agree that Connecticut, Rhode Island, Maine, Massachusetts, New Hampshire, and Vermont constitute New England. (And Robert Frost included only the last three.)

Stubbornly independent, New Englanders revere education and value religion, and possess a deep sense of history and place. All are shaped in some way by the region's gentle, yet insistent, character.

New England's writers, thinkers, and artists, in turn, have shaped American culture. Their works are displayed in museums ranging from Boston's Athenaeum to local library basements where townspeople lovingly assemble everyday objects—churns, lanterns, quilts, and scythes—that speak movingly of the past.

There is a feeling that all New England is a repository of the values upon which the nation was founded. This book introduces natives and newcomers alike to the displays in this living museum: scenic wonders, historic sites, dynamic cities, and rural towns where traditional ways survive.

A state map and numbered list of tours introduce each New England state, followed by detailed descriptions of the walks. An area map keyed by number to each point of interest in the text provides a flexible itinerary of museums, parks, historic houses, churches, wharves, greens and other attractions. The tours range from an hour's casual stroll to a full day's walk. Some points are clustered within a few city blocks; others are side trips of up to a mile. They can be enjoyed whole or in part, with one thing in mind: New England is not a place for hurrying. It is a place to stop to breathe deep of salt air or mountain spruce, a place for shunpiking, poking, picnicking, rambling, remembering history, and savoring timeless pleasures.

New England Architecture

Along each of the walking tours are buildings—from homes and hovels to mansions and manses—that represent New England's architectural tradition. From survival to elegance they were a response to the vast and varied New England landscape and America's changing culture.

Nearly eighty seventeenth-century buildings still stand in New England and provide an eloquent record of colonial life. The simplest had one main room in which the entrance door opened into a vestibule with a steep staircase against the immense chimney wall. The main room, usually about sixteen by eighteen feet, was both living and dining room and kitchen. Above was a single sleeping room, often under a sloping roof. Later houses had two rooms on the first floor: the hall and the parlor. The single, central chimney and fireplaces heated both. The two bedrooms above were called the hall and parlor chambers respectively. The classic Colonial style is the saltbox. The design originated in England, where the plaster and framing were left exposed. In New England, clapboards sheathed the exterior. On the cold north side was a pantry; on the warmer southern side was a downstairs sleeping room, the only one called a bedroom in colonial times.

By the turn of the eighteenth century, parts of New England had been settled for almost a century. An aristocracy, or at least an upper class, had formed, and society was looking more and more to Europe for culture. American architects, many of them gifted amateurs such as Thomas Jefferson, adopted England's Georgian style. The typical Georgian house was brick. Stone trim, popular in England, was expen-

Colonial (1630s–1720s). A gable roof, central door, and evenly spaced windows identify this type of austere, two-story clapboard dwelling.

sive in America, and was replaced with painted wooden pilasters, capitals, and cornices. Windows were located symmetrically, but often at the expense of sound engineering, and Georgian roofs were pitched so as to give the effect of a Greek temple. On top was a flat, narrow roof deck called a widow's walk. According to tradition, the roof was invented in some seaport town so that captains' wives might watch for returning vessels, but its design had actually appeared in earlier English homes far from the sea.

Following the Revolution, American architecture sought to reject the past as symbolized by Europe. As the Georgian style waned, the Federal style flowered. Still, its influences were Roman classicism, and remnants of French and Georgian styles. Federal facades were restrained and dignified. Walls were smooth and white. Circular or octagonal rooms were popular. Perhaps the most distinctive feature of the period was the Federal doorway, with its narrow sidelights and elliptical overhead fanlight.

Georgian (1720s–80s). Formal symmetry characterizes Georgian architecture: gambrel roofs, columns and pilasters framing doors, and pediments crowning Palladian windows.

Federal (1780s–1820s). Delicate balustrades, thin columns and pilasters, fanlights, and low-pitched roofs distinguish this American variation of English architect Robert Adams's style, derived from domestic Roman architecture.

In the early 1800s, Greek neoclassicism swept the country. The dominant feature of the period was the classical portico, usually Doric or Ionic. The portico fronted churches, meetinghouses, commercial buildings, and homes. However, most buildings did not try to imitate an entire temple, so the effect was not very Grecian. Neighborhoods, even entire towns such as Nantucket, were built in this style.

Gothic architecture, with its towers, pinnacles, and rib-vaulted ceilings, became a strong competitor of Greek Revival, especially in churches where there was strong sentiment against "pagan" architecture. It faded, however, during a period of eclectic architecture in the nineteenth century when buildings ran the gamut from Tuscan villas to Moorish synagogues.

Victorian, although it borrowed many Gothic elements, was a step in a new architectural direction, although architects disagree whether or not it constitutes a true "period." The overall effect of the style, popular around the turn of the century, was sometimes French, sometimes Italian, and usually neither. Through each of these periods, New England houses—like the Yankees who built them—retained a distinctive regional character.

Greek Revival (1820s–60s). Popular for its connotations of refined culture and democracy, this style with its templelike columns, gables, and triangular pediments became widespread in America during the Greek war of independence from Turkey in the 1820s.

Victorian (1850s–80s). Eclectic and cluttered, this style typified its materialistic era. It borrowed steeply pitched roofs, pointed arches, and towers from Gothic Revival, popular for its monumentality, and from lavishly ornamented classical Italianate.

Walking Tours of New England

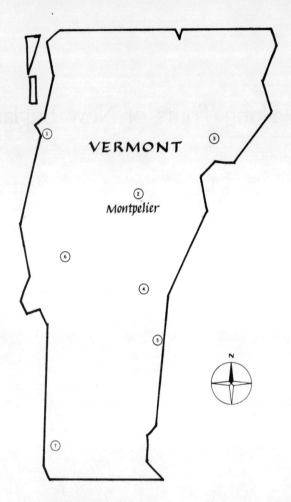

VERMONT

Montpelier

N

VERMONT

Rock-ribbed and resilient, Vermont consists of regions almost as autonomous as her citizens: the rolling farmland and evergreen empire of the Northeast Kingdom, the breadbasket of the Champlain Valley, the terraced industrial towns along the Connecticut River, and the historic southern counties. A spine of verdant peaks ripples north-south; the French, who saw these forested contours first in 1609, named them *Verd-Monts*—the Green Mountains.

In the 1800s Vermonters put their countryside to work for industry, and dammed every creek and river worthy of a waterwheel. Meanwhile, inventive wizards designed and patented everything from jointed dolls to ball-point pens. A stretch of Vermont riverbank along the Connecticut was known as the "precision valley" for its machine-tool industry.

Late in the nineteenth century, new industry in the southern states and the development of farmland beyond the Mississippi brought hard times to Vermont. Many heeded the advice of Horace Greeley, who honed his editorial pen in Poultney, and went West. Textile mills along the riverbanks slowed to a halt; woodworking plants closed as markets for spools and bobbins disappeared. Farm buildings sagged and stone-wall fences melted into the forest.

Today the trend has been reversed as city dwellers flock north, some to ski in winter and admire the foliage in fall, others as full-time residents in search of a simpler life. They discover what Robert Frost learned during the twenty-three summers he spent in a hilltop cabin near Ripton: that Vermont inspires the mind and replenishes the soul.

Burlington

Vermont's Big City: A Small Town at Heart

William Dean Howells wrote that sunsets he watched over Lake Champlain from Burlington's **Battery Park** (1) were second only to those over the Bay of Naples. Many Vermonters think the Ohio-born author saw one of the sun's rare poor showings, or else he would have reversed his preferences.

Perched on a steep lakeshore escarpment, Battery Park overlooks spruce-tufted islands strewn like stepping stones across the lake. To the west New York's Adirondacks loom hazy and blue like humpback whales sporting to the horizon.

This park saw a particularly bloody sunset during the War of 1812 when a battery of thirteen guns repulsed three British warships anchored below the cliff. A cannon from the skirmish and a plaque set in a boulder commemorate the victory. The stirring strains of band concerts resound in the park Sunday evenings in summer.

The park also overlooks Burlington's waterfront, which in the 1800s was cluttered with coal and lumber yards. A creative urban renewal project centered along Battery Street has revitalized the entire area. The program is typical of Burlington, which blends pragmatism and imagination to concoct a feisty brew acclaimed by old and young, conservative and liberal.

Big city by Vermont standards (it boasts the state's only escalator), Burlington is still small-town New England in its friendly, open ambience. Once an important mill town and lake port, it is now the state's cultural and educational center. Much of the activity revolves around the University of Vermont (known as UVM to locals), which occupies a splendid hillside setting above the city and lake.

BURLINGTON

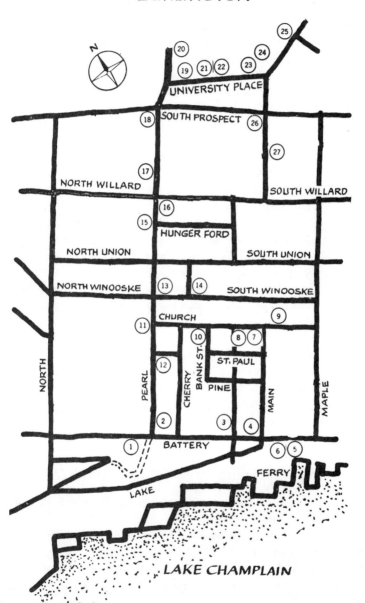

Back down by the waterfront is the modernistic **St. Paul's Episcopal Church** (2), a poured-concrete structure with stark towers and a boxlike form. Industrious Burlingtonians with green thumbs can be seen gardening at community plots on the church grounds.

The imposing **Timothy Follett House** (3), with its broad Ionic portico, occupies a knoll overlooking the lake. This 1840 Greek Revival mansion was designed by Amni B. Young and built for the president of the Rutland Railroad. At one time its terraced grounds, with winding paths and flower gardens, extended down to Battery Street, affording a romantic stroll for party guests at the Folletts' frequent entertainments. A habitué in the 1920s noted that "nearly every evening it was the scene of a dinner or dance. Hoop-skirted young ladies glided over the polished floors, and a hundred candles twinkled in silver candelabra along the walls of the big parlor facing the lake." A bit worse for wear, the house is now owned by the Veterans of Foreign Wars.

A lakefront stroll passes the site of the **Collamer House** (4) on the northwest corner of Battery and Main streets. Widow Collamer raised three sons here, including Jacob, who later became a U.S. senator. She raised money by spinning thread, and spun enough to buy the future politician shoes for college. In autumn and spring Jacob walked barefoot up the hill to school, found his shoes where he kept them in a pine bush near the classroom, wore them to lectures, then hid them again and walked home barefoot. With this careful wear, the shoes lasted through four years of college.

On the southeast corner of Battery and King streets, overlooking a wharf and marina where yachts and Lake Champlain ferries dock, is the site of the **Burlington Shipyard** (5). Here *Vermont,* the first steamboat on Lake Champlain, was built in 1808. On its launching day the vessel slid down the ways, stuck in the mud, and lay on its side until freed by owners James and John Winabs. Its eventual maiden run was a more successful eight-mile-an-hour, 120-mile cruise to St.-Jean, Quebec, on the Richelieu River.

A fine restaurant, offices, and an art gallery now occupy the **Ice House** (6), a three-story warehouse built in 1868 to store Lake Champlain ice. Interior hand-hewn beams and the original masonry have been exposed.

A walk up Main Street leads to a lovely park in front of the **City Hall** (7). At noon on warm summer days people flock there to eat a leisurely lunch amid grassy knolls, apple trees, and a cooling fountain. The City Hall is an impressive brick structure with marble pilasters and a gold dome. The tower of the 1888 **Ethan Allen Fire House** (8) next door was used to dry hoses. The station now contains offices and a community education center.

The elegant Victorian **Old Courthouse** (9), built in 1872 of purple sandstone quarried in town, now houses the sheriff's office. The mansard roof of its tower is topped by a coronet of railing.

In 1879 the **Howard Opera House** (10) offered Donizetti's *Lucia di Lammermoor* as its first presentation. "The curtain was painted by a tramp," recalled a disgruntled citizen, "who roamed about, once in a while doing some fine piece of work, and then squandering the money." A dome of gas jets in crystal globes dazzled audiences before performances and during intermissions. Ushers lit the jets with tapers on long poles. The opera closed in 1904 and the building now contains Magram's Department Store. The only reminders of divas and Donizetti are two half-moon doors on Bank Street, and carved French horns and masks under the cornices above arched windows on Church Street.

The tour now enters an area of fine churches, built on the edge of the business district perhaps to remind bankers and merchants of an eternal debit and credit ledger. The imposing brick **First Unitarian Church** (11) was built in 1816 from plans drawn by Peter Banner, the designer of Boston's Park Street Church, and approved by senior architect Charles Bulfinch. Its square, balustraded tower supports a porch, octagonal belfry, and lantern. The original communion silver, which predates completion of the church, is displayed. *Open Mon.– Fri., Sun.*

The bell of the modernistic **Cathedral of the Immaculate Conception** (12) is supported by two beams, which frame the more traditional spire of the First Baptist Church.

In spring the fragrance of lilacs wafts over the shady yard of the **First Congregational Church parsonage** (13), cloistered by an iron fence and tall pines and brightened by tulip beds. The adjacent 1842 church is fronted by six imposing columns and topped by an ornate tower.

Next door is the ivy-covered Georgian-style chapel of the **First United Methodist Church** (14), a stone structure more somber than its gleaming white Congregational neighbor.

Pearl Street, with its gentle grade, shady sidewalks, and distinguished residences, is perhaps the city's loveliest area. Three bomb-

Old Courthouse

proof rooms with vaulted masonry are in the basement of the **Deming House** (15), built after the War of 1812 and now a doctor's office.

At the rear of a service station on Hungerford Terrace visitors can see the remains of a hundred-foot-deep ravine that once bisected Burlington. Formed by spring-fed streams, this gorge was spanned by a wooden bridge on Pearl Street. Near Green Street the ravine was filled in with wood shavings and sawdust from lakefront lumber mills; the lean of some buildings there reflects this unstable foundation.

On the northwest corner of the **James H. Hills House** (16) is one of Burlington's original street signs (1871). Now a UVM infirmary, this 1820 frame dwelling was built by James Hills, who engraved the illustrations for Zadock Thompson's monumental *Natural History of Vermont* (1842), and the first Bible printed in Vermont (1812).

Flagged sidewalks laid in 1885 can still be seen along Pearl Street above Willard Street.

The 1800 **Horace Loomis House** (17) is named for a tanner with uncertain politics. "He commenced his life as a Democrat but soon discovered his mistake and joined the Federal party and became a great admirer of Hamilton," noted a contemporary. "He afterward belonged successively to the National Republics, Whip and Republican parties and had an unwavering confidence in Abraham Lincoln." His extravagant Victorian house is now owned by the Klifa Club, a women's social organization.

Urban Woodbury was more consistent politically. He entertained Presidents McKinley, Teddy Roosevelt, and Taft—all Republicans— in his 1815 home. A bronze plaque on the **Urban Woodbury House** (18), now a UVM fraternity, commemorates Governor Woodbury and his guests.

The University of Vermont campus has a lovely location on a hill high above Burlington. A long, broad green shaded by elms, lilacs, and pines and graced by a fountain is conducive to contemplation and study. The most imposing structure here is the **Ira Allen Chapel** (19), now used for meetings. The ashes of philosopher-educator John Dewey and his wife are in a granite memorial. Nearby is a statue of Lafayette by J. O. A. Ward. The French major general presided over the unveiling of his own likeness during an 1825 rally. "He was a man of fine stature and commanding presence," noted a contemporary account, "but a little lame."

The **Robert Hull Fleming Museum** (20), a handsome brick building dedicated in 1931, contains the art of many American, European, and Asian cultures. An Egyptian mummy and Sitting Bull's scalping regalia are popular attractions. There are works by Winslow Homer,

Robert Hull Fleming Museum

Albert Bierstadt, a collection of ivory portraits by Edward Malbone, and a charcoal drawing of John Dewey by Henri Matisse. *Open daily.*

The **Billings Student Center (21)**, built in 1886 as a library, was converted to its present use in 1963. Frederick Billings of Woodstock commissioned Boston architect Henry Haleson Richardson to design this Romanesque sandstone masterpiece, with its handsome interior woodwork, massive open beams, brass fixtures, and great fireplace. At the dedication Billings said, "My love is built in it." Architect Richardson considered it "the best thing I have yet done."

Williams Hall (22) next door, home of UVM's art and anthropology departments, is another impressive Romanesque sandstone structure. The Francis Coburn Gallery on the third floor features student exhibitions throughout the college year.

Lafayette limped over from his statue-unveiling ceremony in 1825 to lay the cornerstone of the **Old Mill** (23), which now contains classrooms and various departments.

A statue commemorates Ira Allen, brother of Ethan and founder of the university (1791). Allen raised £1,650 from benefactors and

Ira Allen statue

pledged £4,000 himself, but financial reverses and imprisonment in France in 1795 for gunrunning forced him to revoke his pledge. He died in Philadelphia in 1814, forgotten and impoverished.

The Old Mill's bell is displayed in front of the **Royall Tyler Theater (24)**, an elegantly converted gymnasium with wood paneling, old beams, and mullioned windows. The Champlain Shakespeare Festival is held here from mid-July to August. On the second floor are costume displays and George Washington's copy of America's first play, *The Contrast*. This comedy was written in 1786 by Royall Tyler, a law student of John Adams and later a Vermont jurist. *Open daily.*

A renowned collection of Ovid's works in **Bailey Library (25)** includes a 1626 translation of *Metamorphoses* by George Sandys, treasurer of Virginia. Also displayed is Ethan Allen's handwritten description of his attack on Fort Ticonderoga in 1775. In front of the library is a sculpture by Paul Aschenbach. *Open daily.*

A walk down Main Street leaves the central part of the campus, passes the history department's **Wheeler House (26)**, designed by Asher Benjamin, and provides sweeping views of the lake and its islands.

Grasse Mount (27), perhaps Vermont's finest Georgian house, was built in 1804 by Thadeus Tuttle on land he allegedly swindled from his partner Ira Allen. Lafayette, who seems to have slept in more American homes than George Washington, stayed here in 1825 as a guest of Governor Cornelius Van Ness. The mansion now contains UVM offices.

Main Street's arching trees provide a shady, downhill stroll back to the center of Burlington. Traffic here is more than offset by pleasant homes with tidy yards, and a view of church spires and the shimmering blue expanse of the lake.

Vermont's Robin Hood

Fiery as an autumn maple, Ethan Allen loved a good fight. He found one in 1770 when a vigilante group called the Green Mountain Boys elected him their "colonel commandant."

Their job was to protect settlers on land sold by New Hampshire's royal governor in what is now Vermont. In 1764 George III decreed that the area belonged to New York, whose governor resold most of it, and tried to run farmers off their hard-won acreages.

Enter Allen and his Green Mountain Boys—a colonial version of Robin Hood and his Merry Men. Resplendent in gold-braided epaulets, Allen led troops distinguished by sprigs of evergreen in their hatbands. They hounded Yorker surveyors, trespassers, and squatters with threats, beatings, and "beech-seal certificates" (whipping welts). The New York governor offered twenty pounds for the capture of one of these Green Mountain outlaws.

Their feud was interrupted in 1775 by a common enemy—the British. Always eager for a fight, Allen plotted to capture Fort Ticonderoga at the southern end of Lake Champlain. That dilapidated bastion was lightly guarded, according to an advance scout who disguised himself as a woodcutter, then wandered into the fort and requested a haircut.

Before dawn on May 10, 1775, an eighty-three-man expedition approached sleeping Ticonderoga by boat, and rushed through a breach in the walls. Allen dispatched a drowsy sentry with his saber, then demanded that Lieutenant Jocelyn Feltham, still in his underwear, surrender the fort "in the name of the Great Jehovah and the Continental Congress." Captain William Delaplace emerged from his

Ethan Allen statue

quarters, saw the halfhearted battle was lost, and surrendered his sword without further fuss. In ten minutes Allen had captured 200 cannons, tons of lead shot, 30,000 flints, and a strategic post guarding a potential British invasion route from Canada.

During his next campaign in Quebec, Allen launched an unauthorized attack on Montreal, was captured and imprisoned in England. He returned to the Green Mountains in 1778 to find Vermont a "free and independent republic." The Yorker squabble was over; Allen retired to a farm near Burlington and wrote essays as a sort of backwoods Aristotle who often signed his letters "The Philosopher."

He published an unorthodox tract on the logical improbabilities of the Bible entitled The Oracles of Reason. Much discussed (but seldom bought), "Allen's Bible" aroused the ire of clergy, including the pastor-president of Yale, Ezra Stiles, who wrote upon the frontier rebel's demise in 1789: "Ethan Allen died today and went to Hell."

Montpelier

A Golden Dome and Steamboat Gothic

Nestled in the Winooski Valley, Vermont's capital has intimate, sometimes hidden charms: clapboard houses perched on steep hillsides, narrow lanes bordered by early office blocks, and former tenements lining
a shady stream that flows beneath Main Street buildings.

And always just around the corner is the gleaming golden dome of
the **Vermont State Capitol** (1), topped by a fourteen-foot-high statue
of Ceres, Roman goddess of agriculture, and set against the verdant
backdrop of Capitol Hill. Modeled after the Temple of Theseus in
Greece, this marble state house is the third such capitol, and incorpo-
rates many features from an 1838 building designed by Amni B.
Young. Amid flower beds and spacious lawns are two Spanish cannons
captured in 1898 at the Battle of Manila Bay. Within the portico a
marble replica of an 1861 statue by Larkin Mead depicts early Vermont leader Ethan Allen in a dramatic pose. A nearby cannon was
captured at the Battle of Bennington in 1777.

The lobby floor is embedded with marine fossils found in black-and-
white limestone quarried at Isle La Motte in northwestern Vermont. A
brooding bust of Lincoln by Larkin Mead stands at the end of a hall
whose walls are engraved with quotes extolling the state's virtues.
Elliptical iron stairways wind past portraits of Vermont notables
and lead to second-floor legislative chambers and executive suites.

The molded plaster ceiling of the 150-seat Representatives' Hall has
an elaborate bronze-and-gilt chandelier. Black walnut chairs and desks
in the distinguished Senate chambers date from 1858. Visitors may
watch the legislature in session.

Seventy-nine battle-worn flags of Vermont regiments are displayed

MONTPELIER

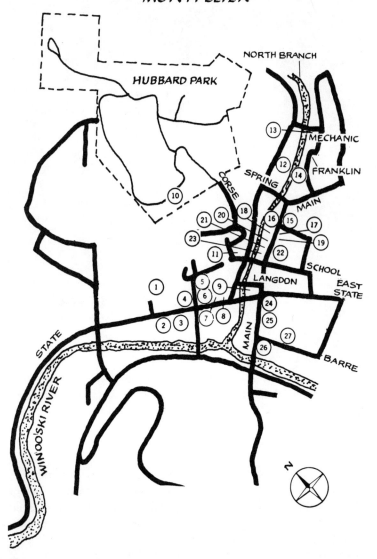

Vermont State Capitol

in second-floor cabinets. The governor's reception room contains a ten-by-twenty-foot mural by Julian Scott depicting the 1864 Battle of Cedar Creek, Virginia, in which Vermont troops distinguished themselves. Nearby is an 1858 chair made of oak timbers salvaged from "Old Ironsides" during a renovation. *Open daily July–early Sept., Mon.–Fri. early Sept.–June.*

Down the walk from the Capitol, the **State Office Building** (2) occasionally serves as a backdrop in summer for theatrical groups entertaining passersby. The main entrance to this granite structure has a bas-relief of Ceres holding the state seal; a frieze encircling the building is engraved with the names of Vermont's counties.

The architectural olio that now houses the **Vermont Department of Agriculture** (3) has 4½ stories of varying heights, windows of different shapes and sizes, and a hodgepodge of roof styles. Described as "palatial" when it opened in 1891 as headquarters of the National

Life Insurance Company, this brownstone structure featured the latest conveniences: quality speaking tubes (with "nonvibrating paint") connecting offices, comfortable quarters on the third floor for the janitor and his family, and a hydraulic elevator with mahogany shafts and brass grillwork.

A charming example of Steamboat Gothic architecture, the **Pavilion Office Building** (4) is a reconstruction of the 1875 Pavilion Hotel which stood on this site until 1971. The original Pavilion was an elegant hostelry that catered to legislators and railroad travelers debarking at a depot that once stood across the street. Parts of the original building that were used in the present structure include bricks made from nineteenth-century molds, veranda railings, and granite sills and keystones.

Four floors are now office space, while the museum and library of the Vermont Historical Society occupy the ground floor. The reception room of the museum re-creates the Victorian ambience of the Pavilion Hotel lobby with period furnishings, a stenciled ceiling, and marble

Pavilion Office Building

floors. A twelve-foot-high grandfather clock in one corner once belonged to Governor Clement. Exhibits, audiovisual presentations, and period rooms tell the state's history. The last cougar, or catamount, shot in Vermont (1881) is mounted and displayed, along with the Stephen Daye Press, thought to be America's first (c. 1638). *Open Mon.–Fri.*

A restaurant now occupies the quaint **Thrush Tavern** (5), built about 1825 and architecturally unique in Montpelier. A combination of Federal and earlier Georgian styles, the tavern has its original marble fireplaces and door moldings.

The **Vermont Federal Savings and Loan Association** (6) has exposed the original bricks of its 1816 structure and furnished several offices with reproductions of period furniture.

Despite the 1828 date above its entrance, most authorities think the **Vermont Mutual Fire Insurance Company** (7) was built about 1810. Lilac bushes on its lawn give downtown a splash of color and whiff of perfume in spring.

Montpelier citizens donated $1,000 to help finance the 1844 Greek Revival **Washington County Courthouse** (8), which replaced an earlier structure destroyed by fire. Behind the courthouse, a former jail now houses the sheriff's office.

A carnival atmosphere prevails during the Saturday morning farmers' market at Langdon Street from June to mid-October. Impromptu musical groups entertain city slickers buying cheese, fruits, vegetables, and crafts. The **Artisan's Hand** (9) sells pottery, colorful quilts, and wooden dolls and toys made by local craftsmen.

A long, steep climb past trim bungalows perched on Capitol Hill leads to **Hubbard Park** (10), a 134-acre wooded refuge with trails and secluded picnic areas. Bear to the left; at the summit is a fifty-foot-high medieval-looking parapet built with fieldstone from fences that crisscrossed the hillside when it was a pasture (remains of other fences can still be seen in thickly wooded areas). A stairway leads to a viewing deck with sweeping views of the Worcester Mountains and the Winooski Valley; tall spruce prevent the city from intruding on this sylvan vista.

After a pause for a rest or a picnic, walkers can better appreciate the scenery while they make a leisurely descent: the distinctive pin-striped steeple of the Congregational Church, lush pastures overlooking the river valley, and fleeting shadows cast by clouds on the hillsides that surround the town.

Farmers' market, Langdon Street

The **Rawsel R. Keith House** (11), set in a natural amphitheater, was built in the early 1800s by a justice and president of the Bank of Montpelier. Judge Keith suffered financial reversals due to bad railroad investments; ". . . a long sufferer from kidney disease, [he] ended his sufferings [in 1874] by taking a dose of laudanum."

The great flood of 1927 caused $30 million damage in the state and claimed forty-five lives. President Coolidge sent Secretary of Commerce Herbert Hoover to assess the disaster. His terse report: "Vermont at its worst, Vermonters at their best."

One of the flood's casualties was Montpelier's **old cemetery (12)**; the North Branch of the Winooski spilled over this riverbank meadow and washed away headstones and monuments. "They had no idea where the graves were when the water receded," said a nearby resident, "so they just put the stones in neat rows. On Memorial Day there are ceremonies, but veterans could be placing wreaths on anybody's grave."

One of the few remnants of Montpelier's industrial past is the **Lane Manufacturing Company (13)**, which established a sprawling eleven-building complex in 1890 along the North Branch to produce their renowned sawmill machinery. (The factory closed in 1960, except for a small part that still manufactures machinery on the north side of Mechanic Street.) Many of the buildings are now vacant; others have been converted to offices and apartments. A seventy-ton winch mounted on a truck tried to move the 1848 Greek Revival **Roger Hubbard House (14)** to its present location at 20 Franklin Street. The truck collapsed; it took a stronger vehicle a month to make the three-block trip.

The town's most elegant dwellings line elm-shaded Main Street, enhanced by graceful church spires. The **James Langdon House (15)** has an extravagant piazza with slender Corinthian columns and delicate rail spindles. The apartment building to the rear was originally a coach house.

The **Constant Storrs House (16)**, built about 1852 by a prosperous State Street merchant, has fine Greek Revival features heightened by Flemish bond brick. The hip-roofed **William Upham House (17)** has a lovely portico and a decorated frieze below the cornice. The last single-family residence on Main Street has a recessed pediment porch, a two-story solarium, and a brick carriage house with a square bell tower. Built about 1850, the **James Spaulding House (18)** is named for a prominent surgeon.

Across the street from the 1874 **Methodist Church (19)** is a splendid Victorian mansion that now houses the **Vermont Education Association (20)**. This striking brick structure with black trim has elegant interior woodwork; a brass lantern with beveled and colored glass still lights the entrance hall. Livestock were kept in the barn with its tilting cupola.

The Second Empire house built in the late 1860s for merchant James French is perhaps the street's most impressive edifice: a projecting central section with Gothic windows towers above a mansard roof. The dwelling now houses the **Vermont State Medical Society** (21).

Surrounded by dignified churches, the **Kellogg-Hubbard Library**

Kellogg-Hubbard Library

(22) is an unecclesiastical Italian Renaissance structure, with pink Vermont granite columns flanking a portico and a second-floor balcony. Endowed in 1895 by Montpelier businessman John Hubbard, it contains 35,000 volumes. *Open daily.*

The Wood Art Gallery on the library's second floor has more than one hundred works by Montpelier's Thomas Waterman Wood, along with other American art of the 1920s and 1930s. The gallery hosts a month-long exhibition of northern Vermont artists in June. *Open afternoons Tues.–Sat.*

The town's oldest church (1865) is on the site of a 1793 tavern built by Montpelier founder Colonel Jacob Davis. Flanked by venerable pines and capped by a pin-striped spire, the **Unitarian Church** (23) was described by a contemporary account as "an intellectual landmark cultivating the best thought and the best taste." The church has tall hand-painted windows with a grape-and-leaf pattern, black walnut pews, and chestnut balustrades.

The tour now enters the downtown business area, where the architecture reflects the city's appearance during the height of its prosperity in the late nineteenth and early twentieth centuries. The fourth floor of the **Blanchard Block** (24) once contained an eight-hundred-seat opera house (1885–1910). A ten-cent, seven-mile trolley ride took Barre residents home after performances.

Civic pride delayed completion of the **Montpelier City Hall** (25) until 1911. Its floor was hastily laid to prevent a governor's ball from relocating in a rival community. The floor eventually buckled and had to be replaced, but as a contemporary report noted, "the advertising that the city got [from] the most elaborate social event that has ever occurred here . . . is worth many times the cost. The damage and injury had the ball been held in Burlington could not be measured in dollars and cents."

On June 20, 1849, a train pulled by an engine named *Abigail Adams* brought the first railroad passengers to town. The **Wells River Railroad Depot** (26) welcomed eight daily passenger trains, plus freights transporting granite and lumber. A train loaded with butter, cheese, eggs, and poultry left early enough each Saturday to reach Boston markets by 8 A.M. The depot now houses a beauty parlor and offices.

In the Gothic **Catholic Church** (27) is a copy of Raphael's "Transfiguration of Christ" by Thomas Waterman Wood. Pope Leo XIII, who blessed the painting, was astounded that a Protestant would travel to Rome to produce a work for a Catholic church.

Colorful Ballads from Cast-off Cloth

Patchwork quilts and cushions splash color—and win admiration for their creator's patience—during a three-day October craft festival at Alumni Hall, Vermont College, in Montpelier. These painstaking la-

Vermont crafts festival

bors of love transform scraps of cast-off cloth into intricate artistry warm enough for a cozy bed, lovely enough to frame.

The craft dates from the earliest colonial days. Quilting flourished in the New World, where travel and entertainment were limited and winters long and cold. Making quilts became a social institution that gave women a chance to gather and to use creative abilities stifled by pioneer living. Patchwork became an American folk art, with designs that were increasingly intricate and imaginative.

Quilts came in many forms. Family record quilts show symbols depicting family events; freedom quilts were made by groups and presented to young men on their twenty-first birthdays. A friendship quilt was assembled from a variety of squares worked by different women and designed to commemorate a friend's wedding or birthday.

Some patterns were handed down from mother to daughter; others, like ballads, moved from place to place until they were repeated all over America. Their names recall American history: Indian Hatchet, Log Cabin, Lincoln's Courthouse, Wagon Tracks.

Unlike these famous patterns, a crazy quilt changed every time it was made. It varied with the scraps that were available, and was made by stitching down colorful, oddly shaped pieces of different prints and textures in whatever design seemed pleasing.

St. Johnsbury

Cultured Capital of the Northeast Kingdom

St. Johnsbury is an anachronism: a working northern New England factory town. Tucked in a remote corner of Vermont's "Northeast Kingdom," this blue-collar community of 9,000 is a thriving reminder of mill towns that once lined virtually every New England stream.

The city's industrial history began in 1815 when the Fairbanks family came here and turned a grist- and sawmill into a foundry. One of the Fairbanks, an introverted genius named Thaddeus, began to work on inventions. At age thirty he designed an iron plow, then went on to accumulate thirty-two patents for everything from refrigeration to cookstoves. His most significant brainstorm was a platform scale to weigh bulky hemp then grown in Vermont for cloth and rope. Fairbanks cornered a worldwide market.

The Fairbanks Weighing Division of Colt Industries still manufactures scales at its plant on the outskirts of town. No Fairbanks is associated with the firm because, as one old-timer put it, "the family was daughtered out."

While other wealthy clans summered at Bar Harbor and operated their holdings in absentia, the Fairbankses stayed in St. Johnsbury to enrich the community that enriched them. "Four generations of Fairbanks lived here," notes Howard Reed, curator of the town's museum. "Not many other families with power and wealth like that would have stayed." Their legacies include a private school, an art gallery and library, a museum, and two Congregational churches.

The remarkably well preserved Main Street has changed little in the past century. Modest business blocks are flanked by steeples and gra-

ST. JOHNSBURY

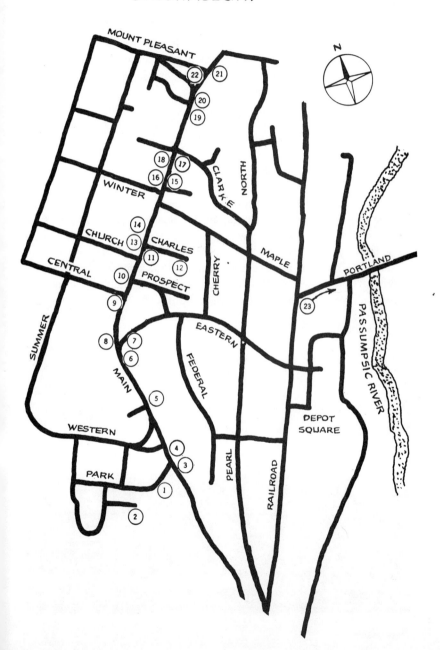

cious houses fronted by spacious lawns. Surrounding wooded hills seem only a short, inviting hike away, even from the center of town.

Dominating the west end of Main Street is St. Johnsbury Academy, founded in 1842 as a private school. It is now an odd institutional hybrid of public and private. The town pays tuition to the academy for local students, while the school also enrolls boarding students, mainly from New York State.

Brantview (1), a dormitory in a Victorian residence with ornate towers, was built about 1885 by William P. Fairbanks, Thaddeus Fairbanks' nephew. On warm spring evenings students hold flag drills for parades on Brantview's front lawn. Nearby playing fields echo with keen competition, while the more studious sit beneath spreading elms and pines.

The Society of Vermont Craftsmen sponsors an arts and crafts fair in mid-July at the academy's **Alumni Gymnasium** (2). Geodes, stone nodules with crystal-lined cavities, fetch reasonable prices (and the most interest).

Near Brantview is the **President's house** (3), a modest white frame dwelling built about 1840. The academy's main buildings seem like typical nineteenth-century Georgian campus architecture, but they are

Brantview

actually of recent vintage. **Colby Hall** (4) is flanked by two impressive brick wings: Fuller Hall to the south and Carl Ranger Hall to the north.

Classic lines and elegant simplicity grace the **South Congregational Church** (5), built in 1851 with funds donated by the Fairbanks family.

The **Caledonia Courthouse** (6) was built in the 1850s on the site of St. Johnsbury's cemetery. "It was too small anyway," says Howard Reed, with classic Vermont pragmatism, "so they packed up the remains and moved them to a new graveyard off Mount Pleasant Street. Quieter there anyway."

The St. Johnsbury Town Band, the nation's oldest (1830), performs Monday nights in summer at a bandshell in **Arnold Park** (7). "They may not always be on pitch," says one resident, "but they're always enthusiastic."

Colorful flower beds, benches, a war memorial by Larkin Mead, and a Civil War cannon from U.S.S. *Magnolia* fill the park. An information booth here is open in summer.

The 1873 **St. Johnsbury Athenaeum** (8), an elegant Victorian building designed by John Davis Hatch of New York, is a peaceful retreat where contemplation in quiet alcoves is disturbed only by the ticking of an antique wall clock. Resplendent with its elaborate woodwork and oak and walnut floor, the Athenaeum was given to the town as a public library by Horace Fairbanks, nephew of the platform-scale inventor and later governor of the state (his father held the office twice).

An art gallery was added to the 40,000-volume library to accommodate the classical paintings Fairbanks bought on his travels in Europe. The room has the feel of a wealthy man's study: rich wood paneling, heavy gilt frames, and marble busts on pedestals.

The gallery's design was dictated by Fairbanks' purchase of the overwhelming "Domes of the Yosemite," by Albert Bierstadt. This ten-by-fifteen-foot oil painting, illuminated by the gallery's massive skylight, seems to transport viewers, who almost hear the waterfall's roar and feel the sting of its spray.

In 1832, at age two, Bierstadt emigrated with his family from Germany to New Bedford, Massachusetts. The influences of both European culture and spacious American landscapes are reflected in his gigantic canvases.

When the painting was acquired in 1873, the New York *Times* sniffed, "It is now doomed to the obscurity of a Vermont town where it will astonish the natives." Fairbanks retorted, "The people who live in this obscurity are nevertheless quite capable of appreciating the dignity it lends to this small village."

Bierstadt's opinion on the matter is unrecorded; however, he returned to St. Johnsbury every summer until his death in 1902 to view his masterpiece and touch it up.

St. Johnsbury Athenaeum

The Hudson River school is well represented in the gallery by artists such as Asher B. Durand, the father of American landscape painting; Jaspar Cropsey, renowned for his autumn landscapes; and Sanford Gifford, the founder of luminism. Many works here were commissioned or purchased directly from the artists. A touring ensemble of students and faculty from Lyndon State College in nearby Lyndonville gives chamber concerts on occasional Sundays in the Athenaeum. *Open Mon.–Sat. except holidays.*

The veranda of the **St. Johnsbury House** (9) is a fine spot to pull up a chair and watch the world go by, at least the world that comes to this corner of the Northeast Kingdom. Henry Ford and Thomas Edison used to sit on this porch while waiting for their orders of St. Johnsbury soda crackers to be filled at a nearby food processing plant, long since demolished. Now known as Montpelier crackers, these delicious biscuits apparently warranted personal trips to St. Johnsbury by Ford and Edison. Fronted by four massive Greek Revival columns, the inn (c. 1850) has beautiful paneling and the original fireplaces in the lobby.

St. Johnsbury's strong religious character is evident from the church spires lining Main Street beyond the Victorian business blocks designed by Lambert Packard. **St. Andrew's Episcopal Church** (10) was built in 1877.

The turreted red sandstone **Fairbanks Museum of Natural Science** (11) was also designed by Lambert Packard and dedicated in 1890 by Franklin Fairbanks, who said, "I wish the museum to be the people's school." The people first must pass snarling lions guarding the front walk. (One of the beasts was made toothless because, according to local legend, a young girl thought it looked too fierce.) The museum has a complete collection of Vermont's flora and fauna, including mounted animals (its hummingbird collection is reputedly the world's largest) along with fossils and minerals. One live avian specimen, a white dove, greets visitors with lively chatter. A museum guide occasionally tucks the bird's head inside his shirt to calm it for a nap.

A prototype of the Mercury space capsule dangles from a vaulted oak ceiling in the Hall of Sciences. Lectures are offered on Saturdays at a planetarium with a twenty-foot screen that produces special effects—from flying saucers to the death of a star.

On the museum grounds are antique farm implements and a modest children's zoo with owls, hawks, ravens, and squirrels. A peripatetic but poky turtle named Tina can often be found snoozing in unlikely corners of the fenced yard. *Open daily except holidays.*

Behind the museum is a former Catholic **rectory (12)**, built in 1916 with delicate Romanesque arches and columns. It now contains museum offices and provides a fine view of lower St. Johnsbury along Railroad Street. This rectory is one of the few reminders of St. Johnsbury's French-Canadian population (once as much as thirty percent). They came here to work in factories after the Civil War, and established a separate community that included a scaled-down replica of Paris' Notre Dame Cathedral, a convent, a hospital, and the flat-roofed rectory (designed by an architect from southern France who knew his buildings, but not the weight of a New England winter's worth of snow). The church was burned in 1966; fire claimed the convent in 1972. The hospital across the street from the rectory now serves as professional offices.

The French-Canadians joined the Irish Catholics in **St. John's Church (13)**, a brick structure built in 1897 with square towers.

The castlelike spires of the **North Congregational Church (14)**, built in 1878 with limestone from Isle La Motte, Vermont, symbolize man's striving for a higher love (and provide convenient roosts for pigeons).

Main Street now broadens, and the pace, although never bustling in the business district, becomes even more leisurely. This part of town, with its fine homes surrounded by large lawns and gardens, reflects St. Johnsbury's prosperity after the Civil War. A walk along either side of the street leads visitors past handsome residences: the 1858 **Dr. David Poll House (15)**, and across the street the brick **Dr. James Russell House (16)**, which dates from the same year. Two doors down on the east side are two **clapboard houses (17)** built in 1874, one with square towers, the other with a large porch. Diagonally across the street is the 1830 **Walter Scott House (18)**, which contains a real estate office.

Perhaps Main Street's finest showpiece is the 1874 **Ide House (19)**, fronted by sweeping lawns. It was once owned by America's first governor-general to American Samoa. His daughter befriended Robert Louis Stevenson, who resided on the same group of islands at the turn of the century. The writer willed Ide's daughter his birthday, since hers fell on Christmas. (Stevenson's official document is displayed in the Fairbanks Museum.)

The Victorian **Billig House (20)**, in immaculate condition, has delightful gingerbread trim and graceful turrets. The Georgian

Ephraim Paddock House (21), the oldest brick dwelling in town (1820), is named for a lawyer and entrepreneur who convinced his brother-in-law, Erasmus Fairbanks, to build a factory here.

At the end of Main Street is a nineteenth-century **fountain (22)**

North Congregational Church

with ram's-head spouts, mirrored by a companion fountain at the other end of the street. From here visitors can look back down this broad boulevard to the church spires and the business district and academy beyond. It's a charming scene that looks much the same as it did to Thaddeus Fairbanks and his kin strolling here on some pleasant summer's evening more than a century ago.

More than 100,000 people a year visit the world's largest maple-candy factory, a ten-minute drive (or a half-hour walk) southeast of St. Johnsbury on Portland Avenue. Year-round weekday tours leave every ten minutes from **Maple Grove, Inc. (23)**, on the banks of the Moose River. Visitors can see maple syrup processed into fondant, the candy's soft center, then poured in molds to make delicious fudges with Vermont themes: covered bridges, pine trees, and maple leaves.

The nearby Maple Museum, housed in a former sugar shack, has exhibits of antique and modern sugar-making equipment. Sap boils all summer and visitors can chat with an old-time sugar maker. Another rustic cabin doubles as a candy shop and a theater with a short film on maple syrup.

Sugarhouse

Sugar on Snow—a Chewy Springtime Delicacy

The season is brief for Vermont's most famous treat: from early March to early April. That's when sap begins to flow in maple groves, and there's still enough snow on the ground to make "sugar on snow"—a maple-syrup delicacy that has long been an excuse for an end-of-winter party.

Each spring more than one hundred Vermont farms open their gates to visitors with a sweet tooth. They can watch farmers gather sap and boil it down, buy maple products (syrup, sugar, and cream), or arrange a sugarhouse party of their own.

To make sugar on snow, boil maple syrup until it reaches 230° F. on a candy thermometer. Pack down a handful of clean snow, and pour a tablespoon of thickened syrup over it in thin strips. When the syrup cools and hardens, it can be wound around a fork. The chewy strands (called "leather aprons") are irresistible. The traditional way to eat sugar on snow is with doughnuts and sour pickles, to offset the sweetness.

Woodstock

A Truce with Time

Woodstock's **Green** (1) seems an unlikely place to exorcise a vampire. Yet in 1830 a strange ceremony was held on this tree-shaded oval of grass. When a Woodstock man died shortly after his brother's demise, all five town physicians diagnosed vampirism. The first brother's body was disinterred: Its heart was still filled with blood. To prevent his troubled soul from haunting local folk, Woodstock officials boiled the heart in an iron pot, then buried both heart and pot on the Green in a grave capped with a seven-ton granite slab. The blood of a young bull was sprinkled over the area for good measure.

Ten years later, curious townspeople dug up the grave: no heart, pot, or granite slab. A roaring noise and sulfurous odors emanated from the excavation. It was hurriedly filled in, but for several days the earth around it shifted. There has been no vampirism since—at least none that has been reported.

The town that flourished around the Green has more to offer than grisly stories. Its splendid architecture is such an important reminder of eighteenth- and nineteenth-century New England that much of the town has been designated a historic district.

Home to an inordinate number of millionaires, including sometime resident Laurence Rockefeller, Woodstock exudes rustic, comfortable affluence. Houses are painted regularly, lawns are neatly trimmed, and downtown flower boxes are kept blooming with geraniums. Although a year-round recreation center, Woodstock seems at its best in spring, when elms quicken with green, and in late autumn when they wear crowns of gold thrust in cloudless blue skies.

WOODSTOCK

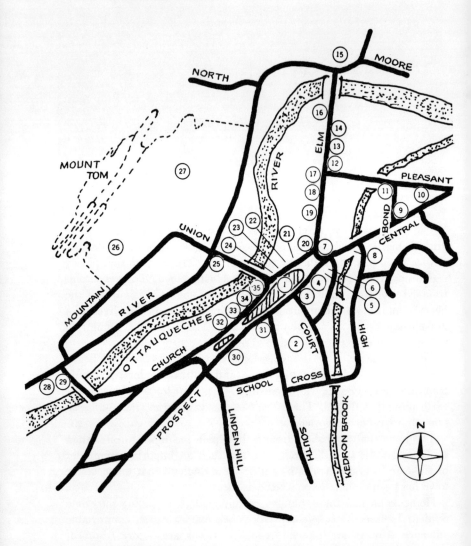

The Green is the starting point for a tour of this venerable community, founded in 1761 and the "Shire Town" of Windsor County. An information booth here is open from June 20 to the end of foliage season (usually the end of October).

Fiddler on the Green

The Eagle Hotel, the town's first inn, was built on the Green in 1793 where the elegant **Woodstock Inn** (2) now stands. Intended to accommodate lawyers serving the Windsor County Courthouse, the building was painted bright red so as not to confuse it with other establishments. It was replaced in 1892 by a larger inn to cater to wealthy tourists. Many frequented the hostelry, whose "riotous parties are the talk of Montreal and Boston." The present structure was erected in 1969. A gilded eagle carved for the Eagle Hotel in 1830 by itinerant cabinetmaker Moody Heath overlooks the Green from the front porch roof.

Festivities were unkind to Woodstock's second courthouse. Built in 1797 to replace a 1787 structure, it burned to the ground when a Fourth of July firecracker ignited its roof. The present **Windsor County Courthouse** (3), which dates from 1854, is open to the public when court is not in session. Its chambers contain benches from the first courthouse, a 1797 document signed by George Washington appointing Woodstock's Charles Marsh federal attorney, and a copy of Gilbert Stuart's unfinished portrait of the first President. *Open Mon.– Fri.*

No unfinished works are in the fascinating nineteenth-century Japa-

Windsor County Courthouse

nese art collection of the Romanesque **Norman Williams Library (4).** When Dr. Williams, a longtime Woodstock physician who endowed the 50,000-volume library, visited Japan in the 1880s he commissioned hundreds of works from artists and craftsmen. Their delicate art, done in precious metals and bronze, includes a 1780 lacquer cabinet with silver sake bowls, Satsuma ware, and a four-hundred-year-old engraved executioner's sword. *Open Mon.–Sat.*

Two houses next to the library were built in 1827–28 with fieldstone

Kedron Brook

intended for an Episcopalian church at the other end of the Green. The **Syz House** (5) is private; the **Wright House** (6), also called "T'other House," contains offices.

A walk along Central Street with its sidewalk flower boxes leads past antique and leather shops and bookstores. **Gallery 2** (7) has works of contemporary Vermont artists such as sculptor Georgia Mitchen and painter Virginia Webb. *Open Mon.–Sat.*

A design studio and more antique shops are found in a nineteenth-century mill along Kedron Brook, which yields trout upstream near the town's golf course.

Down the street from the 1821 **Ora E. Paul American Legion Post** (8) is a plaque commemorating the **Justin Morgan Horse** (9), Vermont's state animal. The progenitor of the Morgan breed was stabled here about 1800 by Sheriff William Rice. The offspring it sired were named after a singing teacher who lost his stallion to Sheriff Rice in payment of a debt.

In **Tribou Park** (10) a life-size Union soldier atop a twenty-five-foot granite shaft remembers Woodstock men who served with the army and navy during "the Rebellion of 61–65."

Two residences, the 1808 **Governor Billings House** (11) and the 1821 **Governor Converse House** (12), are reminders of the dozen or so men that Woodstock has sent to the state house at Montpelier. The soft rose brick of the Converse home is enhanced by a portico carved by local craftsmen. Jesse Williams and Charles Marsh, Woodstock's first lawyer, opened Elm Street in 1797 as a private enterprise. In the early 1800s rows of houses were erected here in the best tradition of New England architecture. Soon it earned a reputation as one of the loveliest streets in America.

Next to the 1832 **Richardson House** (13) is the **Congregational Parsonage** (14), built in 1828. Across the Ottauquechee River is Woodstock's most impressive dwelling, screened by hedges and plants. The **Charles Marsh House** (15), built in 1806, was declared a national historic site in 1967 by Mrs. Lyndon Johnson, mainly because George Perkins Marsh was raised there. While a congressman (1843–49), Marsh helped to found the Smithsonian Institution, and he was considered one of America's earliest environmentalists. He was later appointed U.S. minister to Italy by Lincoln.

The Greek Revival **Chapman House** (16) was built in 1829 by merchant Charles Dana for two spinster sisters from Canada, daugh-

Charles Marsh House

ters of a Boston Loyalist who fled the United States during the Revolutionary War. Dana had four huge white pine logs drawn by sled from Canada to use for portico pillars. On the front lawn is a small fountain graced by a copper statue of the angel Bethesda.

The distinguished 1808 **Congregational Church** (**17**) was designed by Woodstock architect Nathaniel Smith. (He also designed the Dana and Marsh houses; only the Dana is unaltered.) Its Revere bell, guaranteed by the Boston silversmith for "one full year," was installed in 1818 at a cost of $319.95. It cracked after summoning worshipers for more than 175 years, and is now displayed on the south porch. Revere bells in the Episcopal, Universalist, and Masonic churches are still in use. *Open Sun.*

A few doors down from the 1809 **Emmons House** (**18**) is the **Dana House** (**19**), containing the Woodstock Historical Society. Restored to the period 1800–60, this nine-room white clapboard residence was built by Charles Dana in 1807. Local cabinetmaker John White crafted the Windsor chairs in the kitchen. A variety of furnishings, portraits, tools, and other historic articles are also displayed. Especially notable are the collections of old costumes, dolls, and silver. *Open daily.*

Facing the triangular intersection known for some reason as "The Square" is the **Titus Hutchison House (20)**, once the residence of a Vermont Supreme Court Justice and now a clothing shop. A stone marker on the front lawn locates the southern terminus of the Royalton-Woodstock turnpike, which opened to traffic in 1802. Next door is the 1825 **Professional Building (21)**, once a hotel called the Churchill House.

Lining the northwest side of the street is more outstanding early architecture, including the 1807 **Ross House (22)**, the 1776 **Williams House (23)**, and the 1827 **Goat House (24)**.

The 1841 **Governor Washburn House (25)** is reached by crossing the Ottauquechee River via a covered bridge. (One covered bridge is

sufficient for any New England community that considers itself "picturesque"; Woodstock has three.) Built with traditional tools and methods in 1969, this 150-foot, one-hundred-ton span was drawn into place across the river by oxen.

Along Mountain Avenue with its canopy of maple and pine, **Faulkner Park** (26) has a broad expanse of lawns dotted with picnic tables. Paths offer a leisurely walk up Mount Tom, crossing a spring-fed creek and connecting with bridle trails at **Billings Park** (27). The south summit offers sweeping views of the town and river valley. On the north summit are iron hitching posts installed by Frederick Billings in the last century.

The basketball courts and swimming pool of the **Woodstock Recreational Center** (28) are housed in an 1835 woolen mill. The nearby **Little Theater** (29) presents shows in what was once a wool storage building, hence the "Woolhouse Players" drama group. This structure was built of stone to prevent fires when storing lanolin-rich, combustible wool. The river below is a fine spot to cool tired feet.

Across the Green the **D.A.R. House** (30) was built in 1807 by innkeeper Tillie Parker to accommodate legislators. In its Hiram Powers Room is a marble bust of "America," personified by a woman with one breast bare and one covered. The statue was intended for the Capitol dome in Washington, but President Franklin Pierce had a different concept of America and refused the work. "Pierce was never popular here anyway," notes an elderly guide. Also in the museum is a miniature of Powers' "The Greek Slave," the first nude female statue displayed publicly in America. Railroad memorabilia include a train bell and conductor's lantern from the short-lived Woodstock Railroad. The company's epitaph: "No collisions, no fatalities, no profit." *Open Mon.–Sat. July–Aug.*

The **General Mower House** (31) is one of the finest examples of Federal architecture in the Northeast. Built in 1823 on the site of Woodstock's first courthouse, the dwelling boasted the town's first bathtub (made of tin).

Across the Green is another row of early nineteenth-century homes: the 1810 **Sharp** (32), 1803 **Williamson** (33), and 1805 **Skinner** (34) houses. The **Church House** (35), built in 1823, was owned by Stephen Powers, Woodstock's first physician. The good doctor was usually attired in buckskin, on which he sharpened his scalpels before operating. He charged twenty-five cents for a tooth extraction and fifteen cents for a suture. Even at those rates Powers prospered, as did the town whose industrious citizens he treated.

Succotash: Fresh Garden Vegetables and Vermont's Thick Cream

Though early New England Indians were indifferent farmers at best, they had one trick that seemed like superstition but was in fact good agricultural practice. They buried three alewives—small herringlike fish that abound in New England streams—in each mound of earth where vegetables were planted. The fish fertilized the soil.

Pilgrims adopted this method and grew bumper crops of native corn, beans, and squashes. These foods still figure largely in New England cuisine.

Succotash is a simple, chowderlike dish that makes the most of fresh garden vegetables and Vermont's abundant cream. To cook it, bring to a boil 1 quart of salted water. Scrape kernels from 4 large ears of corn, and cut 1 pound of fresh green string beans into 1-inch lengths. (Fresh lima beans are also good.) Place both vegetables in the water and simmer until tender but still slightly crisp. Drain, then plunge into cold water to cool, and dry on paper towels.

Melt 4 tablespoons butter in a heavy skillet, add the corn and beans, and cook and stir for 1 or 2 minutes. Add salt and pepper to taste, and 1 teaspoon sugar. Pour in 1 cup heavy cream, ¼ cup at a time, stirring until it almost cooks away. Serve hot (some cooks sprinkle crisped salt pork over the dish).

Windsor

Vermont's Stormy Baptism

Not many states were born in a tavern, but then Vermont's not like many states. In July 1777, some seventy delegates from across Vermont gathered in Windsor to ratify a constitution. They endured a long, dry sermon entitled "A well tempered Self-Love, a Rule of Conduct towards others," by Rev. Aaron Hutchison, then adjourned to Elijah West's tavern to quaff ale and discuss politics. The constitution they hammered out required many drafts (and draughts). Articles included a ban on slavery and a guarantee of universal male suffrage (the first such acts in the colonies) and a name change, from the derivative New Connecticut to the more descriptive Vermont.

They were about to put quill to parchment when word arrived that British troops led by General John Burgoyne had advanced to Hubbardton, about forty miles northwest. The historic document might have been left unsigned had not a violent storm rumbled over the Green Mountains. While waiting out the deluge, delegates inked the constitution amid "a baptism of thunder, lightening and rain." The storm abated and they galloped off to defend their "free and independent republic."

Elijah's tavern is now a museum called the **Old Constitution House** (**1**), considered the state's oldest building (1774) and the birthplace of Vermont. The table around which the delegates parlayed is displayed in the Tap Room, along with period furniture and documents relating to the historic convention. The first percolator and cookstove made in Vermont are also here, along with a rare doll col-

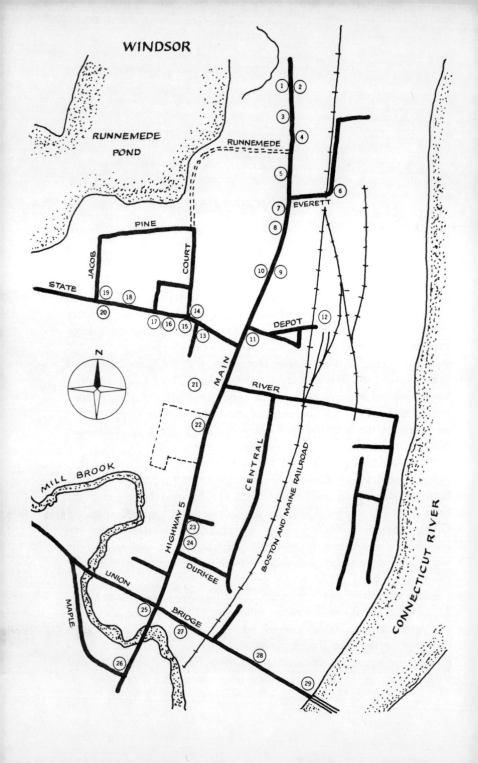

lection and old tools. A backyard garden features common colonial herbs. *Open daily mid-May–mid-Oct.*

History seems to live on here in white clapboard houses and church steeples. There are fewer clues, however, to indicate that this small town dominated by the furrowed, spruce-clad slopes of Mount Ascutney was once one of America's great industrial centers.

Windsor broke all economic laws to reach that status: It was far from markets and most raw materials, with no apparent labor or transportation advantages. Its predominance was due to the fertile imaginations of Yankee inventors who built factories here; their wizardry developed the American system of mass production that changed the world.

Windsor is less earth-shattering today. In the classic design of

Old Constitution House

major Vermont towns along the Connecticut River, it ripples over residential, commercial, and industrial terraces down to the water's edge. Windsor's compact community seems a mile long and only a block wide, perhaps because many of its fine dwellings line a Main Street that doubles as Highway 5.

One of these gracious residences is the 1806 Federal-style **Colonel Jesse Lull House** (2), named for a distillery magnate noted for his generous dispensation of the company's product at frequent and elaborate entertainments. In 1825 Colonel Lull escorted Lafayette through Windsor on a white steed.

The **Simeon Ide House** (3), once a girls' school, was later the residence of engineer Daniel Linsley, who supervised construction of the Windsor post office. Built in 1818 by printer and publisher Simeon Ide, this handsome home encircled by elms and neatly trimmed hedges has a cozy third-floor balcony, slender Ionic columns, and Greek Revival windows.

Unusual chimney arches in the south parlor of the **Dr. Nathum Trask House** (4) form a "courting alcove." This 1796 Georgian house has a splendid doorway framed by pilasters. Dr. Trask was a physician and Revolutionary War hero.

A side trip on Runnemede Road past an 1825 brick dwelling leads to a hundred-acre park creased by deep ravines and shaded by stands of pine and maple. Runnemede Pond was created by Senator William Evarts on his estate for the recreation of a son wounded in the Civil War. This old-fashioned swimming hole yields walleye, bass, and carp. Most travelers rushing through town on Route 5 never sample this delightful part of Windsor, with its secluded picnic areas.

The 1796 **Zebina Curtis House** (5), almost hidden by a front-yard grove of trees, was dubbed the "White House" during the occupancy of Senator Evarts, Secretary of State for Rutherford B. Hayes. Also a prominent lawyer, Evarts defended Andrew Johnson at his Senate impeachment trial in 1868. Ironically, his direct descendant Archibald Cox was the special Watergate prosecutor fired by President Nixon in 1973, prior to impeachment hearings in the House of Representatives.

In 1903 Evarts entertained Theodore Roosevelt at his Windsor home. When the Rough Rider returned in 1911 as a Republican presidential candidate, Evarts had changed his political persuasion, and greeted Roosevelt's train with a sign that proclaimed: "We're farmers and we're for Taft." Roosevelt never left his car.

Along the east side of Main Street sprawls the **Cone-Blanchard**

Company (6), where gears, spindles and valves are manufactured in Windsor's venerable precision-tool tradition. Founded by Frank Cone in 1916 as a one-story shop, the plant has expanded eighteen times to accommodate its burgeoning trade. *Prearranged tours are available Mon.–Fri.*

Ministers of Windsor's **Baptist Church** (7), now known as the Trinity Evangelical Free Church, have often put politics before patriotism. In 1917 Rev. Clarence Waldron stood on the steps of an earlier Baptist church at the corner of Main and River streets to face his angry flock. He had ignored President Wilson's request that congregations sing "The Star-Spangled Banner" and ring church bells at 10 A.M. to inaugurate the first Liberty Bond drive. Rev. Waldron resigned that November. A month later the former pastor, "whose pro-German utterances and sentiments have been notorious," was arrested for sedition. He was convicted and sentenced to fifteen years' imprisonment; President Wilson pardoned him after a year's incarceration. (Across the street is the 1846 Unitarian Church, now a day-care center.)

The **Stoughton House** (8), once the town's showplace and now a senior citizens' home, saw several occupants brought to financial ruin. It was built in 1833 by a shrewd promoter and businessman named Thomas Emerson, who lost his fortune and those of several other Windsor investors in an 1837 financial panic. His property was attached and he was imprisoned in Woodstock. A later owner, Sewall Belknap, known as the "Napoleon of Railroads" for his Vermont Central line, also lost his fortune. He died in 1849 at age thirty-seven, $89,000 in debt. Edwin Stoughton, ambassador to Russia in 1877, survived the vagaries of politics and finance to transform this house into Windsor's most elegant residence.

The **Courthouse and Post Office** (9), the oldest continuously used courthouse in the United States (since 1857), was designed by Amni B. Young. Wide side doors in this brick and granite edifice accommodated ladies with billowing bustles. There are federal courtrooms on the second floor and a jail in the basement. *Open Mon.–Fri.*

With its six massive Doric columns, broad porch, and tiled floors, **Windsor House** (10) still has the aura of a grand hotel where Presidents and royalty slept, and where a Swedish soprano named Jenny Lind belted operatic offerings from a second-floor balcony. Built about 1840, "the best public house between Montreal and Boston" is now one of Vermont's two state craft centers (the other is in Middlebury). More than two hundred Vermont craftsmen display and sell their work in bright, airy galleries. Colorful quilts drape second-floor balcony rails. Upstairs in studios, bearded resident blacksmith Dick Sargeant hovers over glowing coals pierced by his blackened tools. The clatter of looms and whirring of potters' wheels show the state's traditional skills are alive and well. The center has monthly exhibits and sponsors craft classes and a July competition for Vermont residents. *Open Mon.–Sat.*

The tour now enters Windsor's modest commercial district. Elijah West's tavern once stood on **Constitution Common** (11), a small patch of green rimmed with brick sidewalks and comfortable wooden benches.

Walkers with their appetites aroused can take a side trip to Windsor's turn-of-the-century **Railroad Depot** (12), now a fine restaurant. The first train chuffed into the station from Boston on January 31, 1849. Windsor women had prepared a great feast for passengers and dignitaries on the second floor of the depot; Governor Coolidge presided over the festivities.

With hunger pangs appeased, walkers might be ready to tackle the gentle grade of Common Hill on State Street. Past the **Bank of Windsor Building** (13), the town's first such institution (1820), is **Carleton Hall** (14), where Vermont's general assembly met every two years from 1791–99 and again in 1804 before Montpelier was named state capital. Mobs of angry farmers gathered here at the hall during Shays' Rebellion (1786–87), threatening to burn the building; militia eventually dispersed the rabble. Windsor County's first courthouse (1784), which originally stood on the Common, now houses the Windsor *Chronicle.*

On a fine spot at the top of Common Hill is **St. Paul's Episcopal Church** (15), designed by Alexander Parris and built in 1820. Decorated with two almost perfunctory Corinthian columns and an unusual pilastered cupola, the church received praise in 1876 from Rev. Sewall Cutting. "Not strikingly ecclesiastical in its type, it has always seemed to me, nevertheless, a creation of genius, simple and harmonious in its beauty, and rarely equated in structure of its class." The oldest church in regular use in the Episcopalian Diocese of Vermont, St. Paul's has a splendid organ in a mahogany case designed and built by inventor Lemuel Hedge.

Each year on June 16 at the State Street common across from St. Paul's, a county fair features the succulent aromas of home cooking at food booths, and the treasures and curios of yesteryear at a flea market.

County fair

The town band performs at the bandshell on Thursdays at 8:00 in summer.

Past the **Windsor Library** (16) is the 1831 **Rufus Emerson House** (17), now a home for the elderly.

Lemuel Hedge once lived in the rather plain clapboard **Phelps**

House (18), built about 1794. An anxious-looking man with a patrician nose, Hedge registered his first patent in 1817, for a machine that lined a ream of paper on both sides in only twelve minutes. He also designed the carpenter's folding two-foot ruler and the band saw.

The 1786 **Stephen Jacob House** (19) was named for a lawyer and judge whose slave, Dinah Mason, was the subject of Vermont's test case against slavery.

Jacob later sold his land to the **Vermont State Prison** (20), the oldest such institution in America (1808). This cluster of buildings was constructed with granite from quarries on the southeast slopes of Mount Ascutney. The original thirty-five cells were later expanded to 170. Local industries used the institution as a source of cheap labor, for which they paid the state twenty-five cents a day per inmate. Convicts manufactured hydraulic pumps, nails, shoes, and cotton clothing. Closed in 1975, the prison is now a ninety-unit apartment complex with voluntary residents. A preserved cellblock is used for storage.

The tour returns to Windsor's main artery and continues past the business district to a shady knoll overlooking Main Street. Steps ascend the sloping front lawn of what was once Josiah Dunham's female academy ("the pride of the town"), now known as the **Leonard-Sabin Mansion** (21). Built by Nathaniel Leonard in 1791 and now a Masonic hall, this white Greek Revival house was visited by President James Monroe in 1817. Next door is the 1791 white clapboard Knights of Columbus Hall.

The 1798 **Old South Congregational Church** (22), probably designed by Benjamin Asher, has a unique louvered belfry in a four-tiered steeple. Tall columns rise majestically from its front steps. Its burial ground contains the grave of Samuel Smith, the first male child born in Windsor, and a granite marker locating the site of the town's first meetinghouse. The earliest grave dates back to 1766.

The modest gray clapboard **Reuben Dean House** (23), built about 1770, is named for a silversmith who cut Vermont's first state seal from Ira Allen's design. He charged twenty shillings for the work. Two doors down is the **Methodist Church** (24), built in 1895 with a $10,000 endowment from Rachel Harlow.

The **Windsor Terrace Apartments** (25), with their exterior wooden rear stairwells sometimes hung with laundry, look like they belong in a more urban setting. This seventy-two-unit complex was completed in 1922 to house workers from the area's burgeoning factories.

The power source for the town's rapidly expanding industry was the nearby dam on Mill Brook, thought to be the oldest masonry dam of its size in America (1834). This National Historic Civil Engineering Landmark was once surrounded by grist- and sawmills, paper and chemical plants, and even a dress manufacturer.

The smell of oil and machinery is still in the air at the former Robbins, Kendall and Lawrence Armory and Machine Shop, now the **American Precision Museum (26)**. This three-story, slate-roofed 1846 factory with its delicate cupola was the birthplace of the "American system" of manufacturing: the use of interchangeable parts, a principle that makes mass production possible. The ingenuity that created the machine-tool industry is represented in the museum's lathes, planers, measuring devices, typewriters, early computers, engines, and dynamos. An eight-hundred-volume set of patents describes American and foreign inventions. *Open daily end of May–mid-Oct.*

A walk downhill along Bridge Street passes the modest green clap-

Windsor–Cornish bridge

board **Sylvester Watriss House** (27), built about 1800 by a blacksmith whose shop was in the backyard, and the painted brick 1812 **James Clement House** (28).

The **Toll House** (29) was built about 1797 to collect fares from travelers using the longest covered bridge in America. The 460-foot span (the fourth on this site) had rates ranging from two cents for pedestrians to twenty cents for a four-horse carriage. The last toll was collected in 1943.

The bridge was built in 1866 by James F. Tasker, a black-bearded and bushy-browed two-hundred-pound native of Cornish, New Hampshire, who had complete faith in his work. He once built an eight-foot-long wooden model to test a new bridge design. Tasker was jeered at when he took his flimsy-looking model into Claremont one Saturday afternoon. He led his detractors to a hardware store, piled ten kegs of nails on his model, then added his own bulk. The model held, and so did the bridge built from it, for more than a century.

An Island of Industry in a Sea of Cows

Visitors to Windsor's Precision Museum are surrounded by evidence of Vermonters' ingenuity: everything from metal planes to gun borers, lathes to screw threaders. It's a long tradition: In 1790 Vermonter

Metal plane, American Precision Museum

Samuel Hopkins was granted America's first patent—signed by George Washington—for his method of making potash.

By that time Windsor was already a manufacturing center—and a hotbed of ideas. In 1835 James Cooper invented a rotating water pump and earned Windsor the nickname "birthplace of the U.S. machine-tool industry."

The industrial growth was a bit anomalous in predominantly agricultural Vermont. Senator Ralph Flanders, himself an inventor with more than fifty patents, once described Windsor as "an island of industry in a sea of cows."

Middlebury

Frog Hollow and a French Château

On August 18, 1802, professors, town and state officials, and spectators gathered at Middlebury College to present Vermont's first academic degree. "From the general satisfaction visible in every countenance," a newspaper reported, "It is fairly to be presumed that on no occasion have similar exercises been received with a more decided approbation."

Satisfied countenances did not include that of Aaron Petty, the hero of the hour. Vermont's first graduate had worked himself ill completing his courses and didn't attend commencement. He never fully recovered and died five months later.

His alma mater had greater longevity. Today Middlebury College, the oldest community-founded college in America (1800), is noted for its summer language program and writers' conference. Many ivy-covered campus buildings were constructed with gray limestone quarried at nearby Cornwall and have a pleasing harmony of style. College Hill overlooks church spires that thrust above treelined streets; Otter Creek glides past mellow brick homes and tumbles over Middlebury Falls, onetime power source for thriving nineteenth-century industries at a riverbank glen called Frog Hollow.

The dominant buildings on campus are known as the Old Stone Row. **Painter Hall (1)**, the state's oldest college building (1816), reflects the town's longtime involvement with academia: Citizens raised $8,000 for its construction and local masons fashioned what looks like millworkers' housing in a Massachusetts factory town. Kappa Delta Rho national fraternity, founded here in 1905, is commemorated with a plaque at the south end of the building.

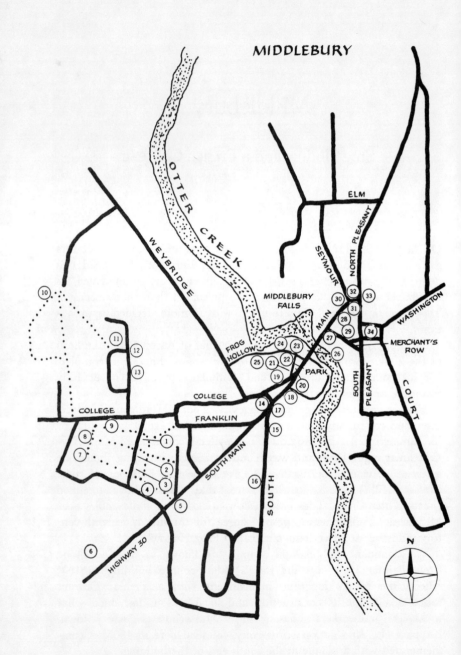

MIDDLEBURY

OTTER CREEK

MIDDLEBURY FALLS

WEYBRIDGE

FROG HOLLOW

COLLEGE

COLLEGE

FRANKLIN

SOUTH MAIN

SOUTH

HIGHWAY 30

ELM

SEYMOUR

NORTH PLEASANT

MAIN

PARK

SOUTH PLEASANT

WASHINGTON

MERCHANT'S ROW

COURT

N

Old Stone Row

Next in the Row is the 1836 **Old Chapel** (2), also in the mill archi-tectural tradition; it is now an administration building.

The interior of **Starr Hall** (3), the Row's third building, burned Christmas night 1864, and was rebuilt inside the surviving walls. It is named for college benefactors Charles and Egbert Starr, as is **Starr Library** (4). Completed in 1900 for the college's centennial, this classic marble structure has a lobby with rich oak paneling and marble man-tel pieces. Its Abernathy Collection has 10,000 volumes, many of them first editions such as Thoreau's 1854 copy of *Walden*. Works by Emerson and Henry Adams are among 1,000 manuscripts here. The Helen Hartness Flanders Ballad Collection catalogues more than 9,500 traditional British and American songs: ballads, hymns, folk songs, and call sets.

About three years after Middlebury College was founded, Emma Willard inherited a "Female Academy," and in 1814–19 she taught classes in what is now the Admissions Office. Usually referred to as the

Emma Willard House (5) in honor of this pioneering feminist, author, and teacher, this 1811 brick dwelling is a National Historic Site.

The oldest grave in the **Main Street Burial Ground** (6) personifies the cemetery's Egyptian theme. Amid obelisks and pyramids is the grave of Prince Amun-Her-Khepesh-Ef, who died in 1883 B.C. This two-year-old son of King Senwoset III and Queen Hawthor-Hotpe was taken from his grave in Egypt's Valley of the Kings to Vermont's Champlain Valley for display in the Sheldon Museum. His mummy deteriorated in New England's damp climate and he was reinterred here.

A. Barton Hepburn (class of 1871) donated money to build the college a dormitory, but specified his favorite type of yellow brick be used in its construction. Diplomatic college officials awaited his demise, then had the conspicuous **Hepburn Hall** (7) painted gray to match other campus buildings. Occasionally used as a theater workshop for student productions, it was once known as "Hepburn Zoo" because its donor's hunting trophies adorn the walls.

"The strength of the hills is His also" is inscribed above the door of **Mead Chapel** (8), whose tower contains an eleven-bell carillon. The college choir performs Sundays, and recitals and concerts are also held here.

In the lobby of **Munroe Hall** (9) is a monumental bas-relief of an Assyrian guardian spirit from the ninth-century B.C. palace of King Assurnasirpal. It was procured by a missionary alumnus who served at Mosul on the Tigris in the 1850s.

Visitors to the **Observatory** (10) can stargaze on advertised nights throughout the year. A telescope from the yacht *America* is displayed along with other nineteenth-century scientific instruments.

A corner of France can be found on campus at **Le Château** (11), the first *maison française* in America. This castlelike language dormitory was inspired by the seventeenth-century Pavillon Henri IV at the Palace of Fontainebleau, France. Its Louis XVI salon contains eighteenth-century furnishings and paneling from the Hôtel Crillon in Paris.

There are other dormitories on campus where only the language studied may be spoken. Middlebury also maintains schools in Mainz, Paris, Moscow, Florence, Madrid, and Oxford, England.

The four-hundred-seat **Wright Memorial Theater** (12), headquarters of the drama department, offers theater, music, and dance productions by student and professional groups.

Le Château

The permanent collection of the Johnson Gallery in the **Christian A. Johnson Memorial Building** (13) includes African sculpture, pre-Columbian artifacts, paintings by Von Aachen and graphics by Dürer, Picasso, and Beckman. The gallery affords vistas of surrounding mountains. A sculpture by George Rickey enhances the grounds. A courtyard is lined with student works displayed on the walls. Music and dance productions are featured here in the "Thursday Series." *Open afternoons daily.*

The tour now leaves the campus, although college and town seem almost to merge. The **Municipal Building** (14), home of the town offices, is on the site of the Old Academy Grammar School. Chartered in 1797 and a forerunner of the college, it was housed in a three-story wooden building similar to Dartmouth Hall in Hanover, New Hampshire. The structure burned in 1867.

The 1854 **President's House** (15), home of Middlebury College's chief executives since 1918, is one of the town's few Carpenter Gothic dwellings. One college president, Cyrus Hamlin (1880–86), won the job with unusual (and unacademic) credentials: While a missionary in Turkey, he had designed earthquake-proof churches and supervised Istanbul's best bakery. As president, he admitted women to the institution and established the first men's dining room (known as "Hamlin's Hash House").

The **Otter Creek Audubon Society (16)** at 40 South Street sponsors field trips to nearby Mount Abraham to observe hawk migrations; nonmembers are welcome.

The 1832 **Seth Storrs House (17)** is named for a prominent lawyer who donated land and money to the grammar school and the college.

Lavius Fillmore designed the lavishly decorated **Samuel Phelps House (18)**, named for a Vermont supreme court justice and U.S. senator. A frieze encircles the building; woodwork details include rope moldings and elliptical sunbursts.

The **Federation Building (19)**, constructed about 1805, has a vegetable cellar which also served as a stop on the underground railway.

Cannon Green (20), one of Middlebury's three commons, is named for a Civil War artillery piece presented to the town in 1910.

A bachelor storekeeper named Henry Sheldon bought a Roman coin in 1875, and kindled what was to become a lifelong interest in history. He began collecting Middlebury memorabilia and stored it in his three-story home. "My time for the past year," he wrote in 1887, "except what was necessary in repairing old buildings, has been devoted to the interests of the museum, which with me takes the place of wife and family and affords me so much pleasure that I never think of being lonely. . . ."

When Sheldon died in 1907, he donated his house and its contents to the town as the **Sheldon Museum (21)**. Its seventeen rooms are furnished to reflect nineteenth-century New England. A formal parlor contains a 1797 clock and a 1780 piano. The kitchen has a 150-piece collection of pewter, and a saloon room is furnished with a marble bar from Middlebury's Addison House. A country store on the grounds is stocked with old-time goods. Also displayed is a turbine from Frog Hollow's Star Grist Mill and a boat-shaped buggy in which President James Monroe toured Middlebury in 1814. A library-research center behind the museum houses early Middlebury newspapers, documents, and photographs. A bell from the old town hall is south of the museum. *Open Mon.–Sat. June–mid-Oct.; Tues., Thurs. mid-Oct–May.*

The **Star Grist Mill (22)**, a woolen mill built in 1837, now contains a shop and a nightclub.

An 1872 sash-and-door factory now houses the **Vermont State Craft Center at Frog Hollow (23)**, the first of its type in America. Visitors can watch glistening hands shape an elegant vase and see fiery molten gold poured into molds. The works of 250 Vermont craftsmen are displayed and sold in a gallery, and in summer on a terrace that overlooks Middlebury Falls. The largest sale occurs August 1–4 during the Frog Hollow Craft Festival. The gallery and terrace overflow with imaginative crafts. There are demonstrations in glassblowing, pottery making, batik, and sculpture, and live music, award-winning short films, and children's theater. *Open Mon.–Sat. Feb.–Dec.*

The 1840 **Old Stone Mill** (**24**) once processed wool from Merino sheep, imported here from Italy in the early 1800s. By 1840 Addison County grazed more sheep per acre and produced more wool than any other county in the country. The mill now contains offices, shops, and boutiques. *Open Mon.–Sat.*

Forges, mills, and Vermont's first nail factory (1796) lined **Frog Hollow** (**25**) in the 1800s. Vermont's marble industry was established here in 1802 when Eben Judd and a ten-year-old boy developed a machine for sawing marble hewn from a riverbank quarry above the falls. Judd's company produced marble "cut and curved with an elegance not surpassed on this side of the Atlantic."

The waterfall that powered this industry can best be seen from a lane between Main Street stores and the craft center. Penstocks which carried water to early hydroelectric plants are still visible.

The **Main Street Bridge** (**26**) is modeled after Rome's Ponte Sant'Angelo, which was built across the Tiber in A.D. 130. Middlebury's more modest version replicated its predecessor's great stone arches but not its Bernini angels. The bridge spans Otter Creek, the longest waterway entirely within the state (one hundred miles). Fishermen familiar with its quiet, shady pools land smallmouth bass, yellow perch, and brown trout.

The **Battell Block** (**27**) with its stone piers, steel girders, and paneled brick upper floors was built by one of Middlebury's most influential, philanthropic, and cantankerous citizens. As publisher of the Middlebury *Register,* Joseph Battell engaged in a spirited but futile campaign to eradicate automobiles. He wrote a weekly column entitled "Chamber of Horrors" which described car accidents across the nation. Perhaps his equestrian passion inspired his hatred of anything automotive. Battell established the Morgan Horse Farm three miles north of town and compiled the breed's first registry. He also built Bread Loaf Inn fifteen miles east of town and bought 30,000 acres of mountains surrounding it. Part of his estate now comprises the Green Mountain National Forest; the rest belongs to the college, as does the

Middlebury Falls

inn, which hosts Middlebury's summer graduate school in English literature and an annual writers' conference.

The Gothic **St. Stephen's Episcopal Church (28)** flanking the Green was completed in 1827 with delicate stained-glass windows and a tower with a Revere bell. This affluent Episcopal parish met all its expenses at the turn of the century "without resorting to fairs, festivals, [and] 'socials.' . . ." (The local Methodist-Episcopalian society might have taken money from any source in 1816. That year they paid their pastor $256, "cheap enough for the pure gospel.")

In the early 1700s Gamaliel Painter donated land near his mills for the village **Green (29)**. Also sheriff of the county, Painter installed stocks and a whipping post (the site is marked by a marble post). The Green was cleared by convicted drunks who were each sentenced to dig up one stump. Concerts are held at the bandstand from June to August.

The 1817 **Community House (30)**, once owned by Senator Horatio Seymour, has forty-foot hemlock beams in its attic, elaborate carvings, and no fewer than ten fireplaces, some with ornate marble mantels.

The **Emma Willard Monument** (31) commemorates a pioneer in women's education. Willard took over Ida Strong's impoverished female academy, founded here in 1803, and taught arts and sciences instead of the usual domestic disciplines. She later established America's first normal school in Troy, New York.

Dominating the Green and the center of Middlebury is Lavius Fillmore's magnificent 1809 **Congregational Church** (32) with its unusual steeple: a spire and two octagonal stages set on top of three square stages. Palladian windows at the front and back and graceful rounded windows along the sides are other distinctive features. Ionic columns made from single tree trunks cut at Court Square support the church's central dome. *Open daily June–mid-Oct.; Sun. mid-Oct.–May.*

Lawyer Samuel Mills hosted a meeting on September 30, 1798, that included Yale president Timothy Dwight, Seth Storrs, and trustees of the newly organized grammar school. With Dwight's advice and encouragement, they applied for a charter for Middlebury College. Miller's residence has since been known as **Charter House** (33).

Middlebury Inn (34), built in 1824 overlooking Court Square, has been remodeled so many times that the only original details are the masonry and a fanlighted doorway facing the Green.

Due to settlers' clearing and the penance of drunks on the Green, Court Street, emanating from the square, was replanted in 1895 by Phillip Battell Stewart, who alternated saplings of oak with balm of Gilead. Similar reforestation elsewhere produced today's pleasant, shaded avenues.

The Morgan: Speed, Strength, and Beauty

Sleek, graceful horses roam 1,000 acres of rolling green pastures and woodlands at the University of Vermont Morgan Horse Farm, 2½ miles north of Middlebury. (This historic ranch is easily reached by car via Weybridge Street and the 1805 Pulp Mill Bridge.)

Morgan horse and colt

A Woodstock singing teacher and composer named Justin Morgan founded America's first native breed (and Vermont's state animal). Although his horse Figure was barely fourteen hands high, it was noted for its speed, strength, and beauty. Colonel Joseph Battell of Middlebury built this farm in the late 1800s, compiled a Morgan registry, and established the breed.

The Morgan's thoroughbred and Arabian ancestry is evident in its deep body, heavy muscles over the quarters and shoulders, and short, fine head. Morgan blood can be traced to the Tennessee walking horse, the English Hackney, and the palomino.

Guided tours from May to November feature an 1878 barn, and an outstanding herd of horses, as well as cattle used in the university's agricultural program. Open daily.

Bennington

Gentleman Johnny and Madame Molly

"The morning of the sixteenth rose beautifully serene," wrote a German mercenary in August 1777 near Bennington, Vermont. The calm would soon be shattered by one of the fiercest battles of the Revolutionary War.

British troops (actually a motley collection of Canadians, Hessians, and Indians) led by General John Burgoyne had invaded New York and were advancing down the Hudson River in an attempt to cut off New England from the other colonies. After victories at Ticonderoga and Hubbardton, "Gentleman Johnny" Burgoyne needed supplies, especially horses for his German dragoons. He was told (erroneously) that 1,300 horses and cattle were at a depot near Bennington.

He sent Lieutenant Colonel Frederick Baum with 1,000 troops to seize the depot. The American militia mustered 2,000 men from New York, Vermont, and New Hampshire, roused Brigadier General John Stark from retirement in Manchester, New Hampshire, and prepared to halt the enemy's advance along the Walloomsac River, about four miles west of Bennington. "There are the Redcoats," said Stark as his troops dug in, "and they will be ours or tonight Molly Stark sleeps a widow."

Madame Molly (her real name was Elizabeth) was spared such a fate, but not Frau Baum, wife of the German commander. A furious two-hour assault "like a continual thunderclap" saw Baum mortally wounded and his troops surrounded.

The Americans captured two cannons and routed the British, who fled under the cover of night. "Had the day lasted an hour longer," said Stark, "we should have taken the whole body of them."

BENNINGTON

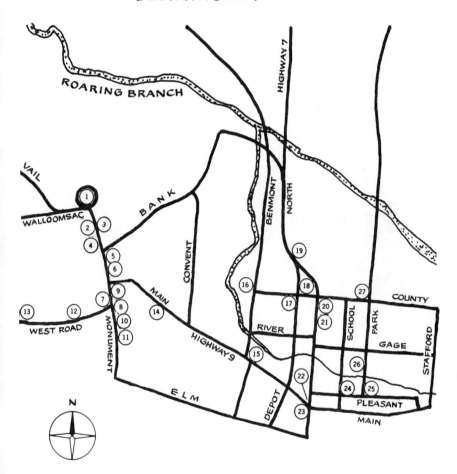

The day was long enough. The British lost about nine hundred troops and their advance was halted. Two months later Burgoyne and his depleted ranks were vanquished at Saratoga, and the tide of the Revolution turned in favor of the colonies.

The **Bennington Battle Monument** (1), an obelisk of blue limestone 306 feet high, was dedicated in 1891 to commemorate this important American victory. An elevator takes visitors to a viewing

Bennington Battle Monument

gallery from which they can see panoramas of the countryside, including the battle site five miles northwest. A diorama in the monument by Vermont artist Paul Winters depicts the conflict. *Open daily Apr.–end of Oct.*

Nearby is a marker on the site of the depot that Baum intended to seize. A life-size statue depicts Seth Warner, leader of the Bennington troops, as rather Napoleonic, with epaulets, cocked hat, and drawn sword.

Local men wear similar colonial garb and charge their neighbors dressed in British uniforms during reenactments of the battle every August. The excitement of the cannons' roar and musket smoke compensates for the certainty of an annual American victory.

Visitors interested in more automotive history can take a 1½-mile side trip east on Walloomsac Road to the Bennington Airport for a September antique car show. Tin Lizzies and sleek Cords compete in slow races and cranking contests, while owners don dapper clothes reflecting their cars' vintage.

There is more to see in Bennington than citizens impersonating Gentleman Johnny or Jay Gatsby. Graced by venerable churches and shuttered colonial houses, this handsome town is cradled between the Taconic range to the west and the Green Mountains to the east. Pine-scented forests hereabouts are the haunts of white-tailed deer, and the region's streams are flecked with trout.

Vermont's first chartered town (1742) is also a half-shire town. When Bennington and nearby Manchester vied for the county seat, a Solomonic settlement from Montpelier gave both centers courthouses and jails; the towns alternate as hosts of twice-yearly court sessions.

Along Monument Avenue is the **Governor John S. Robinson House** (**2**), once owned by one of Vermont's few Democratic governors; he was an early and vocal advocate of building a suitable monument to commemorate the Battle of Bennington.

The **Fay-Brown House** (3), a stone dwelling built in 1781, was originally a blacksmith shop.

The **General David Robinson Home** (4), a handsome 1795 Georgian structure, was built to give the general a more elegant residence. The general's mother, a stubborn matriarch and widow of Bennington pioneer Samuel Robinson, refused to move into the new accommodations. The old home stood until her death, then the family shifted residences.

Bennington's public library was originally the **Old Academy** (5), built in 1821 with Dutch-step architecture, rare in this region. *Open daily.*

A bronze statue of a fierce cougar marks the site of Stephen Fay's **Catamount Tavern** (6), headquarters of the Green Mountain Boys. The yard of this public house once displayed a stuffed catamount, or cougar, snarling west toward New York land speculators from atop a twenty-five-foot pole.

The **Walloomsac Inn** (7), with its gambrel roof and shady front porch overlooking the Green, is perhaps Vermont's oldest hostelry (1766). It has changed little over the years, and is still in business. British prisoners from the Battle of Bennington who were imprisoned in a nearby meetinghouse were fed from the inn's kitchen. Illustrious guests have included Thomas Jefferson and James Madison, who both spent a weekend here in 1791 because Vermont didn't allow travel on Sundays.

Bennington schoolchildren placed a "bowlder" and plaque on the Green at the site of the town's first schoolhouse (1763). Another stone marker is found where William Lloyd Garrison published his

Journal of the Times. This renowned abolitionist was lured here in 1828 by the town's liberalism: He could attack slavery, alcohol, and immorality as long as he also assailed presidential candidate Andrew Jackson (Vermont's favorite candidate was John Quincy Adams). Garrison stayed a year, then moved to Baltimore.

The 1805 **Old First Church** (8), designed by Lavius Fillmore, has a fine Palladian window in its facade and intricate detail on its arched belfry. Plaques honoring Vermonters from all walks of life hang inside the church, which serves the state's oldest Protestant parish (1762). The church was restored to its original appearance in 1937 and declared Vermont's Colonial Shrine. *Open daily June–mid-Oct.; Sun. mid-Oct.–May.*

Poet Robert Frost is interred in the church's **Old Burying Ground** (9). His epitaph: "I had a lover's quarrel with the world." Other names and dates on his stone record how often tragedy and early death

Old Burying Ground

struck his family. Also buried here are five Vermont governors; a common tombstone honors fallen soldiers from the Battle of Bennington.

The 1875 **Blackmer-Meagher House** (10), now owned by novelist John Gardner, boasts thirty-three Ionic columns, seventeen pilasters, and an unusually carved Palladian window.

The **Parson Dewey Home** (11), reputedly Vermont's oldest frame dwelling (1713), was built by a minister of the First Meeting House who also was an accomplished carpenter. This fire-breathing pastor lies in the Old Burying Ground beneath a tombstone inscribed with a fatalistic quote from *Richard II:*

> *Let's talk of graves, of worms and epitaphs;*
> *Make dust our paper, and with rainy eyes*
> *Write sorrow on the bosom of the earth.*

The 1792 **Governor Isaac Tichenor Home** (12) is named for a Princeton graduate who settled here in 1777. Dubbed "the Jersey slick" for his courtly manners, he became a U.S. senator and a governor.

The **Old Bennington Country Store** (13) has served customers from various locations since 1793. It still offers traditional New England general store goods: penny candy, cheeses, old-fashioned wooden toys, and cast-iron cookware. *Open Mon.–Sat.*

The oldest Stars and Stripes in existence flew above the Continental Storehouse during the Battle of Bennington and is now displayed in the **Bennington Museum** (14), a short walk down the hill and one of New England's finest regional museums. It's apparent that the faded and tattered banner has been to war: The top stripe is missing. Also exhibited is an extensive collection of Bennington pottery and plated amberina glassware, named for its radiant amber color. The museum's sculpture includes a gilded eagle with a five-foot wingspan carved in 1790 by Simeon and John Shillings, and a bust by Jacob Epstein of Vermont-born philosopher and educator John Dewey. The artist considered his subject "absolutely straightforward, simple and loveable." Dewey thought Epstein's work made him look like "a Vermont horse-dealer."

The museum's furniture collection includes a Hadley hope chest with shallow, intricate carvings and floral motifs. This rare and uniquely American furniture (only 115 examples survive) was made in the seventeenth century by craftsmen along the Connecticut River. The children's gallery displays a dollhouse inhabited by antique dolls and decorated with tiny furniture. More than thirty Grandma

Gilded eagle, Bennington Museum

Moses paintings are in a re-creation of a schoolhouse the artist once attended.

The **St. Francis de Sales Church** (15), the county's largest Catholic church, was built in the 1890s. Its tall steeple was removed in the 1920s because it swayed in high winds. This limestone structure has retained its stone arches and stained-glass windows.

Bennington's early industry was dominated by the **Holden-Leonard Mill** (16), which manufactured paisley shawls and wool and cotton underwear. Much admired for its beauty and proportion, this structure has a seven-story tower with arched recessed windows and an octagonal cupola. It now houses a dozen companies.

The exquisite brick **Bennington Railroad Station** (17) is a depot with a broad wooden canopy, brick corbeling, and a delicate mansard roof inset with four clockfaces and covered with stamped copper tiles. Restored to its original elegance, it now houses an architectural firm and municipal offices (a town trustee works behind the ticket counter). Opposite the depot is a charming Gothic **cobblestone house** (18) built in the 1850s.

A side trip to **Deer Park** (19) offers walkers a shady picnic spot. A herd of white-tailed deer is in a pen adjacent to the park. *Open daily June–mid-Oct.*

Many venerable downtown buildings have been converted or refurbished in Bennington's imaginative version of urban renewal. The **Stone Feed Mill Store** (20) was once a tack factory operated by industrialist Henry Putnam. The **stone garage** (21) next door was erected as a gristmill in 1842.

Putnam Square (22) is the junction of Highways 9 and 7. A twelve-foot-tall free-standing clock graces the front of the Chittenden Trust Company Bank. Overlooking the square is **Putnam Hotel** (23), built in 1868 and now a men's dormitory for Southern Vermont College.

The 1838 **Norton-Fenton House** (24) was built for Judge Luman Norton, son of the founder of Bennington's first pottery. His son Julius, also a proprietor of the company, built the nearby **1846 dwelling** (25).

Renowned **Bennington Pottery** (26) was produced from 1834 to 1894 in a long, low brick factory beside a waterfall on the Roaring Branch of the Walloomsac River.

The tradition is maintained at **Potter's Yard** (27), which specializes in mat-glazed stoneware fired at high temperatures. Sophisticated, award-winning designs by owners David and Gloria Gil have been exhibited in the Guggenheim Museum. The building also houses a fine restaurant. *Open daily.*

An Explosion of Color and Shapes:
Bennington's Prized Pottery

Bennington is as famous for its ceramics as for its battle. Captain John Norton first established a pottery here in 1793, and for the next century it produced functional stoneware jugs and crocks. Christopher Fenton, a sometime employee and partner in the Norton firm, started his own company in 1847 and manufactured some of America's finest decorative stoneware with an explosion of innovative design, color, and variety. Examples on the opposite page include: 1. Granite ware. Cuspidors, water pitchers, and toilet sets were often embellished with color; 2. Scroddled ware. Its variegated patterns were formed by using multicolored clays; 3. Rockingham ware. Its yellow body and splotched brown glaze resemble tortoiseshell. Hound-handle pitchers and cow creamers were popular designs; 4. Parian ware—hard porcelain named for its resemblance to Parian marble.

1.

2.

3.

4.

NEW
HAMPSHIRE

⊙Concord

NEW HAMPSHIRE

From Mount Washington's glacier-scarred summit to the swampy banks of the Squamscott, New Hampshire cares little for consistency. Hot-headed patriots once fomented revolution in Exeter's taverns, while fifteen miles away in Tory Portsmouth the royal governor desperately clung to power.

Today, many historic southern towns just over the border from tax-ridden Massachusetts are commuter communities for Boston (no state or sales tax is collected in New Hampshire). Up north Granite Staters stay put, and let people come to them for the natural wonders in the White Mountains, and the splendor of autumn foliage—a red blaze of hard maple and the gold and green of oak and ash.

Early towns such as Portsmouth and Exeter looked to the sea and south to Massachusetts. But as settlers moved west and north the state diversified. Industrial Manchester on the Merrimack had more textile spindles than any other American city in the 1860s. Farms along the fertile Connecticut River valley raised rugged, pragmatic types who cleared hillside pastures, bounded them with stone-wall fences, and resisted anyone who tried to chip away their hard-won freedom.

Most Granite Staters are employed in manufacturing, yet New Hampshire has the purest air in America (forests carpet eighty percent of the state). The economy derives additional strength from craftsmen and artists. Statewide outlets market their products, ranging from goat cheese to fine lace, from quilts to leatherwork.

Hanover

The College on the Hill

In 1770 Rev. Eleazar Wheelock was looking for a well for his college, founded the previous year. He struck water and began to build his fledgling institution on a knoll overlooking the Hanover plain above the Connecticut River.

The site of Wheelock's well is now occupied by **Dartmouth Row** (1), three white brick buildings that have come to symbolize "the college on the hill." They seldom fail to produce nostalgia in alumni (and larger donations to the nation's ninth oldest college). Strong, almost fierce loyalties to their alma mater draw graduates back to Hanover "though round the girdled earth they roam" (in the words of a college song).

Hanover is a quintessential college town: ivy-covered campus buildings, streets shaded by huge elms and maples, white frame houses, and students seemingly in perpetual motion.

The best place to observe this swirl of activity is Dartmouth Row, whose architecture reflects the discipline and simplicity of academic life. The central structure of this complex of classrooms and offices is Dartmouth Hall, a replica of a 1784 structure that burned in 1904. Two small ground-floor windows flanking the center door were salvaged from the first hall. A bronze plaque at the southern end of the building was cast from the metal of a tower bell that melted in the fire.

Flanking black-shuttered Dartmouth Hall are the smaller Greek Revival Wentworth Hall to the north and Thorton Hall to the south, both designed by Amni B. Young.

The row overlooks the **College Green** (2), which in Wheelock's time "resembled nothing so much as a giant jackstraw game in progress."

HANOVER

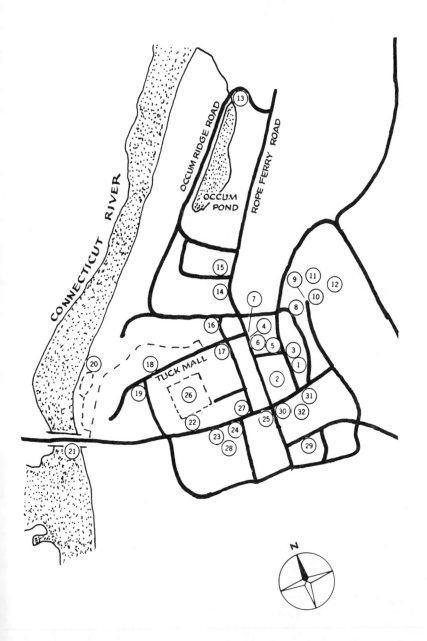

Dartmouth Row

Here, towering white pines were felled in the 1830s, and this 7½-acre clearing became Hanover's common pasture. Students who had to dodge "nuisances" deposited by cattle eventually protested by impounding cows in the basement of Dartmouth Hall until villagers agreed to graze their livestock elsewhere. Today, walkers on the Green only have to dodge errant Frisbees, and weave past soccer, football, and softball games.

Rustic symphonies of fiddles, mandolins, and guitars enliven warm July afternoons during Celebration Northeast, a three-day folk festival on the Green. Toes tap and feet fly in impromptu square dances as jug bands and other musical groups from as far away as Louisiana perform traditional songs and dances.

The Romanesque **Rollins Chapel** (3), with bell tower and immense hinged doors, offers occasional organ recitals; a welded iron-and-steel sculpture by Judith Brown entitled "Noah's Ark" decorates the chapel. *Open daily.*

Winter carnival ice sculpture on the Green, Dartmouth College

Massive **Baker Library** (4), with its two-hundred-foot tower soaring above the Hanover plain, dominates the campus. Built in 1928 from designs by Frederic Jens Larsen, the library takes its inspiration from Philadelphia's Independence Hall.

Those who tire of the pursuit of knowledge in Baker's basement reading room can lift their eyes from books and see the 3,000-square-foot mural "An Epic of American Civilization" marching along the walls. These magnificent frescoes, painted in 1932–34 by Mexican artist José Clemente Orozco, depict Latin American history from the Mayan and Toltec Indian civilizations through 5,000 years of growth and decline. Artistic commentary can be heard on telephone recordings across from the reserve books desk.

Baker is flanked by the imposing classical **Webster Hall** (5), used for special events, and the English department's **Sanborn Library** (6), with its elegant paneled rooms and reading alcoves.

A modernistic metal-and-wood sculpture entitled "Chi Delta" contrasts with the traditional arched windows and Georgian lines of Sanborn. Mark DiSuvero's I-beam work includes a swing irresistible to children—and occasionally faculty and students.

Eleazar Wheelock journeyed up the Connecticut River in 1770 with a Bible, a drum, five hundred gallons of New England rum, and a book called *Gradus ad Parnassum* (A Step to Parnassus). Wheelock's possessions—except the rum—are displayed in the second-floor Woodward Room at Baker, along with his chair and early books.

Orozco frescoes, Baker Library, Dartmouth College

Daniel Webster's oversize copy of John James Audubon's *Birds of America* is in the special collections room on the first floor. (Audubon only delivered three of a four-volume set because Webster never paid him.)

The Robert Frost Room (opened by the special collections librarian on request) contains Frost's handwritten notation on how he started writing poetry, some of his possessions, and a bronze bust of the poet by Walker Hancock. *Open Mon.–Fri.*

The Dartmouth College Museum and Galleries in **Carpenter Hall** (7) adjoining Baker display massive sixth-century B.C. Assyrian reliefs uncovered from the Nimrud Palace in 1847, along with an outstanding collection of Greek and Russian icons from the fourteenth to the nineteenth centuries. *Open daily.*

On the lawn of the **Fairchild Science Center** (8) are triangular enameled-steel panels thrust up from the grass. This sculpture by Beverly Pepper is entitled "Thel," for William Blake's poem on the mystery of the source of wisdom. Pepper intended the white panels to disappear under snow in winter and emerge fresh and vital in spring. Students use the sculpture's sloping grass sides for studying or sunbathing. A symmetrical sculpture by Charles Perry at the foot of the steps leading to the center is based on a mathematical formula explained on a plaque.

In the lobby of the glass-walled Fairchild tower, which connects Steele and Wilder halls, a pendulum proves to even the most skeptical that the earth rotates. Based on experiments by French physicist Jean Foucault in the 1830s, the pendulum consists of a seventy-six-foot cable attached to a 260-pound bronze bob which seems to rotate a fraction of a degree with each arc. It is the floor, and ultimately the earth, that rotate.

Off the central lobby is a globe showing the topography of the continents and ocean floors. From a second-floor balcony the globe appears as the earth would look to astronomers 6,300 miles in space. Artwork from the college's permanent collections is displayed throughout the building. *Open daily.*

A **plaque** (9) on a granite outcrop behind the science center explains that in 1810–11 the first—and for a long time, the only—building of the Dartmouth Medical School was constructed here. It was torn down in 1961. Nearby College Park was designed by Frederick Law Olmsted, who also planned New York's Central Park.

The **Shattuck Observatory** (10), built in 1853 using Amni B. Young's design, once had an elaborately paneled wooden dome mounted on six cannonballs, which acted like giant ball bearings as the dome rotated. Using the observatory's twelve-inch telescope, Professor Charles A. Young made pioneering discoveries in the 1860s by studying light spectrums of stars. *Open Mon., Wed., and Fri. nights.*

On the highest point on campus rises **Bartlett Tower** (11), a medieval-style turret built by students in 1885–95. A circular staircase leads to a viewing platform with splendid panoramas of the Connect-icut Valley, Hanover, and the surrounding hills. In autumn a stunning blaze of color splashes the hillsides in scarlet and yellow. *Open daily.*

Nearby is the Old Pine Stump, the artificially petrified remains of a bent and twisted white pine under which Eleazar Wheelock reputedly taught classes. An earlier legend tells that the hunting grounds of three Indian villages overlapped here. Before the seasonal move to other ter-ritories, the village chiefs smoked peace pipes, then broke them on the old pine.

That tradition is remembered in a moving ritual each June on the day before commencement, when seniors smoke clay pipes together at Class Day ceremonies, then smash them on the stump as a symbol of breaking their immediate ties with Dartmouth.

Class Day and other college functions are held at the **Bema** (12), a natural amphitheater formed by rough-hewn granite walls and shaded by tall pines.

A lovely walk on Rope Ferry Road passes the Mary Hitchcock Hos-pital (on warm summer days patients and nurses sun themselves on the landscaped grounds) and Dick's House, a hospital for students. Farther along this shady avenue is the golf course and Occum Pond, scenes of skating in winter. The **Dartmouth Outing Clubhouse** (13), a rustic fieldstone hunting lodge adorned with moose, deer, and elk trophies, houses a restaurant in summer.

A stroll along Occum Ridge Road, overhung with birches, weeping willows, and pines, passes stately white frame dwellings nestled back among the woods. Sylvanus Ripley, a member of Dartmouth's first graduating class (1771), built **Webster Cottage** (14) in 1780 for his bride, the daughter of Eleazar Wheelock. The cottage is named for its most illustrious tenant, Daniel Webster, who roomed here as a student. The local historical society has refurnished the humble dwell-ing with period pieces and Webster memorabilia. A steep staircase leads to his garret bedroom and an alcove. A black leather barrel chair from his home in Franklin, New Hampshire, is in the sitting room/library; bookshelves hold the orator's inkstand and autographed copies of his speeches. Henry Fowle Durant, founder of Wellesley College, was born here in 1822; the Durant bedroom is furnished with family pieces. *Open Tues., Thurs., and Sun.*

Sylvanus Ripley also built **Choate House (15)** in 1786. After an unsuccessful stint as a tavern, it became the residence of Mills Olcott, a wealthy lawyer who entertained President James Monroe here in 1817. It is now occupied by visiting professors.

Eleazar Wheelock erected his log cabin near present-day **Silsby Hall (16)** (a plaque behind nearby Russell Sage dormitory marks the exact spot). Dr. Dixie Crosby's and Professor Oliver Hubbard's analysis of oil-bearing Pennsylvania rock in 1853 developed at **Crosby Hall (17)** led to the sinking of America's first oil well at Titusville, Pennsylvania, six years later.

The **Tuck School of Business Administration (18),** the nation's first such institution (1900), was founded with gifts from banker and financier Edward Tuck (class of 1862).

The nearby **Thayer School of Engineering (19),** also the nation's first (1871), was founded by Sylvanus Thayer (class of 1807), an engineer, soldier, and superintendent of the U. S. Military Academy in 1817–33.

Summer strollers along Tuck Mall may be drafted into volleyball games with graduate students relaxing from demanding curricula. An escape route for the nonathletic branches off Tuck Mall and winds down a shady ravine lined in places with mossy masonry.

Near the Connecticut River are the crew boathouses and the **Ledyard Canoe Club (20)**. A stone tablet here commemorates adventurer and explorer John Ledyard (class of 1776), who as a freshman hollowed out a log canoe and paddled to the mouth of the Connecticut. He later served as an officer with Captain Cook in the Pacific, and died at age thirty-seven in Egypt while preparing to cross the Sahara. (More conventional craft than Ledyard's log canoe can be rented at the clubhouse.)

Ledyard Bridge (21) replaced the first toll-free covered bridge across the Connecticut. At the dedication of the wooden span in 1859, Professor Sanborn declared: "Let no vandal hand be raised to deface this noble structure, or injure one fiber of its timbers." Despite this bombastic threat, the bridge was unceremoniously torn down in 1934 and replaced with this modern structure.

A steep climb up West Wheelock Street offers physical rewards, along with the 1790 **Samuel McClure House (22)**, once the home of a village cabinetmaker, the 1774 **Comfort Seaver House (23)**, residence of Wheelock's carpenter, and the 1839 **First Church of Christ, Scientist (24)**.

The oldest dwelling in town is **Wheelock House (25)**, built in 1773 and Eleazar's first permanent home. Once the town library, it is now owned by the American Universities Field Staff.

Past Psi Upsilon fraternity and behind the college dining hall is the secluded **Dartmouth cemetery (26)**. Tall white pines and birches shade the graves of Eleazar Wheelock (d. 1779) and his wife, Mary (d. 1783), along with students and faculty, many claimed by consumption in the college's early years.

On the Green in front of **College Hall (27)** run parallel rows of fences, remnants from the days when this was an enclosed pasture. The "Senior Fence" was once the exclusive perch of upperclassmen.

Down South Main Street is Hanover's small business district, usually thick with shoppers. Browsers leaf through books displayed outside the Dartmouth Book Store. **AVA Gallery (28)** exhibits paintings and etchings by local artists. *Open Mon.–Sat.* Crafts are displayed and sold in an outlet of the **League of New Hampshire Craftsmen (29)**. *Open Mon.–Sat.*

The play's the thing during the August Shrine Game, which pits New Hampshire's and Vermont's best high school football teams at Dartmouth's Memorial Field. But a parade highlights the day for many, with floats, balloons, and thousands of spectators lining the route to watch the antics of Shriners from all over the northeastern United States and Canada.

The **Hanover Inn (30)** is a gracious hostelry on the site of Brewster's Tavern, which operated in Wheelock's time. Front porch rocking chairs invite weary walkers to rest before proceeding to the last stops of the tour.

A stroll across a flagstone patio leads to Romanesque **Wilson Hall (31)**, an anthropological museum emphasizing North American native culture. Artifacts of pre-Columbian North American Indians include a collection of ninth-century southwestern pottery, colorful head-dresses, intricate sculpture and baskets, a wooden dugout, and a kayak. *Open daily.*

Artists, musicians, actors, writers, dancers, and artisans practice, perform, and create at the **Hopkins Center (32),** the cultural focus for the entire region. Named for Ernest Martin Hopkins, president of the college from 1916 to 1945, this sprawling complex (it has 4½ acres of floor space) was designed by Wallace K. Harrison (he also planned Rockefeller Center) and dedicated in 1962. Its three galleries have about forty shows a year of works drawn from college, private, and public collections. *Open daily.*

Dartmouth Players' productions are held in Center and Warner Bentley theaters; Spaulding Auditorium doubles as a lecture and con-

Hopkins Center

cert hall. Workshops offer outlets for students creative with pottery, woodworking, and jewelry.

Sculptures and fountains tucked in unlikely nooks and alcoves afford reflective respites from the center's continuous creative bustle. Deep, comfortable couches cluster around a fireplace on the rotunda's second floor—known as the Top of the Hop—where students often give impromptu recitals on a grand piano. Soaring arched windows overlook the Green with Baker's tower rising majestically above the elms. Eleazar's vision for a great college has been fulfilled.

Franconia Notch

The Old Man's Notch

Men hang out signs indicative of their respective trades: shoemakers hang out a giant shoe; jewelers a monster watch; and a dentist hangs out a gold tooth; but up in the mountains of New Hampshire God Almighty has hung out a sign to show that there He makes men.

That's what Daniel Webster reputedly said of the Old Man of the Mountains: a rock formation that is the Granite State's most spectacular natural attraction. This craggy visage stares stonily into eternity at the northern end of an eight-mile-long mountain pass called Franconia Notch.

Rich in geological wonders and stimulating in climate, this narrow defile is the most popular site in New Hampshire's White Mountains. Along with the Old Man, other natural marvels include Cannon Mountain's sheer cliffs, a fractured rock canyon called the Flume, and lakes cradled in rough-hewn settings.

God's advertisement may have been hung out for all to see, but not necessarily via a walking tour. A series of trails, connected by short drives on Route 3 are required to appreciate the Notch fully.

One of nature's most impressive works is the **Flume (1)**, a seventy-foot-deep gorge extending for eight hundred feet along the southern flank of Mount Liberty. All family members can hike this trail along paths and wooden walkways that crisscross the canyon. In fact, it is said that a ninety-three-year-old woman looking for a place to fish discovered the Flume in 1808.

The walk begins in a broad valley that narrows rapidly to twenty feet as it passes a granite behemoth called the **Great Boulder (2)**. The

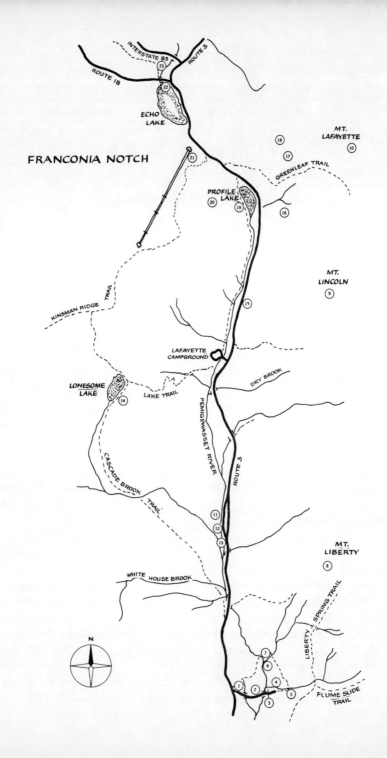

FRANCONIA NOTCH

MT. LAFAYETTE

MT. LINCOLN

MT. LIBERTY

ECHO LAKE

PROFILE LAKE

LONESOME LAKE

LAFAYETTE CAMPGROUND

INTERSTATE 93

ROUTE 18

ROUTE 3

ROUTE 3

GREENLEAF TRAIL

KINSMAN RIDGE TRAIL

LAKE TRAIL

CASCADE BROOK TRAIL

PEMIGEWASSET RIVER

DRY BROOK

WHITE HOUSE BROOK

LIBERTY SPRING TRAIL

FLUME SLIDE TRAIL

N

Old Man of the Mountains

appropriately named Boulder Path (.6 mile) passes through a quaint
covered bridge (3) built in 1820. Visitors can stock up on souvenirs at
the nearby Boulder Store.

Along the Flume Path (.3 mile) perpendicular walls of 200-
million-year-old Conway granite rise seventy feet. A forest of gnarled
pines darkens this lush fissure; moist mosses and luxuriant ferns flour-
ish in ancient fractures. The Flume Brook tumbles over boulders and
eases past **Table Rock** (4), an immense granite outcrop 250 feet long
and seventy-five feet wide. The brook then rushes into the Pemigewasset River.

Pictures taken in the Flume before 1883 show a huge boulder that

The Flume

glaciers had wedged between the walls of the cleft high above the canyon floor. In June of that year, following several days of heavy rain ending with a cloudburst, the Flume Brook became a thundering torrent. Tourists at a nearby guest house thought they heard a mighty blast. When they ventured into the gorge a few days later, the great boulder had tumbled from its perch and smashed into small pieces. The same storm also added two new waterfalls to the Flume.

Cool, misty air and the roar of rushing water signal the nearby **Avalanche Falls** (5), a ragged cataract that tumbles twenty-three feet into a deep pool.

The Ridge Path (.7 mile) meanders through scented pine forests to the **Liberty Gorge** (6), threaded by a foaming mountain torrent called the Cascades. Tree trunks are tumbled along the precipitous edge of the gorge.

The nearby **Pool** (7), a crystal-clear basin forty feet deep and 150 feet wide, was formed some 25,000 years ago during the Ice Age. The Pemigewasset River twists through rapids spiked with granite rocks eroded from surrounding 130-foot-high cliffs, then eases into the pool. On a high precipice above this tranquil basin, a lone pine stood guard for almost three centuries until a great hurricane toppled it in 1938. This same 175-foot tree now supports a covered bridge which spans the Pool.

The Wildwood Path (.4 mile) winds through forest and past huge glacial erratics (boulders deposited by melting ice sheets).

Back at Route 3, near the entrance to the Flume Trail, a stagecoach recalls New Hampshire's contribution to winning the West—and countless exciting chase scenes in cowboy movies. This type of Concord coach was manufactured in the state capital during the 1800s.

A nearby trout pool teems with tempting fish, but unfortunately, visitors are not allowed to drop a hook (the pond is used to stock lakes in the Notch). Those who have packed a lunch will find picnic tables across the highway.

Visitors can test their imaginations as they drive past **Mount Liberty** (8). Some claim they can see George Washington lying in state at the peak: His nose is the summit, his forehead the rocky ledge to the south, and his weak chin points north toward **Mount Lincoln** (9).

The majestic 4,000-foot peaks along the east side of Route 3—Liberty, Lincoln, and **Lafayette** (10)—constitute the Franconia Range, almost as familiar as Mount Washington and other political cronies in the Presidential Range to the east. Cannon and Profile mountains in the Kinsman Range form the west wall of the Notch.

The **Basin** (11), a granite pothole at the foot of a waterfall on the Pemigewasset, was shaped during the Ice Age by melting glaciers. Small stones and sand whirled by torrents of the river polished the sides of this bowl. South of the basin rests the **Old Man's Foot** (12), a self-describing granite formation, and through a narrow trough tumbles the **Baby Flume** (13), a miniature of its namesake. A picnic area here nestles amid tall pines.

A 1.5-mile trail of moderate difficulty leads from the Lafayette Campground to **Lonesome Lake** (14), according to Charles Dudley Warner "a mirror for the sky and the clouds and the sailing hawks." The Appalachian Mountain Club maintains huts in summer on a ridge under one of the shoulders of Cannon Mountain. Unsurpassed views from Lonesome's shore reveal Mount Lafayette and the Franconia Range.

A teamster named Thomas Boise from Woodstock, New Hampshire, was trapped here by a sudden snowstorm in the early 1800s. Desperate for shelter in the impassable Notch, he killed and skinned his horse, wrapped himself in its hide, and crawled beneath the overhang of a large boulder now known as **Boise Rock** (15). When rescuers found him the next day they had to cut away the frozen horsehide blanket that had saved his life.

A long wound on the eastern side of Mount Lafayette was slashed by a **landslide** (16) on June 24, 1948. Trees, earth, and boulders up to fifty feet high blocked Route 3 for several days.

On the west side of the highway opposite the landslide, look with binoculars up Mount Lafayette's rugged western slope to see the **Watcher** (17), a small rock profile also known as the Old Woman of the Mountains. A precipitous foothill called **Eagle Cliff** (18), also visible from here, is named for a legend that tells of eagles that once inhabited this rocky knoll 1,500 feet above the floor of the Notch.

A short drive leads to the **Old Man of the Mountains** (19), the Granite State's official symbol. The Old Man inspired Nathaniel Hawthorne to write his story "The Great Stone Face"; the hyperbolic P. T. Barnum considered it the greatest show on earth—next to his circus—and wanted to take the formation on tour with him.

Discovered in 1805 by highway workers (they thought it looked like then-President Jefferson), this craggy countenance broods on the sheer east cliff of Cannon Mountain 1,200 feet above Profile Lake. It was formed about 200 million years ago when Conway granite crystallized into five separate ledges, arranged horizontally by the caprices of nature to form a man's profile. A twenty-foot-long block weighing thirty tons forms part of the forehead; other massive formations pro-

Cannon Mountain

duce lips, chin, and nose of a profile forty feet high and twenty-five feet wide. The likeness vanishes into a granitic jumble when observers move one hundred yards to either side of a vantage point on Profile Lake.

"The pieces [of the Old Man] are liable to fall at any time," wrote a geologist who surveyed New Hampshire in 1870. "I would advise any persons who are anxious to see the profile hasten to the spot, for fear of being disappointed." But since then, whenever the Granite State symbol has threatened to tumble from the precipice, face-lifters have attached supports, clamps, and pins.

Cannon Rock (20), a formation resembling the barrel of an artillery piece that juts from a fortresslike parapet 1,800 feet up the side of Cannon Mountain, can be seen from the Old Man parking lot on the west side of Route 3.

Echo Lake

Paths encircle Profile Lake, a small, blue gem that has been called "the Old Man's Wash Bowl." Fly fishing lands trout in this headwater of the Pemigewasset River.

The great stone profile's man-made rival, the **Cannon Mountain Aerial Tramway (21)**, was the first such lift in America (1937). Cable cars whisk visitors 5,500 feet in five minutes to views of the valley floor and the folded, forested peaks of the White Mountains. Trails wind about the rock-strewn summit. Visitors can spot Lapland rosebay or wild geranium, flowers usually found in the Arctic.

Like a jewel set in granite, Echo Lake occupies the northern end of this mountain pass. Boating, swimming, and trout fishing are popular on this tiny lake, which also boasts a fine sandy **beach (22)** with picnic areas.

A 1.5-mile path winds up **Artist's Bluff (23)**, a rocky palisade with splendid lookouts. The mountain scene unfolds: the distant rugged slopes of the Franconia and Kinsman ranges looming over the narrow ribbon of road.

Wolfeboro

America's First Resort

Sheltered in a snug horseshoe-shaped bay on a blue-water gem that Indians called "Smile of the Great Spirit," Wolfeboro boasts a charming setting in New Hampshire's scenic lake district.

Perhaps the best way to become acquainted with this town is aboard M/V *Mount Washington*, a 1,250-passenger motor vessel that stops at **Cate Park** (1) in town during its 3½-hour cruises on Lake Winnipesaukee. (Other ports of call include Alton Bay, Weirs Beach, and Center Harbor.) The vessel eases away from the waterfront park, and

M/V *Mount Washington,* **Lake Winnipesaukee**

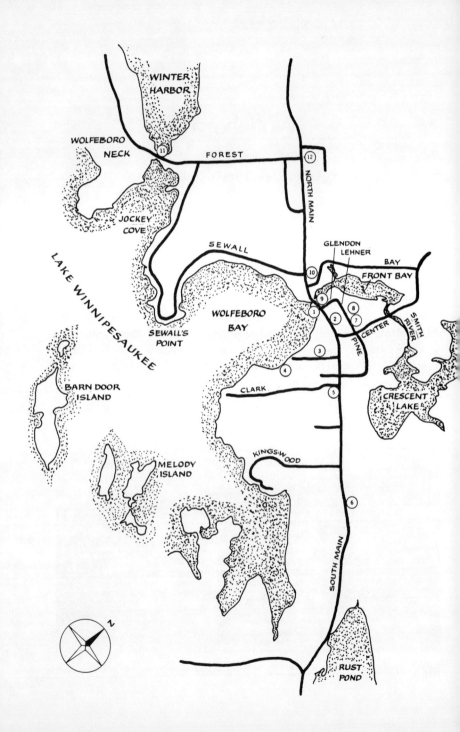

unfolds a splendid panorama of hills cradling what Whittier called the "mountain-sea."

North of town rises the encircling frame of the Ossipee Mountains, to the east slants the gentle slope of Copple Crown Mountain, and to the west the billowing folds of the Belknap Mountains stretch soft and blue to the horizon. And on the shore, the town nestled in a wooded lakeside hollow still earns the acclaim given it by Lady Wentworth: "Wolfeborough is a place to recover appetites. . . ."

Her husband, Governor John Wentworth, gave the town its reputation as America's oldest summer resort when he discovered in 1763 that his vice-regal quarters in Portsmouth lacked the invigorating summer freshness of Wolfeboro. On the northeast shore of Lake Wentworth he established a lavish 4,000-acre estate with servants' cottages, stables for his Arabian horses, mills, barns, shops, and storehouses.

His summer mansion boasted a ballroom and landscaped grounds with flower beds and lawns. Wentworth conducted agricultural experiments here to improve New Hampshire farming methods, and introduced new species of birds and fish to the region. The mansion and outbuildings burned to the ground in 1812; all that remains of colonial America's most extravagant summer home is a cellar hole. A nearby plaque explains its significance.

Cate Park

Visitors who haven't recovered all their appetites aboard *Mount Washington* might try a stroll through Cate Park's lovely grounds. Paths wind past maples and mountain ash, and across broad lawns stretching down to the water. It's a fine place to watch the sun ease behind lakeside hills, as sailboats glide through the gathering dusk. A local high school jazz band occasionally performs here to attentive audiences lounging on park benches or in boats moored offshore.

The Dockside Restaurant on a wharf adjacent to the park is a remodeled turn-of-the-century depot. From the 1880s to the 1920s, the Boston and Maine Railroad offered excursions from Boston to the lake district with connections here to *Mount Washington*.

Fishermen land bass and perch from the docks at the mouth of the Smith River. Salmon can be taken from ice breakup in spring to the end of May; lake trout are landed all year from deeper waters.

A stroll along South Main Street leaves the waterfront and climbs a gentle slope past the impressive **Town Hall** (2), with its Victorian flourishes, tower, and large clock. A Revere bell that once summoned students to class at Wolfeboro's Brewster Academy now tolls the hour. A canopy of elms shades the architectural interplay of the street's well-kept residences: Turreted Victorian homes stand beside comfortable bungalows, a graceful Congregational church, and handsome Federal houses with intricate fanlights.

Sixty-five acres of waterfront lawns dotted with trees and scored with walking paths inspire students at the **Brewster Academy** (3), founded in 1820 and one of New England's finest preparatory schools. In summer physicians from around the world hold research seminars on campus.

A stroll across the grounds leads to **Brewster Beach** (4), patrolled by a lifeguard. Winnipesaukee's waters average a comfortable 70° F. in summer.

Wide hemlock floorboards, massive hand-hewn oak beams, and gunstock corner posts enhance the **Clark House** (5), a 1778 Cape Cod-style dwelling with five fireplaces, period furniture, and a fine pewter collection. Special exhibits of paintings, glass, and pottery are sometimes held.

The house is decorated with many pieces of stick-leg, or Windsor, furniture, the most popular style in the colonies. It originated in seventeenth-century England (near the town of Windsor) and was first used in gardens and on verandas. Other folding and collapsible furniture in the house is based on designs dating back to the Middle Ages. The home and the adjacent refurnished Pleasant Valley Schoolhouse are maintained by the Wolfeboro Historical Society as a museum. *Open Mon.–Sat. July–Aug.*

Farther along South Main Street, past the golf course, is the **Kingswood Regional High School** (6), where the Wolfeboro Playhouse offers five weeks of musicals, dramas, comedies, and a special dinner theater package beginning in mid-July. Theater buffs should check at the information booth in the Chamber of Commerce on Main Street for performance schedules.

For just a taste of Wolfeboro, without strenuous uphill walking, try a circular tour from Cate Park down Center Street with its shops and businesses, then follow Lehner Street past **Father John's Pub** (7), noted, incidentally, for its steamed clams.

Beyond lies **Foss Playground** (8), with playing fields, public tennis courts, and a jungle gym for children more interested in climbing than walking.

Two four-story brick factory buildings that now house a lumberyard and an automotive shop were once thriving shoe factories.

A stroll along Glendon Street, with its stately colonial architecture and well-kept grounds, takes one through Wolfeboro's oldest and most gracious neighborhood.

The **Railroad Station** (9) has been restored by the Wolfeboro Railroad Club to its original condition, including a classic platform awning and gingerbread trim. Unfortunately, the fabled railroad that once skirted lakes, river, and forest on a twenty-four-mile round trip between Wolfeboro and Wakefield has been derailed until new owners are found. Those disappointed over its demise may find solace in the excellent fudge sold by a candy shop in the depot.

Walkers eager for more ambitious expeditions, with the reward of a dip in Winter Harbor at the halfway point, can hike over the bridge spanning the Smith River to the old colonial **Christian Church** (10), adorned with a traditional New England spire.

A four-mile round trip along what locals call the "Gold Coast" passes lavish homes, once summer cottages and now year-round residences, and also more modest modern accommodations set back amid pines, poplars, and beeches. Sewall Road offers occasional glimpses of sparkling Wolfeboro Bay through the trees.

Navy vessels were once built at a boatyard on Sewall's Point. Today visitors can stroll about the docks, look back toward the lawns and ivy-covered buildings of Brewster Academy, or watch pleasure craft scudding across the lake.

An island for every day of the year flecks seventy-two-square-mile Lake Winnipesaukee at the southern flank of the White Mountains. The islands sport colorful names like Barndoor and Melody; some 270 of them are inhabited.

A copy editor's nightmare (there are 130 spellings of Winnipesaukee) and a fisherman's dream, the lake's waters teem with trout, black bass, and a strange creature called the horned pout. Winnipesaukee is a nesting area for the common loon, a diving bird noted for its haunting call that can sound like a lonely wail, a frenzied laugh, or an eerie yodel. Mallard and merganser ducks and great blue herons also summer here.

Indian Beach (11), a short side trip on Forest Road, was once a portage that avoided a three-mile paddle around Wolfeboro Neck for Indians canoeing between Wolfeboro and Tuftonboro Neck farther west. There is a fine stretch of sandy beach on this narrow strip of land, plus a lifeguard and bathhouses.

A walk with a gentle uphill grade along Forest Road leads back to North Main Street and the **Lakeview Cemetery** (12), which marks the western extent of the original Wolfeboro colony. Nestled among early nineteenth-century graves is one large stone capped by a fez that recalls the touching story of a little girl who went down to Cate Park in the late 1920s to greet *Mount Washington,* which was chartered for an annual Shriners' convention. She captured more than a few hearts with her warm welcome to Wolfeboro. When she died of an unrecorded childhood illness, the Shriners commemorated their small friend with this tombstone.

A three-quarter-mile stroll down North Main Street affords views of the town, spread out below with its verdant streets and parks; and the tranquil waters that lap the shores of this peaceful village by the mountain sea.

New England Boiled Dinner

Early Americans relied on winter to keep meat fresh. Cows and pigs were slaughtered in late fall, then the meat was frozen out-of-doors. At winter's end the settlers had to turn to other means. Farmers smoked and salted pork, and made their own corned beef by burying great hunks of meat in stone crocks filled with brine. Though this home-made specialty was tasty, its color was less than appetizing: Instead of pink, the meat was grayish brown.

New England boiled dinner is a simple, hearty meal made of foods that were left after long winters—preserved meat and stored root vegetables—cooked in a single pot. Even though we now can keep next month's meal in a freezer, this is still a popular dish across the country.

To make boiled dinner, simmer a 4-pound brisket of corned beef about 4 hours. (Some cooks add ½ pound salt pork.) Remove the meat and cook the vegetables in the same water. Simmer for 30 minutes 3 parsnips, 6 carrots, 3 yellow turnips, and 4 onions. Add 6 potatoes and cook 15 minutes longer; add 1 head of cabbage cut in wedges and cook 15 minutes. Meanwhile, cook 10 beets separately so they don't color the whole dish. Reheat the meat, and serve it on a big platter surrounded by the vegetables.

Concord

Garrisons, Coaches, and a Restaurant in Jail

Strung along a terrace above a broad bend in the Merrimack River, tiny Concord boasts superlatives and influence far greater than its size: The New Hampshire capitol here houses America's largest state legislature; stagecoaches manufactured at the south end of Main Street were the most familiar vehicle on the western frontier; and a local lawyer became the only Granite Stater to reside at the White House.

This community of 34,500 also has more immediate and accessible attributes. As seat of state government, Concord boasts interesting architecture, a fine library and historical museum, and more cosmopolitan flair than most New England towns its size. A stroll along Main Street with a few side trips east and west reveals charming neighborhoods with historic homes and sites, the bustling capitol area, and the more sedate north end where a jilted lover's house still stands near a renowned tavern.

America's fourteenth President, **Franklin Pierce** (1), lived in this French Second-Empire-style house from his retirement in 1857 until his death in 1869.

A nearby plaque marks the site of the **Timothy Walker, Jr., Garrison** (2), one of seven log forts built in town to protect settlers from Indian raids. Another plaque farther along Main Street is at the site of the **George Abbott Garrison** (3). When Indians threatened, three gunshots sent settlers scurrying from the fields for cover in the garrisons. In those days even meetinghouses were fortified.

The **Capitol Shopping Center** (4) below Main Street hosts an Oktoberfest arts and crafts sale which features the works of forty-five skilled local artisans. The plaza is on the site of the Boston and Maine

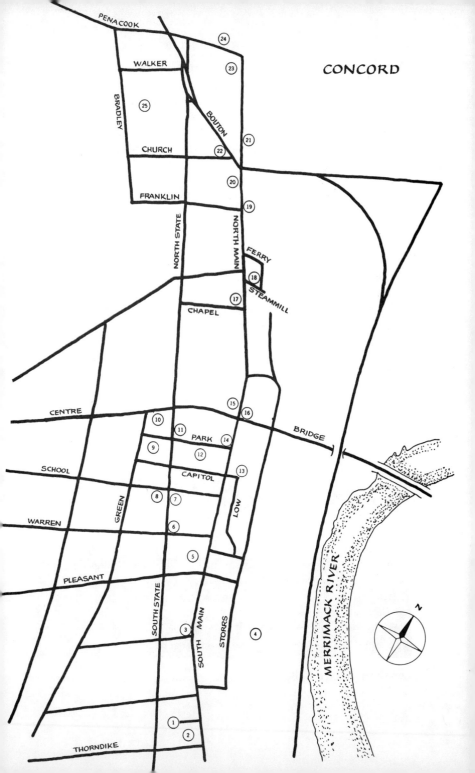

Railroad Station, once one of the largest buildings in northern New England. A 2½-acre train shed behind the three-story brick-and-granite structure was reputedly the longest ever built in America. The depot inspired the design for Grand Central Terminal in New York City.

Bicentennial Square (5), a former parking lot, has been renovated into a pedestrian mall with a fountain, brick sidewalks, and wrought-iron lampposts. Few patrons of Chuck's Steak House on the square sneak out without paying. This restaurant, housed in the former police station, offers meals in cells with barred windows and doors—usually left open. A magistrate's desk in the bar is now cluttered with condiments instead of writs and subpoenas. Narrow Warren Street, a quiet retreat lined with a bookstore, boutiques, and shops, is a contrast to nearby broad avenues.

The ninety-foot Romanesque tower of the **Central Fire Station** (6) looms above State Street. Completed in 1875, this imposing two-story firehouse has an attached barn where horses were once stabled.

Perhaps New Hampshire's finest Romanesque church is a massive symmetrical structure, stuccoed and scored to imitate marble. Pyramidal roofs cap twin bell towers. The 1856 **White Memorial Universalist**

Legislative Office Building

Church (7) overwhelms with arched doors, intricate corbeling, and recessed wall panels.

The more traditional spire of the First Baptist Church, Concord's oldest (1825), looms directly behind its later, more ostentatious neighbor.

Mary Baker Eddy donated funds for the **First Church of Christ, Scientist** (8), built across the street in 1903. Born in nearby Bow in 1821, Eddy founded Boston's First Church of Christ, Scientist, in 1879. She returned here in 1892.

Across the street from the State House is the **Legislative Office Building** (9), an eclectic Victorian structure built in 1889 as a post office and courthouse. Gothic windows and doorway arches pierce granite walls capped by steep roofs with delicate iron railings. *Open daily during legislative sessions.*

The **New Hampshire Historical Society** (10), founded in 1823, moved in 1912 into this large granite building designed by Guy Lowell. The front entrance is graced with a sculpture by Exeter's Daniel Chester French entitled "Ancient and Modern History." Many lovely examples of old New Hampshire furniture, silver, ceramics, and glassware are shown in changing exhibits. The Prentis Collection, compris-

New Hampshire Historical Society

ing four eighteenth-century period rooms, has displays of New England antiques and portraits that re-create the domestic surroundings of a wealthy colonial merchant. A restored 1853 Concord stagecoach is in a rotunda built of imported marble. On the second floor are Franklin Pierce's 1780 Chippendale slant-top desk used in his Concord law office, and the figurehead from the nineteenth-century Lake Winnipesaukee steamer *Lady of the Lake. Open Mon.–Fri. except holidays.*

The **New Hampshire State Library** (11), built in 1894, blends Beaux Arts classicism of smooth gray pilasters with rough Romanesque walls of red Conway granite. *Open Mon.–Fri.*

Built of native granite, the impressive **New Hampshire State House** (12) was completed in 1819 and is the oldest state capitol with original legislative chambers. In 1866 it was remodeled after the Hôtel des Invalides in Paris, and a cupola was replaced with a more elaborate gilded dome. In 1910 a third story was added. A six-foot copper eagle installed in 1957 replaced the original butternut bird, now in the historical society's museum.

The State House accommodates 424 legislators, the largest body of its kind in the United States. Senate chambers were painted in 1942 by New Hampshire's Barry Faulkner with murals depicting state history.

Franklin Pierce statue, New Hampshire State House

A collection of 157 portraits of New Hampshire notables hangs in offices and corridors. Old provincial and state regimental banners are displayed in the rotunda's Hall of Flags, along with a pine sculpture of Revolutionary general John Stark by Harry Donahue. Colorful dioramas by Dudley Moore Blakely depict pivotal moments in the War of Independence. A basement exhibit features birds and wildlife native to the state. *Open Mon.–Fri.*

A two-acre park in front of the capitol is dotted with statues of Daniel Webster, Franklin Pierce, John Stark, abolitionist senator John P. Hale, and a replica of the Liberty Bell. A Civil War memorial arch frames the capitol.

This park was thronged with six hundred people at a luncheon reception in 1825 for French Major General and Revolutionary War hero Lafayette. A commemorative elm was planted, since claimed by disease, and local bachelor barrister Philip Carrigain composed a spirited but awkward seven-stanza song sung to the tune of the Scottish ballad "Scots Who Ha' Wi' Wallace Bled." The homage to the aging, red-headed soldier was memorable only for a line that coined a nickname as enduring as the state's bedrock:

> *North and South, and East and West,*
> *A Cordial welcome have addressed,*
> *Loud and warm, the nation's guest,*
> *Dear son of Liberty . . .*
> *He comes, by fond entreaties moved,*
> *The Granite State to see.*

For more than a century, the Grecian Hall of the 1852 **Eagle Coffee House and Hotel (13)** was a social gathering spot of legislators, and resounded with festivities and dramatic entertainments. Guests included Andrew Jackson, Sam Houston, and Jefferson Davis. The hostelry now houses a convalescent center.

Laid out in 1726, Main Street acquired its red-brick character in the second half of the nineteenth century. The state house and a railroad boom inspired businessmen to replace fading wooden storefronts with dignified brick Victorian facades.

The only remaining Federal-style residence in downtown Concord was built in 1831 by lawyer Nathaniel G. Upham. The charming **Upham-Walker House (14)** has a fanlit doorway, square portico columns of local granite, and an arched gable window.

Two eighteenth-century forts once flanked Main Street. Concord's first white child was born in 1728 in the **Edward Abbott Garrison** (15). A plaque near the Elks Club identifies the site of the **Stickney Garrison** (16), which sheltered twenty families.

A stroll along Main Street beyond the business district passes the site of the town's first **blockhouse** (17), a crude log structure built in 1726. It served as church, town hall, and school until a larger meetinghouse was completed in 1751.

Franklin Pierce worked as a lawyer on the second floor of the 1826 **Merrimack County Bank Building** (18), long a Concord landmark. Designed by local architect John Leach, this brick structure with high recessed arches is a fine example of northern New England commercial Federal style. It now houses an insurance company.

Carrigain, the lawyer, map maker, and amateur poet who coined the state's nickname, built the imposing **Philip Carrigain House** (19) in 1791 for his intended, the daughter of a Dartmouth College president. She later jilted him, and Carrigain was forced to sell his mortgaged mansion. He died in poverty.

What is thought to be the **First Eagle Hotel** (20), John George prop., was a popular watering hole from 1814 to 1840. It now houses the headquarters of the League of New Hampshire Craftsmen.

Fronted by neatly trimmed shrubs and tall shade trees, the **Kimball-Jenkins House** (21) has a charming setting for one of the state's best preserved examples of late Victorian architecture. The tall, symmetrical 1883 dwelling with its brick-and-stone-trimmed walls took nine years to complete.

Across Main and Bouton streets, a plaque marks the site of a two-story **meetinghouse** (22) where state delegates ratified the U. S. Constitution. New Hampshire was the ninth, and key, state whose approval led to the adoption of the document.

The **Rev. Timothy Walker House** (23) was begun in 1733 by Concord's first minister, "a blue-eyed, portly parson" who packed a gun in the early years, even at the pulpit. He also erected a palisade around his home for the protection of nine nearby families from Indians.

The only Concord home owned by Franklin Pierce has been restored and furnished in 1840s style with many of the President's belongings. The **Pierce Manse** (24) also contains furniture from the estate of Lewis Downing, manufacturer of Concord coaches. *Open Mon.–Sat. June–mid-Sept.*

The **Old North Cemetery** (25) contains the tomb of Pierce and his immediate family. The President's eleven-year-old son was killed in a train wreck en route to Washington for his father's inauguration. Pierce returned here to bury his child, and became the only President to deliver an inaugural address extemporaneously.

A Cradle on Wheels That Won the West

In 1813 J. Stephen Abbott and Lewis Downing founded a carriage company in Concord with a box of tools and sixty dollars. By the end of the century one of their products had earned a worldwide reputation as the classic stagecoach that helped to open the American West.

The four-horse, nine-passenger vehicle owed its popularity and durability to superior suspension. Cowhide slings between front and rear axles gave the coach body a rocking, swaying motion over rough

Concord Stagecoach

western roads, unlike the jarring vertical movement of spring suspension. Mark Twain likened the stagecoach to "an imposing cradle on wheels."

Abbott and Downing's outfit supplied Wells Fargo with coaches during the Civil War, and sold thousands more throughout the world. Those shipped to South Africa had steel safes beneath the seats to transport gold and diamonds.

Manchester

Mill Yard of the Merrimack

Most people who drive through New Hampshire's largest city (pop. 96,000) on Interstate 89 are left with one overwhelming impression: the seemingly endless brick facade of a factory along the turbulent Merrimack River. This was the home of the Amoskeag Manufacturing Company, and those who forsake their car for a walking tour will find the remnants of a planned community that this industrial juggernaut laid out in 1838 with great taste and imagination.

Shade trees were planted along broad avenues that paralleled the river (Elm Street was renowned for its mile-long "forest"). Six parks were planned, two with ponds; land was set aside for churches, schools, and libraries. Perhaps most remarkable were the seventeen blocks of company housing. These rows of tenements can still be seen on the gentle slope up from the mills, and many have recently been renovated.

Planning an attractive community was important to Amoskeag, but the mills came first. By the 1880s they extended for three miles along a graceful curve of the Merrimack like the ramparts of some great industrial fortress. Canals, passages, and courtyards threaded a labyrinth of factories and machine shops.

At the height of its prosperity near the end of the nineteenth century, the company was the largest textile producer in the world, and along with its associated industries employed some 15,000 people, one third of Manchester's work force.

The tour begins at the power source for this industrial explosion, **Amoskeag Falls (1)**. At one time a series of rapids here thundered with a roar that could be heard a mile away. Today the cataracts are

MANCHESTER

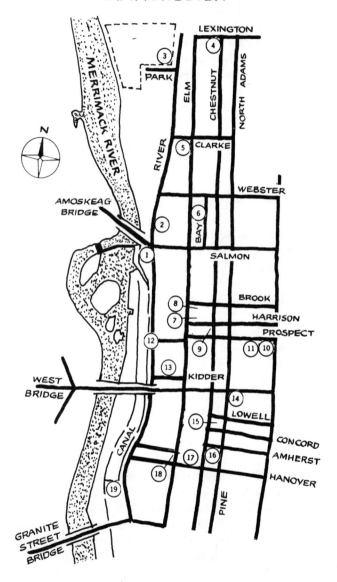

hidden behind a dam, but their former power can be judged by the city that grew up around them.

At the east end of the falls Archibald Stark built a house in 1737 to protect the fishing rights of New Hampshire settlers from Massachusetts poachers. The cataracts were a hindrance to navigation. A canal built in 1807 by Judge Samuel Blodgett bypassed the rapids and made the Merrimack navigable between Concord, New Hampshire, and Boston. The canal was obsolete by the 1850s with the advent of railroads.

Amoskeag Village, where Manchester's manufacturing began, was founded on the west side of the river near the present-day Holiday Inn. Woolen and cotton mills, machine shops, and workers' housing once lined the far bank of the Merrimack. An eight-hundred-foot-long covered toll bridge nicknamed Old Amoskeag stood here from 1856 to 1920. This arch-truss span had an advertisement from a local shoe store running its length to entice shoppers entering town from the north. The bluff at the east end of the bridge once stood twenty feet higher than today and was used for thousands of years by Indians as a fishing platform. Excavations here have uncovered storage pits and fire-cracked stones, possibly used for drying salmon in spring.

A wide variety of artifacts found at what is known as the **Smyth site** (**2**) indicate that several tribes used this riverbank as neutral territory during fishing season. Nearby is the Nevill archaeological site, once a continuation of the same Indian camping grounds. (Many items found here can be seen in Harvard's Peabody Museum.)

A verdant umbrella of maples, elms, and evergreens shades the grassy brow of a hill in **Stark Park** (**3**), a quiet retreat that was once part of John Stark's farm. A handsome equestrian statue of the Revolutionary hero by Richard H. Recchia dominates the hill's crest, which also affords fine views overlooking the river and the Uncanoonuc Mountains. A short walk north leads to a marker at the site of the general's house; its well can still be seen.

At the bottom of the knoll are the graves of Stark and his family, his wife, Elizabeth, usually known as Molly and immortalized in Stark's rallying cry at the Battle of Bennington: "There are the Redcoats, and they will be ours or tonight Molly Stark sleeps a widow." Always quick with a well-turned phrase, in 1809 Stark also contributed the command now on New Hampshire license plates: "Live free [from tyranny] or die." The rest of the vigorous quote: "Death is not the worst of evils."

An imposing mansion in Norman French château style houses the administration offices of **Notre Dame College** (4), a liberal arts school operated primarily for women by the Sisters of Holy Cross.

Notre Dame College

The red, two-story **Archibald Stark House** (5), built in 1737 by the father of the general, was moved here from near the falls in 1970. Surrounded by a white picket fence, this humble abode has period furnishing. *Open Wed. and Sun. mid-May–mid-Oct.*

Trees that etch leafy margins to the contours of Elm Street were planted in the nineteenth century by the Amoskeag company; many have succumbed to disease. Fine **Victorian residences** (6) here and on both sides of Chestnut and Bay streets were built by Amoskeag executives and transformed this area into one of the city's best neighborhoods.

An amphitheater with a ceiling painted to simulate a night sky

Archibald Stark House

serves as a meeting hall of the **Masonic Temple** (7), a classical structure designed by C. R. Whitcher. *Open Mon.–Fri.*

The handsome Italianate **Straw Mansion** (8) was once the home of
Governor Ezekiel Straw, a longtime agent of the Amoskeag company
who designed the master plan for Manchester. His estate included the
area occupied by the Masonic Temple and the nearby Christian Science Church.

Straw joined Amoskeag at age nineteen and for the next ten years
learned the trade—everything from building a dam to repairing a
loom. In 1844 he went to England, stole a method of printing patterns
on woolen fabrics from manufacturers there, and returned to corner
the American market. His son Herman followed in his footsteps at
the mill, as did his grandson William Parker. In fact, Straws supervised company operations from its inception to its closing.

Bald men built the **Herman Straw House** (9), now a funeral home.
This extravagant mixture of Gothic Victorian and Tudor was constructed about 1867 by one Mr. Tubbs, who made his fortune in hair
restoratives. A few years later the Amoskeag company purchased the
house for Herman Straw.

The **Currier Art Gallery** (10), one of New England's finest, is housed in a Renaissance-style limestone-and-marble building. Ground-floor displays are devoted mainly to decorative arts, and include excellent examples of eighteenth- and nineteenth-century New Hampshire furniture. Works by the elder and younger Reveres as well as Samuel Edwards, Jacob Hurd, and other colonial silversmiths are represented, along with Early American pewter and glassware.

On the upper floor an excellent collection of Flemish and Italian Renaissance paintings features Pietro Perugino's "Madonna and Child." Other canvases are by Monet, Homer, and Andrew Wyeth. Pablo Picasso's "Woman Seated in a Chair," painted in Nazi-occupied Paris in 1941, shows a subject depicted from several viewpoints. One of the most important works of sculpture here is Henri Matisse's "Seated Nude," number four in an edition of ten cast in 1925. *Open Tues.–Sun.*

North of the gallery, the Kennard House, built in 1868 by a Manchester businessman, now serves as the gallery's art school. To the west of the Currier is the lavishly Italianate 1872 **Alpheus Gay House** (11).

For walkers overcome with the urge to shop, a side trip leads to the **Pandora Factory Store** (12), a discount outlet for a renowned

Currier Art Gallery

clothing manufacturer. Hand-hewn beams can be seen inside this former locomotive works, renovated to its original condition. *Open daily.*

Amoskeag company housing (13) on both sides of Kidder Street between Elm and Canal streets recalls the appearance of Manchester in the late nineteenth century. Textile mill workers here may have thought themselves fortunate, lodged in the company's brick row houses and employed in a job that was far safer and cleaner than many other industries. But by today's standards hours and wages were exploitative. French-Canadians came here in the 1840s and replaced New England farm girls in the mills. The immigrants established their own society with French-language newspapers, schools, and clubs. This fragmentation, along with that caused by other ethnic groups, created a Canadian-style cultural mosaic in Manchester rather than an American melting pot, and prevented the city from becoming a cosmopolitan force in New Hampshire. Instead, its influence was measured in profits and payroll.

Maples and flower beds enhance the grassy confines of **Pulaski Park** (14), named for General Brygady Kazimierz Pulaski. This Revolutionary hero emigrated to America after Russia invaded Poland, and helped to found the American cavalry. An imposing equestrian statue of the general by Lucien Gosselin was unveiled in 1935.

Several important Manchester institutions are clustered around the former Concord Common, now known as **Victory Park** (15) for its World War I statue of winged victory by Gosselin. Just north of the common the 1869 St. Joseph's Cathedral and the 1860 Grace Church, designed by Richard Upjohn, face each other at the corner of Lowell and Pine streets. The Manchester Institute of Arts and Sciences at the corner of Concord and Pine is an art and music school with many exhibits, films, and concerts open to the public. *Open Mon.–Fri.* The Manchester Historic Association at the corner of Pine and Amherst is renowned for its fine collection of nineteenth-century fire-fighting equipment, along with tools, costumes, paintings and furniture from the Stark homestead. *Open Tues.–Sat.*

The **Manchester Opera House** (16) was considered the most elegant pleasure palace north of Boston when it opened in 1881. Edwin Booth and all three Barrymores once graced its stage. After showcasing glittering dramatic productions for two decades, it was converted to a movie theater.

The opera had dazzling competition, when in 1915 the 960-seat **Palace Theater** (17) opened with excellent acoustics and a bigger stage than most Broadway theaters. One of the nation's earliest air conditioners cooled patrons strolling amid potted palms during intermission in vaudeville revues. The New Hampshire Center for the Performing Arts restored and refurnished the theater in 1974; the Palace again offers musical, theatrical, and dance productions. *Open Tues.–Sat.*

Manchester's **City Hall** (18), designed by New Hampshire-born Edward Shaw, is older than the city; it was constructed in 1844 of local red brick (like the Amoskeag company buildings) the year before Manchester received its charter.

The **Amoskeag Manufacturing Company** (19) produced more than a mile of cotton cloth a minute during its heyday in the last half of the nineteenth century. Clattering shuttles are silent now; the mill yard, once a testament to unbridled industrial growth, has been altered in the decades since Amoskeag's decline. Although about twenty of the company's forty buildings remain, the distinctive narrow factories and the canal they lined are gone, changing the character of the yard completely. Monumental towers with complex brick corbeling and delicate iron railing are still intact, as is the impressive clock in the Jefferson mill building.

Founded in 1830, the company built its first mill in Manchester in 1838. Booming sales diversified the company. Not content merely to swathe the world in cotton, Amoskeag had its own printshop and machine shops, which manufactured locomotives and ornate fire engines. During the Civil War when the supply of southern cotton dried up, Amoskeag made Springfield rifles and filled a U. S. Government order for 4,000 American flags. When the company folded during the Depression, a citizens committee bought its buildings and began attracting new industries to the great mill yard on the Merrimack. Company housing at the south end of the yard and along the eastern side of Canal Street between the Amoskeag and Granite bridges dates from 1838 to 1914; many tenements have been renovated into attractive apartments.

The transformation of Amoskeag's buildings exemplifies the resiliency of one of the few planned towns to survive the company that nourished it.

Exeter

Seeds of History Along the Squamscott

The shire town of Rockingham County has several claims to fame: home of a prestigious preparatory school, birthplace of the Republican party, and site of a widely publicized UFO sighting in the 1960s dubbed "the incident at Exeter." But it also has a wealth of history, embodied in early taverns and fine Colonial, Federal, and Victorian homes. And although Exeter is one of New Hampshire's manufacturing centers, it has retained the quiet beauty of another era.

This town of 12,000 only eight miles from the ocean, was not so tranquil during the Revolutionary War. Then it was a hotbed of radicals. And since Portsmouth was too Tory and vulnerable to attack during those stormy years, Exeter functioned as the state capital. On January 5, 1776, the first constitution for popular government in the United States was adopted here along the marshy banks of the Squamscott.

In the heart of town the river is spanned by the **String Bridge** (1), which takes its name from the days when the bridge was a single log, or "stringer." A fish ladder between String and Great bridges helps salmon swim upstream to spawn.

The **Exeter Craft Center** (2), an outlet for the League of New Hampshire Craftsmen, displays and sells stoneware, pottery, wood furniture, and stained glass. *Open Mon.–Sat.*

The **Gilman Garrison** (3), the state's oldest dwelling on its original foundations, was built by John Gilman in the 1670s as a log house and fortification. In 1772 Gilman's grandson added clapboards and a wing in preparation for Governor John Wentworth's council meetings here.

EXETER

The sumptuous paneling and classic woodwork of the addition contrast with the rough-hewn log walls and puncheon floors of the original structure. Rooms in the new wing are furnished as they were in the late eighteenth century. Also displayed is a crude desk once used by Daniel Webster, who boarded here while a student at Phillips Exeter Academy. The Society for the Preservation of New England Antiquities, which restored the structure, has plans for a "homespun approach" to the museum, including live demonstrations of colonial domestic skills, occasional seventeenth-century banquets with period food and costumes, and community events. *Open Tues., Thurs., Sat., and Sun. May–end of Oct.*

Gilman Garrison House

The **Exeter Town Hall** (4) was originally a courthouse, as shown by a statue of justice atop the cupola. A plaque at the intersection of Court and Front streets is on the site of the original **Town House** (5), a 1732 building flanked by stocks and a whipping post "erected in the most public position as a terror to evildoers." The state's 1776 constitution was signed here.

The **Congregational Church** (6), completed in 1801, was the first in the state to blend Georgian refinements with meetinghouse style. The hipped roof, cornices, and Doric pilasters and entablatures are all noteworthy; a tower over the entrance supports a fine octagonal belfry and dome. A Palladian window can be seen at the rear of the second story. *Open daily.*

A plaque at **Gorham Hall** (7) commemorates the 1853 founding of the Republican party here by Exeter lawyer Amos Tuck, who later became a supporter and personal friend of Lincoln. (Others consider Ripon, Wisconsin, the birthplace of the GOP for an 1854 meeting in which Free-Soilers, Whigs, and dissident Democrats joined to denounce an act to extend slavery into free territory.)

The **Exeter Historical Society** (8) is housed in an 1831 brick bank building. Well proportioned with its arched, recessed doorway balancing two Dutch-style gables and chimneys at either end, the structure appears today very much as it did when completed. The historical society's museum contains artifacts and documents relating to the town's past, including a 1638 document between settlers and Squamscott Indians, who ceded land hereabouts but retained fishing rights at the falls. Chief Wehanownowit signed with his totem, or mark. *Open Tues. and Thurs. afternoons June–Aug.; Tues. afternoons Sept.–May, and by appointment.*

Strains of music waft over Exeter's busiest intersection on summer nights when bands perform at **Swasey Pavilion** (9). This bandstand has delicate columns supporting a roof whose intricate mosaic ceiling was designed by Henry Bacon. Copper lions' heads spout rainwater; a floor inlaid with signs of the zodiac reflects the astrological bent of industrialist Ambrose Swasey, who donated funds for the pavilion.

A riverbank path behind Water Street stores begins between Lopardo's and Haley's (watch for traffic), and leads to a machine shop that once housed Exeter's **Academy boathouse** (10). Visitors can often see the rhythmic rise and fall of oars propelling skulling shells, like giant water bugs, along the Squamscott. Those more interested in fishing than walking can drop a line here or farther north at the **Swasey Parkway Landing** (11). Between nibbles look across the river north of Clemson Fabrics, Inc., housed in an 1825 brick mill building; a square brick structure with a peaked roof there is a 1771 **powder house** (12) which held gunpowder manufactured at an Exeter mill during the Revolution.

The **Water Street parking lot** (13) is peaceful now, except for the odd careless driver, but in 1734 it was the site of the Mast Tree Riot. Colonials dressed as Indians clashed with royal forest inspectors who came to town to ensure no tall white pines fit for navy masts were cut for other purposes. Exeter men threw the scoundrels out of Gilman Tavern, which once stood here, scuttled their boats and cut the sails. The inspectors walked back to Portsmouth.

The owners of what is now **Cincinnati Memorial Hall** (14) believed in bringing their work home. Town sheriff Nathaniel Ladd built his two-story home in 1721 with two rooms flanking a central hall. In 1752 Colonel Daniel Gilman added a more elaborate porch and two great fireplaces, and covered the brick walls with clapboard. During the Revolution, state treasurer Nicholas Gilman, Daniel's son

Cincinnati Hall

and Ladd's cousin, turned one room into his office, where bills were
paid and currency signed to make it legal tender. He kept receipts in
a black iron chest, still in the refurnished room along with its huge
key. The vault is open (but empty). Also displayed is a 1752 table
and Gilman family possessions such as a sampler, a coat of arms, and
Nicholas Gilman's draft copy of the constitution from the 1787 federal
convention. The building is now owned by the Society of Cincinnati.
Open Tues., Thurs. May–Oct.

The society was formed by Revolutionary War officers in 1783 at
Folsom Tavern (15), built in 1775 and now owned by the group.
George Washington stopped here in 1789.

The **Exeter Public Library (16)**, fronted by Civil War memorials,
has works such as "Crossing the Brook," by Exeter-born Elizabeth
Gardner Bouguereau. *Open Mon.–Sat. Oct.–mid-June; Mon.–Fri.
mid-June–Sept.*

The 1735 **Nathaniel Gilman House (17)**, named for a son of state treasurer Nicholas Gilman, is now the home of the Phillips Academy principal.

The campus of Phillips Exeter Academy on both sides of Front Street is a pleasing blend of Georgian brick, white clapboard, and modern architecture. In spring the grounds are abloom with sweet-smelling lilacs; students with books in hand amble off to classes, while others jog to athletic fields south of Front Street. The students infuse the community with infectious energy and enthusiasm. Many of their cultural, social, and sporting events are open to the public; lectures and concerts are held most Sunday evenings. The academy was founded in 1781 by John Phillips, a Harvard graduate at age sixteen who also sponsored a school with his brother at Andover, Massachusetts. Its teaching is based on the Harkness classroom: Twelve to fourteen students and a teacher engage in Socratic discourse.

The **Academy Building** (18), with its handsome white cupola topped by a ship weather vane to recall Exeter's shipbuilding days, is one of the main classroom structures. It contains Assembly Hall, where musical and cultural events are held for students and townspeople.

Crafty architects discovered a design to increase student art appreciation: They put Lamont Gallery in **Alumni Hall** (19) above the cafeteria. There are student art exhibitions, along with workshops and studios.

Across from the gallery is the **First Academy Building** (20), a 1783 clapboard dwelling where the first class of fifty-six attended their lessons. It is now the dean's residence. **Fisher Theater** (21), the academy's center for the performing arts, has a four-hundred-seat hall where concerts and plays are held, many open to the public.

The **academy library** (22), designed by Louis I. Kahn and dedicated in 1971, includes more than books: Concerts are held in Michael Rockefeller Hall, poetry readings in McConnell Fiction Lounge. The Lamont Special Collection has early American maps and documents including a 1776 copy of the New Hampshire constitution, considered the first document of a state government. *Open daily.*

Sixteen lovely acres of shrubs, trees, and lawns laced with footpaths were once the grounds of the **Robinson Female Seminary** (23), a private girls' school founded in 1867. They now form a park.

A historic district lined with venerable homes extends along Front Street between the city center and Gale Park. The **Edward Tuck House** (24), the street's oldest residence (1730), is named for a phi-

Gale Park

lanthropist and son of Amos Tuck. Edward donated funds for the nation's first business school, at Dartmouth College, the New Hampshire Historical Society, and many Exeter institutions.

George Whitfield preached his last sermon from a pulpit built of planks and hogsheads in front of a tavern, now the **Thing-Lovering House (25)**. This leader of the Great Awakening, a religious revival that swept the American colonies in 1740–45, died in Newburyport, Massachusetts, the following day. (The present owners didn't want a gravestonelike marker commemorating the event in their front yard, so it was placed next door in front of an 1857 Baptist parsonage.)

Abraham Lincoln was entertained at the 1853 **Tuck-Nelson Home (26)**, while visiting his son Robert at the academy in 1860.

Across from the Exeter Inn is the **Moses-Kent House (27)**, built in 1868 for wool merchant Deacon Henry Moses. The lovely landscaped grounds were designed by Frederick Law Olmsted, who also laid out the Boston Common.

A war memorial in leafy **Gale Park (28)** was sculpted in 1922 by Exeter's Daniel Chester French, whose work includes the Lincoln Memorial in Washington and the Minute Man statue in Concord, Massachusetts.

The **Winter Street Cemetery (29)** has seen better days. Originally the Gilman family plot, this graveyard was donated to the town in 1743 and used for about a century. It contains the remains of the illustrious Gilman and Folsom clans.

A hatter named **Jeremiah Leavitt (30)** built a tavern/hat shop here about 1744. The tavern was later headquarters for the "White Cap Society," a group of prominent citizens who skulked about town at night digging for buried treasure. They had been duped by a con man and "became heartily ashamed of themselves and prayed that their folly might never be mentioned."

All that remains of the **town pound (31)**, moved here in 1793 from where Swasey Pavilion now stands, is a low enclosure of granite blocks.

"A Thankless Job at the Village Zoo"

Most early New England towns were clustered around a central green where livestock grazed during the day. By the early 1700s this communal pasturing led to innumerable damage suits when animals wandered into neighboring fields and gardens.

The practice was ended, and towns constructed corrals on the outskirts to impound strays until owners paid a fine. These enclosures were usually built with thick granite walls "horse high, bull strong, and hog tight."

But not farmer-proof. Owners sometimes reclaimed their stock on dark nights and liberated other animals along with their own. Poundkeepers, who were paid a percentage of the fines, were not above opening pasture gates and rounding up strays when business was slow.

Guarding these menageries was a thankless task. Poundkeepers paid for fodder and had to contend with stray hogs, wild horses, and irate bulls (and their owners).

In some communities the job went to the most recently married man, determined at that year's town meeting; in others the post was made an apprenticeship for aspiring politicians.

Portsmouth

Lone Port on a Brief Shore

In 1630 eighty colonists aboard *Pied Cow* landed on the banks of the Piscataqua River. They were looking for sarsaparilla, believed to have medicinal properties; instead they found strawberries, their first fresh food in three months. They settled here in lush riverbank meadows, and named their colony Strawbery Banke for its profusion of fruit. Today, the strawberries are gone (the colonists never did find sarsaparilla) but this area in downtown Portsmouth retains much of its prosperous colonial atmosphere.

The centerpiece of New Hampshire's only seaport is **Strawbery Banke (1)**, a ten-acre restoration dotted with the homes of sea captains, merchants, and craftsmen; many of the buildings are on their original sites. A reception center welcomes visitors to the Banke with a film and information on activities. *Open daily May–Oct.*

Meander along narrow cobbled streets where militia and fife-and-drum corps occasionally parade, then wander into almost any rustic dwelling or shop and discover a wealth of activities.

A silversmith works his trade in the James Marden House (c. 1700), and traditional salt-glaze stoneware is fired in the Hutchins House (c. 1810). The hammer rings in the Dinsmore Blacksmith Shop (c. 1800), while a spinet maker produces melodious instruments in the Deacon Penhallow House. (Prudence Penhallow's "Penny Shop" here was once patronized by John Paul Jones.) Ralph Lowell, a seventh-generation member of a boat-building family, supervises construction of rowboats, skiffs, and seven types of dories at the Boat House.

A shallow tidal creek here called Puddle Dock was once lined with

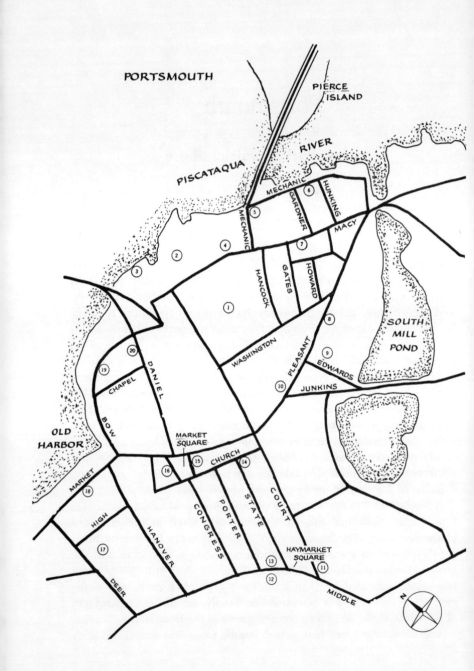

Governor Goodwin Mansion, Strawbery Banke

homes, shops, and warehouses. The region decayed and the waterway was filled in about 1900 when nearby residents complained of the mud flat's noxious odors. Perhaps it was the area's nocturnal activities that turned up noses: At that time this was Portsmouth's red-light district with flophouses, saloons, and dance halls. The dock's warehouses and wharves are now outlined in stone.

The "Earl of Halifax public house" sounded a bit too Loyalist during the Revolution, so its proprietor renamed it the William Pit Tavern after a British statesman with colonial sympathies. The 1776 alehouse is being restored.

Notable dwellings restored with period furnishings and open to visitors line the restoration. Outstanding workmanship and detailed wood carvings characterize the Captain Keyran Walsh House on Washington Street. This Federal "double house" is one dwelling with two chimneys and a central hall.

The 1762 Chase House on Court Street, a handsome mid-Georgian structure with unusual exterior lines, has ornate doorways and impressive woodwork in several rooms. The 1785 Daniel Webster House on Hancock Street has an unusual roof hipped at one end and gabled at the other where a two-story addition was once attached. The great orator and statesman rented this unpretentious dwelling in 1814–16.

Visitors to the Thomas Bailey Aldrich Memorial on Court Street might recognize this 1790 residence as the Nutter House in Aldrich's *The Story of a Bad Boy* (1868). First editions of the author's books and his autographed letters are displayed, along with fine silver.

Lovely **Prescott Park** (2), a waterfront garden filled with flowers and shrubs typical of colonial America, is the scene of uncolonial activities such as picnics, a children's art festival, and dance and music productions. Theater-by-the-Sea, Portsmouth's resident professional troupe, performs at the park in summer, and the rest of the year at their theater in a restored Bow Street warehouse. Boat tours of Portsmouth harbor leave three times daily from the park.

John Paul Jones reputedly outfitted his sloop *Ranger* in 1777 at the **Sheafe Warehouse** (3), a carefully restored 1709 wooden building. It now contains a fine collection of ship models and folk art relating to Portsmouth's maritime heritage. *Open daily June–mid-Sept.*

The **Liberty Pole** (4), a 110-foot staff of Oregon pine, commemorates the unfurling of a banner in 1776 to protest the Stamp Act. A 3½-foot-tall wooden eagle and a carved wooden shield made in 1857 decorate the mast.

Just beyond Prescott Park is Portsmouth's oldest cemetery, known as **Point of Graves** (5). This half-acre plot was donated in 1671 by Captain John Pickering, who was granted exclusive permission "to pasture his neat cattle there." It contains a fine collection of early slate gravestones, including one monument to Tobias Lear, George Washington's personal secretary. A chart near the entrance locates the markers of various stonecutters.

A lovely waterfront stroll along Mechanic Street passes weathered fishing shacks overlooking the broad harbor, busy with dories, pleasure boats, and gunmetal-gray cutters from the navy yard.

The dockside is graced by the **Wentworth-Gardner House** (6), a splendid example of Georgian architecture. Its fifteen-paneled doorway is crested with gilded pineapples, traditional symbols of hospitality. This mansion was presented in 1761 to the nephew of the last royal governor as a wedding present from his mother. Three master carvers are said to have toiled for eighteen months on the interior trim alone. Outstanding cornices, medallions, and fluted pilasters can be seen

Fish pier

throughout the house. One of its owners, the Metropolitan Museum of Art, wanted to move this masterpiece to Central Park. *Open Tues.–Sun. May–Oct.*

Rev. Samuel Haven dug soil rich in nitrate from beneath his **Old South Meeting House (7)**, and extracted saltpeter to make gunpowder during the Revolutionary War. The Strawbery Banke Chamber Music Players perform here Saturday and Sunday evenings in summer. *Open daily.*

In 1775 patriots in pursuit of Loyalist Captain John Fenton gathered in front of the **Governor John Wentworth House (8)** and threatened to blow up New Hampshire's last royal governor along with his dwelling if he didn't hand over the Tory rebel hidden within. Fortunately, Wentworth was persuaded by a cannon, delivered Fenton, and preserved his 1763 mansion for our enjoyment.

Nearby **Haven Park** (9) is a shady enclosure of oaks, maples, cedar, and pine.

In 1789 George Washington remarked that his host had "the handsomest house in Portsmouth," no mean compliment considering the fine residences in this prosperous town. Built in 1784, the **Governor Langdon Mansion** (10) has a striking Chinese Chippendale balustrade crowning the roof and a front portico graced by four Corinthian columns. Inside are fine carved paneling and period furnishings. Landscaped grounds are brightened with flower gardens tucked amid shrubs and stately trees. *Open Tues.–Sat. June–Oct.*

Along Middle Street are some of New England's finest residences, including the three-story **Pierce House** (11), a Federal-style mansion with elaborate woodwork. Its central hallway has an elliptical stairway climbing two flights in a graceful spiral. Crossed dueling swords of some owner's distant ancestors hang on the wall. The house is now owned by the Middle Street Baptist Church, to which it is attached, and is used as an education center. *Open Mon.–Fri.*

Just off Haymarket Square, where hay was sold as far back as 1755, is the **Portsmouth Public Library** (12), housed in a red brick building. The attached Benedict House was built about 1800. *Open daily.*

From the window of a Portsmouth home, John Paul Jones could see his seventy-four-gun sloop of war *America* being built in 1782 on Badger's Island in Portsmouth Harbor. On a visit in 1777 Jones had supervised construction of the eighteen-gun *Ranger,* the first vessel to fly the Stars and Stripes on the high seas. The noble banner was made from the silk dresses of Portsmouth's young ladies (a wedding gown provided the white stripes). The 1758 **John Paul Jones House** (13) contains period furniture, china, and silver. Guides in colonial costumes conduct tours of the house, including Jones's bedroom, where a model of *Ranger* is displayed. *Open Mon.–Sat. June–mid-Oct.*

A stroll toward downtown passes the 1826 **South Church** (14), where records dating back to 1714 are displayed. A bell cast by the Revere foundry in Boston summons worshipers.

The massive white steeple of the **North Church** (15), decorated with elaborate ornamentation and a clock, towers above the busy intersection at Market Square. Daniel Webster was a church warden here in 1815–16.

The 1805 **Portsmouth Athenaeum (16)** across the square contains rare books, pamphlets, and manuscripts. Its reading room, lit by arched windows, is decorated with paintings of Portsmouth's early days. A collection of ship models includes *Clovis,* carved in full rig from whalebone, and a 1749 model of H.M.S. *America. Open Thurs.*

Fourteen houses (half of them built before or during the Revolution) have been relocated and restored on **The Hill (17)** as offices. The buildings are grouped around a courtyard and connected with brick sidewalks. The 1770 Richard Shortridge House is now a senior citizens' home.

Overlooking the Old Harbor area is the **Moffatt-Ladd House (18),** a superb 1763 Georgian structure modeled after Captain John Moffatt's home in Hertfordshire, England. Surrounded by a picket fence, this house is noted for its richly ornamented stair hall and original "Bay of Naples" wallpaper, printed in Paris in 1815. William Whipple, a signer of the Declaration of Independence, lived here from

Moffatt-Ladd House

1768 to 1785. A countinghouse (1830) and coach house are on the property.

The oldest English garden in its original form (1763) descends behind the house in four lush terraces shaded by fruit trees. A path wanders through a vegetable garden, past a terrace fragrant with damask roses and a broad bed of candidum lilies to the lower grassy level lined with beehives. The house is now owned by the Society of Colonial Dames of New Hampshire. *Open Mon.–Sat. mid-June–mid-Oct.*

Nearby Ceres Street is a quaint harborside thoroughfare with narrow sidewalks and restored brick buildings that house taverns, shops, and offices. Lining the piers are tugboats, their smokestacks emblazoned with giant "P's," their sides battered from thousands of pushing and shoving matches.

Tugboats, Portsmouth Harbor

The handsome 1808 **St. John's Church** (19), focal point of the waterfront, contains a bell captured at Louisbourg, Nova Scotia, in 1745 and recast by Paul Revere in 1807. Also displayed is a chair in which George Washington sat while attending services here in 1789 (other pew owners included Benjamin Franklin and Daniel Webster), and a 1717 "Vinegar Bible" (one of four in America) printed in Oxford, England. (An editorial error substituted "vinegar" for "vineyard" in the Parable of the Vineyard.) A Brattle pipe organ, imported from England prior to 1708, is the oldest such instrument in the United States. It is exhibited in its mahogany case. *Open daily.*

A graveyard behind the church contains fine slate stones, including an early urn-and-willow design on the marker of Elizabeth Turner (d. 1790). Just down the street Theater-by-the-Sea offers productions staged in its converted warehouse.

The **Macphaedris-Warner House** (20), one of the most magnificent brick town houses in America, is protected with lightning rods installed in 1762 under the supervision of Benjamin Franklin. Built in 1716 by Scottish merchant Archibald Macphaedris, the house is decorated with unusual and eclectic frescoes depicting Governor Phipps on a charger, a lady at a spinning wheel, and Isaac and Abraham. On a stair landing are murals showing two of the Indian sachems (chiefs) presented to Queen Anne in 1710. The woodwork is outstanding, particularly the marbleized paneling in the dining room. The house is furnished with period pieces, including fine portraits of the Warner family by Joseph Blackburn. *Open daily mid-May–mid-Oct.*

MAINE

Serrated by surf-scoured granite headlands, Maine's coastline twists and turns for 3,500 miles, though by air it's only 320 miles from Kittery northeast to Quoddy Head, where the sun first shines on America each morning. Sailors coasting downwind from Boston gave the battered shore its nickname, "Down East."

This rock-bound realm nurtures a hardy people, renowned for a taciturnity occasionally broken for a dollop of salty humor or an odd pronunciation. The state's northernmost coastal town, Calais, becomes "Callus" on Maine lips, and a charming resort called "Bah Habah" perches on the rocky shoulder of Mount Desert Island, which sounds like an after-dinner treat, not a sandy wasteland.

Both natives and tourists treasure the beauty of this region, first seen by Champlain in 1604. Originally part of Massachusetts, Maine achieved statehood in 1820 and began a half century of unbridled growth nurtured by maritime trade.

A third of Maine's one million people live within smelling distance of the sea, and ninety percent of the state's vast interior is forested, much of it wilderness. The backwoods of New England's last frontier fuel a $1.2-billion-a-year pulp and paper industry. The capricious Gulf of Maine also yields a bounteous catch. Mud flats north of Wiscasset abound in clams; their harvest was once called "Down East welfare" because it traditionally supplemented the incomes of Mainers.

An independent lot, most Down Easters would rather rely on a humble mollusk than government handouts. "Hard to tell who's more meddlesome," they say, "politicians in Augusta or Washington." These self-reliant folk prefer to look to their own ample resources.

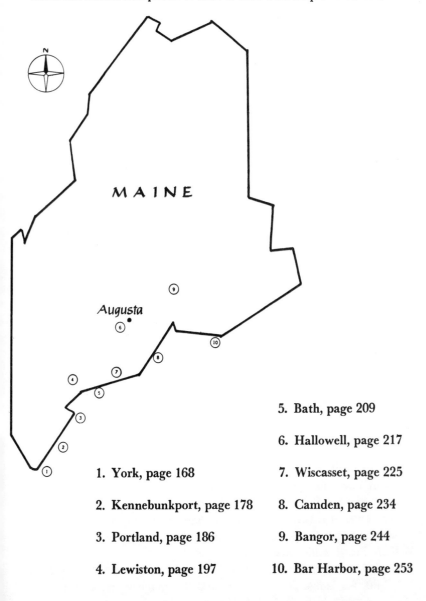

MAINE

Augusta

York

Wayside Along the Old Post Road

America's first chartered city (1641) was named Gorgeanna for Sir Ferdinando Gorges, an English colonizer who once owned much of what is now Maine. Many settlers of this village (it was a city in name only) were English prisoners who chose to remain here when they became freemen.

Today, this peaceful coastal community is known as York, but its captivating charm remains. Many summer residents would gladly serve year-round terms near its broad white beaches. Excellent fishing and boating abound, and the town is unmistakable for its quiet historical aura. Almost every street has eighteenth-century homes, many occupied by descendants of the original owners. The village green, shaded by tall elms planted in 1753, is the heart of historic York village. America's second church (after Jamestown, Virginia) was built here about 1636. The **First Parish Congregational Church** (1) was built in 1747, and has been remodeled often. Its steep roof line and a weathercock atop the spire are two of the original details.

That venerable New England institution, the town meeting, was held here until recently in the **Town Hall** (2). This renovated 1734 structure now contains municipal offices.

The adjacent **Benjamin Stone House** (3) was built in 1720 as a tavern. Later it was the home of Dr. Alexander Bulman, who accompanied colonial troops to Louisbourg, Nova Scotia, in 1745 as Sir William Pepperrell's physician.

Beyond the Civil War monument are the handsome **Coventry Hall** (4), built for Judge David Sewall, and the **Emerson Homestead** (5),

YORK

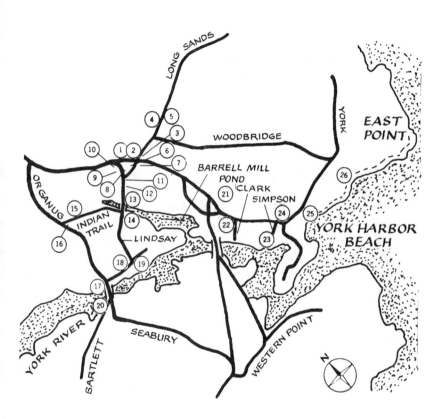

another venerable nineteenth-century dwelling with a widow's walk. This residence once operated as Woodbridge Tavern. John Adams, a circuit judge here in 1770–74, was a frequent guest. Paul Dudley Woodbridge specialized in "entertainment for the sons of liberty."

The 1740 **Emerson-Wilcox House** (6) won't have to move for a while—a parish lease for its lot expires in 759 years. This former home, post office, and tavern (its cook also fed inmates of a jail across the street) is now furnished with antiques. The central fireplace has an unusual passageway formed by the flues of six chimneys. *Open late May–Sept.*

On a knoll overlooking the green is the **Old Gaol** (7), the oldest royal public building still in use in America (1720). This brick-and-wood structure, which looks more like a barn than a jail, is now a museum. Its rooms are furnished with period pieces, including the jailkeeper's elegant dining room and his even more luxurious bedroom. The more austere dungeons have windows barred with saw blades and contain instruments of punishment such as manacles, leg chains, and thumbscrews. In a tiny second-floor attic, a bored prisoner named Edward Grant neatly carved into the floor the numbers one to twenty and the year of his confinement for assault and battery: 1846. *Open daily mid-June–end of Sept.*

A classic New England setting makes the **Old Burying Ground** (8) one of the most attractive cemeteries in Maine. Enclosed by a stone wall, this triangular graveyard has many well-preserved slate markers, including the elaborate headstone of Jonathan Sayward (d. 1797). A huge boulder here caps the grave of Mary Nasson (d. 1774). Local legend told that this woman had been executed for witchcraft, and the boulder prevented her troubled soul from leaving its worldly confines. The truth, however, is more prosaic: Nasson's husband installed the boulder to protect the grave from roaming livestock before the fence was built around the cemetery.

Jefferds Tavern (9), a colonial watering hole built in 1750, is now a museum. In front of this austere red building is a 1765 granite milestone from the Old Post Road between Boston and Portland—a marker for the tavern's days as a stagecoach stop. The mileage inscription—"B81, P11 and ⅞"—means 81 miles to Boston and 11⅞ miles to Portsmouth. Hostesses in period costumes account for much of Jefferds' charm. Ruffled lace caps, aprons, and billowing hoopskirts allow visitors effortless transitions to the eighteenth century. The hostelry smells of wood seasoned with a century of guests, including notables such as France's Louis Philippe and Prince Charles Maurice de Talleyrand in the 1790s. A paneled taproom has a horseshoe-shaped wicker chair by the hearth and massive dark tables scarred by years of use (one of them is an original). The tavern's five fireplaces, which converge in a central chimney, originally enclosed a five-by-nine-foot secret refuge that secreted inhabitants during Indian raids.

The tavern's vast kitchen, or "keeping room," extends the width of the building and centers around a huge hearth with beehive and reflector ovens. Colonial hardware displayed includes ironware, pewter, whale-oil lamps, and tole candle lanterns. A partitioned section of the kitchen was once a dairy shop where milk and butter were sold.

An upstairs parlor, or "retiring room," is decorated with murals of York scenes—the First Parish Church, Sewall's Bridge, and the John Hancock wharf—painted by York's Adelle Ells in the early nineteenth-century style of itinerant artist Rufus Porter. Furnishings include a cradle for two, a wooden baby walker, and a 1784 chest with a secret compartment that served as the family safe. *Open daily end of May–mid-Sept.*

A schoolmaster and pupils in colonial costume welcome visitors to the restored 1745 **Old Schoolhouse** (10), perhaps the oldest in Maine. This simple saltbox has also served as a tool shed and a chicken coop in its day. *Open daily end of May–mid-Sept.*

Along Lindsay Road, once part of the King's Highway and later the Boston-Portland Old Post Road, are the 1727 **Hugh Holman House** (11), named for a soldier in the Louisbourg expedition, and the 1719 **Nicholas Sewall House** (12), whose namesake established a tannery on this site.

A **parsonage** (13) built in 1699 for Rev. Samuel Moody is near the site of York's second church (1667). Barrell Mill Pond, once known as Meeting House Creek, was dammed in 1726 to power a sawmill. Nearby is the site of the first house in York, built in 1630 by the town's founder, **Edward Godfrey** (14).

Beyond several modern dwellings on Indian Trail is the **General Jeremiah McIntire House** (15), built in 1737. Another colorful York legend has it that the general used to ride his horse onto the front porch. Apparently, hoofprints are still visible to those with keen eyesight (or vivid imaginations).

On the corner is the 1785 **Dr. Job Lyman House** (16), once occupied by York's leading nineteenth-century citizen, Nathaniel Grant Marshall. He developed the town as a summer resort.

For adventurous walkers, a hike on Organug Road past a country club leads to the tidal York River, spanned here by **Sewall's Bridge** (17). It is an approximate replica of the world's first pile drawbridge, built in 1761 by Major Samuel Sewall. This engineer invented a trip-hammer to drive piles deep into the bed of the turbulent York River. (He used the same technique to span the Charles River in Boston.) Once part of the King's Highway, the bridge now affords an excellent fishing platform. River cruises can be arranged here.

A side trip along the riverbank leads to the **George Marshall Coun-**

try Store (18), once the commercial center of York and now a wharf-side museum and shop. The original New England country-store flavor has been retained along with traditional craft items such as pewter, tin, and wooden dinnerware. *Open daily June–mid-Sept.*

The **John Hancock Warehouse** (19), owned by the patriot at the time of his death in 1793, is now a museum that re-creates the atmosphere of a colonial commercial building. Exhibits on the second floor reflect early life on the York River with photographs of early fishermen, model ships, and a replica of a batteau. Steps lead down to the original Hancock wharf. *Open daily mid-June–end of Sept.*

John Hancock Warehouse

The central part of the **Elizabeth Perkins House** (20) was built in 1626 and survived an Indian raid in 1692 when most of York's buildings were burned. The front section was added in 1732. The windows throughout the house have protective "Indian shutters," which close from the inside. The Victorian furnishings belonged to the last owner, Elizabeth Perkins, who bequeathed the house to the Society for the Preservation of Historic Landmarks, which she founded. *Open daily July–mid-Sept.*

Elizabeth Perkins House

The **Sayward House** (21) was built about 1719 by Jonathan Sayward, a wealthy merchant who commanded *Seaflower* during the capture of Louisbourg in 1745. His booty included candlesticks, end irons, tableware, and brass tongs, all of which now furnish his mansion. His granddaughter Sally Sayward Barrell (also known as Madam Wood) was born here in 1759. She was one of the first authors to adopt an "American" style of writing. *Open Tues., Thurs., and Sat. June–mid-Sept.*

Next door is **Market Place** (22), established as a center of local trade in 1642 by a decree from Sir Ferdinando Gorges, who also proclaimed that two annual fairs be held "forever" on St. James' and St. Paul's days. Time ended, according to this schedule, in the early 1700s when the last market fair was celebrated.

Boats can be chartered for cruises or fishing expeditions at York's colorful **Waterfront (23)** between Simpson and Clark lanes. Visitors can watch fishing fleets return to the harbor at about 4 P.M. Dockside anglers land flounder, striped bass, and harbor pollock, particularly when the tide comes in.

Along York Street is the 1795 **Job Wells House (24)**, onetime residence of Revolutionary War hero Captain James Donnell.

A half-mile crescent of sand at **York Harbor Beach** (25) offers safe swimming and relaxing sunbathing. Lovely summer homes are perched along the rocky shore. The Agamenticus Yacht Club sponsors sailboat races three times a week, and small craft can be rented.

The **Marginal Way** (26) between York Harbor Beach and East Point skirts ocean bluffs and rocky ledges wet with spindrift, headlands pounded by surf, and pines twisted by winds and salt spray. Marine creatures such as periwinkles, barnacles, starfish, and hermit crabs are shrewn on shores littered with kelp and sea grasses.

An Oasis of Roistering Cheer
Along a Bone-rattling Road

Summer visitors are always welcome to Sam Jefferds' tavern in York, but in the eighteenth century one unidentified New England hostelry was more discriminating:

Rules of the Tavern
No more than five to sleep in one bed
No boots to be worn in bed
Organ grinders to sleep in the wash house
No Razor Grinders or Tinkers taken in

Despite such strictures, most public houses were "oases of frolic and roistering cheer." Those like Jefferds on the Old Post Road between Portland and Boston were particularly welcome to weary travelers on bone-rattling turnpikes.

Stagecoach drivers, usually nattily attired in fancy overcoats, driving gloves, and bright sashes, heralded their approach with blasts on six-foot-long horns, one toot for each passenger.

Tavern keepers renowned for their ability to remember names greeted guests to inns "simple to the point of crudity." This spartan ambience was reflected in menus: Cornmeal mush was a staple, although Sam Jefferds offered distinguished visitors venison, grouse, lobster, and trout.

Bars were more imaginatively stocked. Rum, ale, cider, and beer were augmented with more exotic beverages such as metheglin (fermented honey and water), toddy (rum with sweetened water), and flip (beer or ale mixed with rum and molasses).

Visitors congregated in a common room to warm their feet by the

Taproom, Jefferds Tavern

hearth, quaff drinks, and relate gossip from the previous turnpike stop. Women withdrew to retiring rooms where they chatted and sipped nothing stronger than sugared tea.

Sleeping quarters were also austere. Beds were wooden platforms topped by ticks stuffed with straw, dried leaves, or corn husks. Next morning at dawn, travelers were back on the road.

Kennebunkport

Rustling Ghosts, Singing Spirits

Dock Square (1) once hummed with wharfside activity as longshore-men unloaded square-riggers' cargoes of rum and molasses fresh from the West Indies. Barrels were hoisted to the second-story loft of a warehouse (now a bookstore) with a huge iron ring that can still be seen. Shipowners watched their vessels return to harbor from a rooftop lookout tower. Today, the square's bustle is confined to visitors browsing in shops and frequenting restaurants housed in nineteenth-century buildings. The activity is more restrained but no less infectious. The smell of hemp, tar, and rum seems to linger.

Dock Square is still the heart of town, as in Kennebunkport's days as a waterfront for Kennebunk, a few miles inland, and a shipbuilding center. (Eight hundred vessels were launched from here in less than eighty years.) Today this fishing village, resort, and artists' colony of 2,500 is one of Maine's most popular vacation areas.

The windjammers are gone but pleasure craft bob at marina berths on the Kennebunk River, along with sturdier lobster boats and their raucous entourage of gulls. Emerald lawns and a canopy of huge old trees frame lovingly restored and preserved captains' mansions. Many homes proudly record their vintage (as early as 1724) over doorways. Grander "cottages" along Ocean Avenue were built by wealthy summer residents from Boston, Philadelphia, and New York, who descended on the port in the 1890s.

But the more animated part of this seacoast town is back at Dock Square, dominated by the Soldiers and Sailors Monument with its fierce eagle perched atop a granite base. It was erected in 1909, largely

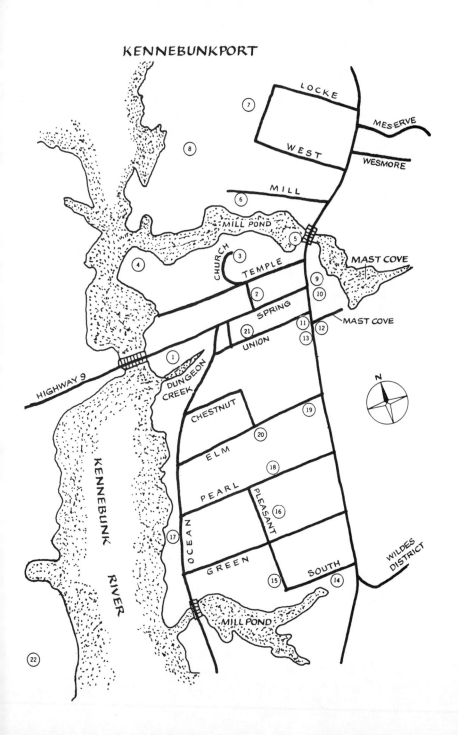

Dock Square

through the efforts of Abbott Graves, an architect and artist who lived here in the early 1900s.

In the **Post Office** (2) is a Gordon Grant mural depicting the brig *Lima* anchored at Kennebunkport. This painting replaced a more controversial work which resident writer and critic Booth Tarkington described as "a mixture of Coney Island and Mexico." *Open Mon.–Sat. except holidays.*

The immense clock tower of the **South Congregational Church** (3), built in 1824, was designed by Aaron Willard of Boston. Behind the church are stables built in 1892, large enough to accommodate the minister's horses and about two cords of wood. Services are held on the second floor. The ground floor is now a gallery for the work of local artists.

Near the riverside **Robinson Memorial Park** (4) are a few pilings and planks—all that remain of a shipyard. A four-masted schooner named *Savannah,* launched in 1901, was the last vessel to slide down the ways.

Mill Bridge (5) spans the entrance to Mast Cove, once a storage basin for trees belonging to the Crown. A 1721 act declared that all trees in British North America fit for masts were property of the King.

A hundred-pound-sterling fine was levied for felling without authorization. Some particularly tall, straight white pines even warranted a guard. (Colonials occasionally used broad pine boards from illegally cut trees on second or third floors, where building inspectors seldom ventured.)

The **Olde Grist Mill Restaurant** (6), housed in a 1749 corn mill, retains its original atmosphere with scales, a hopper, a conveyor belt, hand-hewn beams, and wooden shutters. An 1821 map of northeastern North America is displayed, and traditional menus include New England dishes such as johnnycake (journey cake), a dry corn bread made of scalded meal, and baked Indian pudding. *Open Tues.–Sun.*

The **Captain Thomas Perkins III House** (7), the oldest residence in town (1724), was used as a hospital for inoculations during a 1787 smallpox epidemic. Second owner Captain James Perkins brought back this virus from the West Indies along with his cargo.

The **Perkins' family burying ground** (8), almost hidden by trees and undergrowth on private property, is near the site of a tragedy ac-

Harbor view

cording to local legend. One evening a fisherman returned here to find his home burned and his wife and children killed by Indians. Every year on that night, spirits of the family haunt the cove; the sweet voice of the wife singing is sometimes heard by boatmen on the fog-shrouded river.

Imposing Greek Revival pillars earned **White Columns** (9) its name. The estate of this 1853 mansion on Spring Street included a three-story barn. (The street takes its name from a freshwater spring that bubbled up in the middle of saltwater Mill Pond.)

Aunt Felicia's Folly (10) was a typical colonial house until 1895, when Felicia Perkins added a vaulted ceiling and quaint gingerbread trim. Children dubbed the fairy-talelike cottage, with its suddenly dark and mysterious yard, "the Witch's house."

Crews from docking ships hurried up a footpath that is now Union Street to wash away salt spray at **Nowell's Tavern** (11), built in 1802. If the old tars had any money left after a swilling session, they might have deposited it in a nearby branch of the Kennebunk Bank, now the **Louis T. Graves Memorial Library** (12). The massive vault door is left open as a reminder of the building's original purpose. The library has a painting and a mural by Abbott Graves, a longtime Port resident. *Open Mon., Wed., Fri., and Sat.*

A ghost called "the rustling lady" haunts the 1803 **Alexander Gould House** (13). This ethereal upstairs tenant reputedly sits in an invisible rocking chair and has a disconcerting habit of opening the guest-room door in the middle of the night to tap sleeping occupants on the shoulder.

Crosstrees (14), a colonial home built in 1818, takes its name from "husband and wife" maple trees planted by the front door. Only one tree survives. Abbott Graves bought the house in 1894 and used its barn as a studio.

The **Port House Inn** (15) is on the estate of a "castle" built in 1882 by Rev. Edward Clark of New York. He brought rock by barge from nearby islands to build a medieval-looking dwelling. The castle was badly deteriorated when Edwin Robinson tore it down and built his gracious home, now the Port House Inn.

The **Nathaniel Lord Mansion** (16), also an inn, was built during a War of 1812 blockade. Idle shipbuilders were put to work completing this mansion, with its distinctive octagonal lookout. It was said to be so carefully constructed that it would float in the event of a second Flood (an unusual but understandable feature, given the occupation of its

Nathaniel Lord Mansion

builders). This house still has some original wallpaper and carpeting. Tours are available.

A short walk down to the riverside leads to the **Arundel Yacht Club** (**17**). Some of the sailboats anchored here seem to strain at their mooring in the tidal river, eager for a strong, fresh sea breeze in their rigging.

Tory Chimneys (**18**) is named for a black band painted on this dwelling's chimney, a sign that supposedly indicated its occupants' Loyalist tendencies. The name is a misnomer, however, since most of the house was built well after the Revolution. The home is comprised of three separate structures, including an ell which dates from about 1740. The third floor was once used as a sail-rigging loft.

A seaman named **Thomas King** (**19**) had a terrible premonition in this 1816 Greek Revival home. He had signed on for the maiden voyage of the barque *Isidore* in November 1842, but a vivid dream of disaster frightened him so badly that he hid for four days. The ship sailed without him in blustery weather. The first night out a northeaster drove the vessel onto shoals off Bald Head Cliff at nearby Ogunquit, and sixteen sailors drowned. King never recovered from the shock.

The builder of the 1799 **Captain Dudley House** (**20**) surrounded himself with mementos of his voyages. He chained two small brass cannons captured during his travels to fluted pillars flanking his front door, and on holidays flew the flags of a dozen countries he had visited from his flagpole.

A **gully (21)** here was once Dungeon Creek. Cargo ships were hauled up the shallow waterway to this spot by hand with ropes winched around trees and posts. Cargoes were stored in the warehouses that once lined this shady avenue. Bowsprits of windjammers anchored here at the head of the cove once extended over Cross Street. Granite blocks form a bulkhead that can still be seen between the yellow barn and the bridge that spans Dungeon Creek gulley.

A long, leisurely walk across a bridge spanning the Kennebunk River rewards visitors with the peaceful repose of sweeping lawns, stately pines and elms, and flower gardens of the **St. Anthony Monastery and Shrine (22)**. A turn-of-the-century Tudor mansion built by a Buffalo, New York, industrialist now houses the monastery and its shrine. On the grounds are Stations of the Cross, a chapel, a grotto of Our Lady of Lourdes, and a monument from the Vatican's pavilion at the 1964 New York World's Fair. A tranquil woodland walk along the river leads to a rock-rimmed bay overlooking the Atlantic. *Open daily.*

America's Number One Dump

Visitors to Kennebunkport in early July may see a strange parade winding through the streets. Residents decked out in castoffs not fit for a rummage sale tow an assortment of junk not even a tramp would salvage. Meanwhile, local beauties compete for the dubious distinction of Miss Dumpy. It's all part of this community's sincere but unorthodox efforts to keep America beautiful.

Artist and longtime Port resident Edward Mayo organized the nation's first garbage dump association, with a "bored" of directors and a credit card that gives its bearer "national dump visiting privileges, making it unnecessary to use the roadside." (Mayo is also the author of the definitive reference work Dump Watchers' Handbook.)

The overcrowded dump, north of town and soon to be closed by its own success, is distinguished only by a weather-beaten sign that proclaims it "America's Number One."

Portland

Black Wharves and Emerald Isles

Often I think of the beautiful town
That is seated by the sea;
Often in thought go up and down
The pleasant streets of that dear old town.

Portland still inspires visitors to wax poetic, though perhaps not as eloquently as Henry Wadsworth Longfellow, who penned these reflections about his boyhood home in "My Lost Youth."

Much of the city's beauty derives from its splendid location atop a swayback ridge on a peninsula in Casco Bay. To the east emerald-chip islands can be seen in the bay; to the west are glimpses of New Hampshire's White Mountains from lookouts along a promenade that encircles the peninsula.

Maine's largest city (pop. 65,000) has been known by many names —Machigonne, Casco, Falmouth, the Neck, Indigreat, Elbow—and for its diverse charms: the commercial bustle of Congress Street; the gracious homes of State Street; and the cobblestones and tangy waterfront along Commercial Street.

Perhaps Portland changed its name so often to improve its luck. This unfortunate city was left in ruins in 1675 during King Philip's War and again fifteen years later during the French and Indian wars. Bombarded by the British in 1775, it has also been destroyed by fire three times. An 1866 blaze left 10,000 homeless and destroyed $12 million worth of property, but fortunately claimed no lives.

The indomitable spirit of this community is perhaps best reflected in the **Old Port Exchange** (1), a once-decaying waterfront area whose

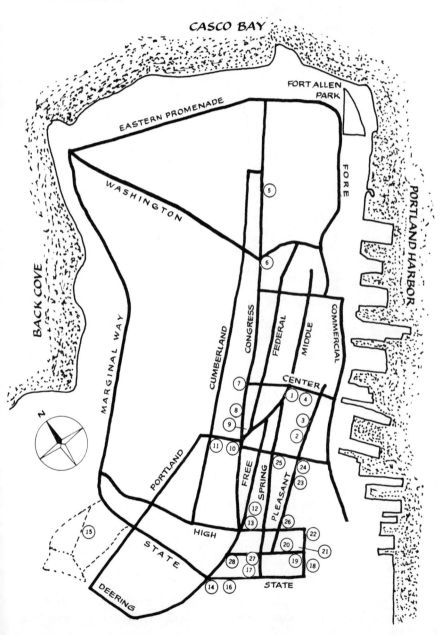

PORTLAND

CASCO BAY

FORT ALLEN PARK

EASTERN PROMENADE

WASHINGTON

FORE

PORTLAND HARBOR

BACK COVE

MARGINAL WAY

CUMBERLAND

CONGRESS

FEDERAL

MIDDLE

COMMERCIAL

CENTER

FREE

SPRING

PLEASANT

PORTLAND

HIGH

STATE

DEERING

STATE

N

Old Port Exchange

restored nineteenth-century buildings now contain boutiques, shops, and restaurants. Brick sidewalks in this old part of town are lined with benches and maples.

The area's exotic atmosphere inspired Longfellow to write:

> *. . . the black wharves and the slips,*
> *And the sea-tides tossing free;*
> *And Spanish sailors with bearded lips,*
> *And the beauty and mystery of the ships.*

Foreign craft still dock along Commercial Street, and Longfellow's bearded Spaniards, along with Italians and Germans, can still be seen wharfside unloading cargoes. On Sunday visitors can tour the more familiar Coast Guard cutters stationed here.

The **U. S. Custom House** (2) was built in 1872 with carved granite. In the 1840s import duties averaged a million dollars a year at this port of entry. A museum here features artifacts and displays related to Portland's rich maritime heritage. *Open Mon.–Sat.*

Visitors can dip wax during tours of the **Spencer Candle Factory** (3), and watch workmen pour and decorate candles. *Open daily.* The **Marketplace** (4), housed in an 1867 Federal-style building, is a craft shop with toys, miniatures, and jewelry. *Open Mon.–Sat.* A mural painted on the side of an Exchange Street building depicts—appropriately enough—another building. This *trompe l'oeil* is three stories high.

The eighty-five-foot-high **Portland Observatory** (5) was built on Munjoy Hill in 1807 for merchants, shipowners, and sailors' wives anxious to see cargoes, ships, and husbands—respectively—make port. *Open daily June–Sept.*

U. S. Custom House

Portland Observatory

The tower affords magnificent views of Casco Bay's Calendar Islands, named in 1691 by a British sailor who reported that there
seemed to be an islet for every day of the year. Potatoes were discovered growing on these islands in 1628, but church elders forbade
their consumption because the American tuber wasn't mentioned in
the Bible. Fort Ferdinando Gorges, built on an island in the harbor

in 1858, can be seen from the tower. Authorized by Jefferson Davis, the fort has yet to be involved in battle.

Greenwood Opera House, America's first summer theater, was established in 1870 on Peaks Island. This same jumble of rock was the scene for Longfellow's "The Wreck of the *Hesperus*," a poem based on the sinking of *Helen Eliza* in 1869. In that wreck, all hands were lost except for a young boy, who promptly retired from the sea (he had also survived a shipwreck in the West Indies). This accident-prone individual later drowned in a stream on his New Hampshire farm.

Eastern Cemetery (6), on a sun-dappled knoll, surrounded by a high iron fence, was established in 1698 and dubbed the "field of ancient graves" by early settlers. A marble monument honors Commodore Edward Preble (1761–1807), who in his flagship *Constitution* ("Old Ironsides") led an American fleet against Barbary pirates. After Preble had scored several victories over infidel pirates, Pope Pius VII declared that the commodore had "done more for Christianity in a short space of time than the most powerful nations have done in ages."

There are free concerts four nights a week in summer at the **Portland City Hall (7)**, which houses the Kotzschmar Memorial Organ. This magnificent instrument has an air chest fifty-three feet long; 6,500 pipes range in size from half an inch to thirty-two feet. The organ was donated by Philadelphia publisher Cyrus H. K. Curtis in memory of Hermann Kotzschmar, who served as the First Parish Church organist for forty-seven years. The Portland Symphony Orchestra performs in an auditorium here.

Maine's oldest stone public building, the **First Parish Church (8)**, dates from 1826 and serves a parish established in 1674. The church is furnished with a carved mahogany pulpit and "slip pews"—polished benches with slight downward slopes that deposit sleeping worshipers on the floor. An exquisite crystal chandelier is suspended from a cannonball found embedded in the church's wall after the British bombardment in 1775.

The bronze figures at **Monument Square (9)** were sculpted by Franklin Simmons, a Maine native. (He was knighted by King Humbert of Italy for one of his works.) Dedicated in 1891, this monument honors more than 5,000 Portland soldiers and sailors who served in the Civil War.

Nearby is the **Wadsworth-Longfellow House (10)**, where the poet was sheltered as a boy by "the peaceful threshold of home." The first brick dwelling in town (its walls are sixteen inches thick), this mansion was built in 1785 by General Peleg Wadsworth, a Revolutionary War hero and grandfather of the poet. The parlor, once the largest in town, contained Portland's first piano. Eight fireplaces swallowed thirty cords of good oak and birch to ward off the chills of one Portland winter.

The home is decorated with furniture from Longfellow's family. Near the parlor couch is a portrait of Longfellow as a professor at Bowdoin College. A small study across from the kitchen contains the desk at which Wadsworth wrote "The Rainy Day" in 1841. On the wall is a copy of the speech his father (Stephen) gave to welcome Lafayette to Portland.

Upstairs is Longfellow's cradle, writing desk, corn-husk bed, and trunk. A second-story window overlooks the mansion's lovely terraced gardens. *Open Mon.–Fri. June–Sept.*

In the adjoining **Maine Historical Society Museum (11)** is a replica of the bust of Longfellow that stands in Westminster Abbey,

Sweat Mansion

London. Also displayed are Indian relics, historical artifacts, documents and portraits of local notables. *Open Mon.–Fri. June–Sept.*

The Portland School of Fine and Applied Arts is in the white **Charles Q. Clapp House** (12), built in 1832. Fluted Ionic columns define a central bay in this templelike residence.

The **Portland Museum of Art** (13) consists of two buildings. The 1801 Sweat Mansion, restored with handsome furniture (Queen Anne, Hepplewhite, and Chippendale), now contains an important collection of American decorative arts from the Federal period. An exhibit of nineteenth-century glass includes rare Portland glass, a local product produced for only ten years (1863–73).

A permanent collection in the adjacent Sweat Memorial Building features artists Gilbert Stuart, Andrew Wyeth, and seventeen works by Winslow Homer. Paul Akers' sculpture "The Pearl Diver" is also displayed, along with Gaston Lachaise's "Standing Nude." *Open Tues.–Sun. except holidays.*

Portland's literary heritage is reflected in the imposing **Longfellow Monument** (14), dedicated in 1888. A seven-foot-high bronze statue of the poet was cast by Portland sculptor Franklin Simmons; the ornate pedestal was designed by architect Francis Fassett.

> *And Deering's Woods are fresh and fair,*
> *And with joy that is almost pain*
> *My heart goes back to wander there . . .*

So wrote Longfellow of what is known today as **Deering Oaks** (15). Portlanders strolling through its quiet woods share the poet's sentiments. Boaters paddle among flocks of white ducks and Canada geese on Deerings Pond; in winter skaters glide past oaks silent as sentinels with frosty patinas.

Fifty-four-acre Deering Oaks is the largest of Portland's twenty-six parks, established after the 1866 conflagration for "protection against the spread of fire and to promote general health."

The **Prentiss Mellen House** (16), a Federal structure built in 1807, was once the home of Maine's first chief justice. Later owned by William Pitt Fessenden, a U.S. senator and Lincoln's Secretary of the Treasury, the house is now the Monastery of the Precious Blood.

The **Cathedral Church of St. Luke** (17) was the first Episcopal church in the United States to serve as a cathedral from the time of its completion. Built of stone in 1868 in Gothic Revival style, it features a carved oak reredos. The octagonal Emmanuel Chapel, built in 1905

Deering Oaks

with a handsome mahogany interior, has as its altarpiece "The American Madonna," painted by John La Farge. *Open daily.*

The 1801 **Joseph Holt Ingraham House (18)** is one of two remaining Portland dwellings designed by Alexander Parris. Graceful pilasters from its orignal facade have been replaced by modern siding, but delicate woodwork can still be seen at the cornices, windows, and doorways.

The **Robinson-Cutter House (19)** was once the home of Levi Cutter, Portland's mayor in 1834–40. This 1820 Federal structure with its careful proportions is now a senior citizens' home.

No luxury was spared on the **John B. Carroll Mansion (20).** The elegant 1851 residence even had a Greek Revival stable. Playboy architect Charles Q. Clapp probably designed it for his daughter.

What appears to be an opulent Italian villa is really the **Victoria Mansion (21),** the city's finest example of high Victorian architecture. Built for New Orleans hotel owner Ruggles Morse, this two-story brownstone topped by a three-story tower is an eclectic blend of the most elaborate aspects of the late English, French, and Italian periods.

A flying staircase has 337 hand-carved balusters of Brazilian mahogany (each was a week's work for one man); the seven Carrara marble mantels were carved in Italy. Completed in 1863, the house has fine woodcarvings and a parlor ceiling decorated by hand-painted roses. Displayed in rooms furnished with period pieces are a square grand piano with mother-of-pearl keys and a rare glass harmonica. *Open Tues.–Sat. mid-June–mid-Sept.*

The **McLellan-Oxnard House** (22), now a nursery, was built about 1830 for two prominent citizens: Portland Mayor Jacob McLellan lived in the left half of the house and shipbuilder Edward Oxnard lived in the right half.

Daniel How forsook a career as a hatter to become one of Portland's leading nineteenth-century merchants. The 1799 **Daniel How House** (23) reflects his success. The adjacent **Joseph How House** (24) was built by his son in 1818; the nearby **John How House** (25) was built by another son in 1817.

Elihu Deering followed the elder How's example. He exchanged his carving tools for a merchant's ledger; the **Elihu Deering House** (26) offers evidence of another successful transition. Later the residence of banker and merchant William Moulton, this 1800 Federal structure has a stable with a facade similar to that of the house.

One of the last dwellings built on Pleasant Street—the **William Wood House** (27)—dates from 1874. This Italianate structure is now the parish house of the **Holy Trinity Orthodox Church** (28), built in 1826. In an adjacent park is a Revere bell from the steeple. This 1,800-pounder, number 250 in a series of four hundred cast by the patriot and his family, is one of Maine's seventeen remaining Revere bells.

American Folk Heroes Born at the Pen of a Beloved Bard

Hiawatha, Paul Revere, Evangeline—all were immortalized by the bard of New England, Henry Wadsworth Longfellow. A noted scholar and linguist who mastered ten languages, this beloved storyteller lured poetry from its garret into a world where it was read and enjoyed by everyone.

Longfellow was born in 1807 in Portland, where his family home is now a museum. From 1829 to 1854 he taught modern languages at Bowdoin College in Brunswick and at Harvard. His anthology The Poets and Poetry of Europe *made foreign verse accessible to Americans, but it was his own poetry that brought him fame.*

Longfellow's popularity was such that The Courtship of Miles Standish *sold 5,000 copies in Boston the day it was published. Poems like "The Village Blacksmith" reveal Longfellow's skill as an artist and his uncanny ability to create American folk heroes.*

Longfellow faced tragedy in his life. He saw his first wife die of fever during a European visit. His second marriage was a happy one, but that wife died in 1861 when her dress caught fire. The flowing beard the poet wore in later years hid scars from burns he received trying to save her.

Two years after Longfellow's death in 1882, he became the first American honored with a bust in the Poet's Corner of Westminster Abbey, London. But perhaps the poet (and father of six) would have preferred this distinction: Longfellow was the first American writer to make a living from poetry.

Lewiston

A Textile Town's Grand Design

Maine's second largest city (pop. 41,000) and industrial center borders the great falls on the Androscoggin River amid rich farmland thirty miles from the sea. Lewiston's one hundred factories produce everything from shoes to spools, incense to incandescent lamp grids.

Textiles still provide most industrial muscle in a city whose first mill was built in 1834. In the 1850s Boston capitalists dammed the Androscoggin and constructed canals that still thread the factories to distribute water power to the great textile mills.

French-Canadians flocked here in the last half of the nineteenth century to work in the factories, creating a lively, French-speaking community in a section of town called "Little Canada." Today, Lewiston's population is sixty percent Franco-American.

This was a planned city whose grand 1857 design, like those in Manchester, New Hampshire, and Lowell, Massachusetts, included treelined canals, public buildings, churches, parks, and attractive row houses lining broad avenues. Many elms have succumbed to disease, but the canals, mills, and tenements illustrate a period when designers and builders combined utility and beauty in industrial structures.

Wealthy mill owners and investors endowed Bates College, the oldest coeducational institution in New England. Bates occupies 125 landscaped acres, with the verdant slopes of Mount David as its showpiece. Stately old maples and ancient pines canopy classic Georgian architecture. Students paddle canoes on the tree-rimmed waters of Lake Andrews in the middle of the campus.

Its classical features almost unchanged, **Hawthorn Hall** (1) was

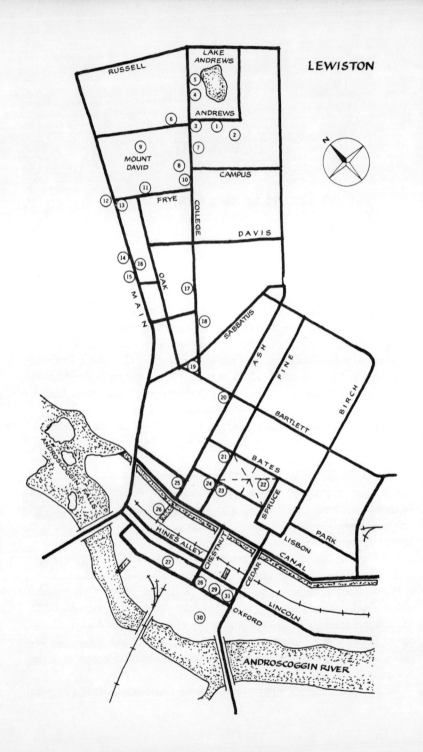

Hawthorn Hall, Bates College

designed by Gridley James Fox Bryant as one of the original campus buildings. Its bell still rings for classes. *Open Mon.–Fri. Sept.–June.*

The imposing neoclassical **Coram Library** (2) boasts massive Ionic portico columns. It contains many rare volumes, an extensive ornithological exhibit, the Phelp collection of signed first editions, and one of America's largest compilations of early Freewill Baptist material. *Open daily.*

North of **Parker Hall** (3) another Bryant building in Greek Revival

style, the **Treat Gallery** (4), features the works of Lewiston artist
Marsden Hartley, and sponsors a full schedule of exhibits. *Open daily
Sept.–June.*

Five major student productions are held annually at the 324-seat
Schaeffer Theater (5), a center for the performing arts. A variety of
cultural events, including modern dance, are held throughout the year.
Open daily Sept.–June.

The 1908 Romanesque **Libbey Forum** (6) contains the social science departments. It was originally an auditorium for commencement
and the meetings of Bates's three literary societies.

Built of granite in soft shades of tan and amber, the **Bates College
Chapel** (7) takes its inspiration from the Gothic King's College
Chapel in England. The intellectual tradition of the West is represented by stained-glass windows depicting Aristotle, Erasmus, Shakespeare, Goethe, and Marie Curie. Services, lectures, and debates, along
with student noon concerts, are open to the public. *Open daily
Sept.–June.*

Bates College Chapel

Behind the 1873 **Cheney House** (8), home of the first president of the college and now a dormitory, rise the wooded slopes of 340-foot **Mount David** (9). Paths lead to a summit lookout with panoramas of the Androscoggin River's ragged cataracts, downtown Lewiston's massive brick mills, and on clear days, the White Mountains of New Hampshire to the west.

The simple colonial features of the **Mitchell House** (10), a college dormitory, are unified with geometric symmetry. Along Frye Street are more lovely dwellings, once private homes and now college residences. The inspired Victorian eclecticism at **10 Frye Street** (11) includes a French mansard roof, Gothic gables, and a doorway with etched glass windows.

Many private homes along Main Street are early nineteenth-century farmhouses that reflect Lewiston's agricultural origins. The 1901 **J. D. Clifford House** (12), now an office building, has a beautiful Palladian window on its south side, and terra cotta decorative trim. A carved front hall staircase may be admired during the week.

The **Senator William Pierce Frye House** (13), named for one of Lewiston's most distinguished sons, is graced with a mansard roof and stylish dormers. Frye served as mayor in 1866, then went on to the U. S. Senate, where as chairman of the foreign relations committee he supervised peace negotiations after the Spanish-American War.

The town's oldest dwelling was built about 1800 for farmer and tanner **Amos Davis** (14), a Quaker settler who made the first survey of Lewiston. His clapboard home is now a variety store and barbershop. His son David's farm extended between Jepson Brook north of the Bates campus to College Street and the river. Davis pastured his cattle and horses amid tall pines on the rocky mount that now bears his name.

A downhill stroll toward the Androscoggin passes the Romanesque **Wallace Public School** (15), built in 1866, and the classic 1860 Greek Revival home at **391 Main Street** (16). The **Captain Daniel Holland House** (17) is an exuberant mixture of European influences: Two Italian-style floors are topped by a French mansard roof.

Down the street a more restrained tradition identifies the 1875 **Quaker Meeting House** (18), whose strong, austere lines reflect the religious beliefs of the sect. Capped by a sharply curved and pointed roof, this building was later Christian Science and is now Presbyterian.

The **Calvary United Methodist Church** (19) was built at the turn of the century with a variety of materials—stone, brick, and shingle.

From a commanding location high on Bartlett Street, twin 180-foot spires of the magnificent **Saints Peter and Paul Church** (20) dominate the skyline. This 230-foot-long Gothic structure of

Saints Peter and Paul Church

Maine granite is the state's largest church and seats 2,000. *Open daily.*

The tour proceeds down Ash Street to Lewiston's commercial district. Nestled amid this mercantile bustle, the quaint 1876 **Dr. William Bradford House (21)**, now an office building, overlooks **Kennedy Park (22)** with its Victorian bandstand and treelined paths. The city's largest ethnic group is feted here the last week in July with a lively Franco-American Festival that features a sidewalk café with French dishes, rollicking Québecois folk music, and handicraft displays.

Opposite the 1890 **City Hall (23)** is the Greek Revival **Lewiston Public Library (24)**, an 80,000-volume institution built with funds donated by Andrew Carnegie. *Open daily.*

Architect George Coombs of Lewiston designed one of the city's most elegant commercial structures, the **Depositor's Trust Company Building (25)**. Four Ionic columns front a portico with tall, arched windows. Coombs's agile imagination and classical bent were responsible for most of the city's major buildings, and shaped the features of present-day Lewiston. The firm he founded is perpetuated as Alonzo J. Harriman Associates in Auburn, across the river.

The tour now enters the industrial heart of Lewiston, where textile mills once clattered with a deafening din of shuttles and looms when cotton was thirty cents a ton and labor a nickel an hour. Boston capitalists Benjamin Bates, Thomas Hill, and others directed the city's economic growth through the Lewiston Power Company. They also constructed canals in 1850 to transfer power from the Androscoggin rapids to their complex of mills.

Two parallel canals fourteen feet deep and sixty-five feet wide, and several cross-channels, constitute a system almost a mile long. Granite locks at the head of the main canal regulated water flow. Early photographs show trees and lawns lining the waterways, giving this area a pastoral charm that has long since disappeared.

The **Bates Manufacturing Company (26)**, a maker of fine fabrics and tent cloth during the Civil War, was built piecemeal along the canal from 1852 to 1920. Tours of the plant can be arranged. *Open Mon.–Fri.*

The first glimpse of Lewiston for many French-Canadian immigrants was the sprawling Bates mill and city hall framed by the iron railroad bridge spanning the Androscoggin. At the end of the line was the **Grand Trunk Railway Station (27)**, Lewiston's modest—and more humane—version of Ellis Island. Relatives and friends greeted thousands of newcomers from Quebec, introduced them to the vigor-

Bates Manufacturing, from Wiseman Bridge

ous French community here, and eased their transition to a new country. Built in 1885 in "stick-style" architecture, the depot now houses a family health clinic.

Once the unofficial city hall of "Little Canada," the **Dominican Block** (28) was the center of the French-Canadian community. This five-story brick-and-granite structure designed by Coombs opened its doors in 1883 to 650 students tutored by the Gray Nuns. It was also used to present French-language plays, operas, and church services (those who worshiped here avoided the uphill walk to Saints Peter and Paul). The block now contains shops and offices.

Brick row housing like the **Oxford Mill Block** (29) once lined this street, in its time a shady thoroughfare that gave this neighborhood character and dignity. These tenements were first built to shelter New England farm girls who provided the first labor in the mills. A director supervised his tenants' morals and health. Most women worked temporarily to pay debts, accumulate a dowry, or finance an education. (The first woman to graduate from Bates paid her tuition with mill wages.)

Although erected quickly and for practical reasons, huge nineteenth-century mills were often graceful, and sometimes even stylish, with a sense of power and grandeur. Looming above nearby row housing, the **Continental Mill** (30) embodies two architectural traditions. Its octagonal towers and steep-pitched mansard roof with dormer windows reflect French Imperial style. Below the roof line Italian Renais-

Continental Mill

sance predominates with arched windows. Once noted for producing fine shirts, the mill now houses five shoe manufacturing companies.

The steeple of **St. Mary's Church** (31) casts its shadow on the other powerful force in Franco-American life—the Continental Mill. This cruciform church of Maine granite has several French Norman features that reflect the origins of French-Canadian parishioners whose ancestors came from Normandy, France. The apse containing the altar is square, in Norman style, rather than round as in most churches. Built for a parish created between Canal Street and the river to minister French-Canadian workers, the church was completed in 1928, just as the mills began to close, and population declined.

Maine's Little Canada

The Dominican Block was the center of a swirl of Franco-American life in Lewiston's Little Canada—a 9½-acre neighborhood bounded by Lincoln and Oxford streets and an Irish-American enclave east of Cedar called the Gas Patch.

About 1,000 people still live here amid an Old World atmosphere. Tiered balconies and porches press close together along twisting, narrow streets and alleys. Soaring above the rooftops and factories is the spire of St. Mary's Church, a reminder of how religion protected Québecois culture during French-Canadians' early years in a new land.

In the 1860s Lewiston mill agents recruited Quebec habitants who had a reputation as hard workers. By 1873 as many as 150 immigrants arrived daily at the Grand Trunk Station, most expecting to stay only long enough to pay off a debt or save money to buy a farm back home. Instead they created an industrious, fun-loving French-speaking community amid canals and mills along the river.

Le Messager, a French-language newspaper established in 1880, featured a feuilleton, or serialized daily romance, and urged its readers to become naturalized Americans. In 1872 francophones organized a social men's club called L'Institut Jacques Cartier, whose members were resplendent in plumed cocked hats, sashes, and swords. Lodge meetings featured a beau parler, or skilled orator who dazzled listeners with stories in French.

Operas and plays were translated and presented at the Dominican Block. Gilbert and Sullivan's H.M.S. Pinafore became the smash hit L'Amour a bord. An annual ballet choreographed by a Swiss nun was a popular fund-raiser for churches and schools in the early 1900s.

The entire community gathered on St. Jean-Baptiste Day (June 24) with boisterous celebrations commemorating the French patron saint. Bands, choirs, and floats paraded through narrow streets arched with red, white, and blue bunting. Festivities were capped with a sumptuous banquet.

Bath

Cradle of Ships

Dreaming of its windjammer glory days, Bath lines the broad Kennebec River thirty miles from the sea. Known as the "cradle of ships," this community of 9,600 retains the colorful atmosphere of the days when "Bath boats" were familiar sights in ports from Rio to Rangoon.

A three-mile stretch of Kennebec riverbank called the Long Reach was ideal for shipbuilding: The shore sloped at an angle just right for laying keels, and the sheltered river channel was deep enough for large vessels. Upstream lay untracked forests with enough lumber to launch a dozen armadas.

The first ship built in America, a thirty-ton pinnace named *Virginia,* was launched here in 1607 by the Popham Colony whose members had landed the previous year south of Bath at what is now Popham State Park. After a severe winter survivors determinedly built *Virginia,* loaded her with furs and sassafras roots, and returned to England. The colony was a failure, but a glorious shipbuilding tradition had begun.

By 1900 half the large wooden vessels sailing under the American flag had been built at Bath. Bustling with rope walks, chandleries, and sail lofts, the town launched the largest wooden ship ever built, *Wyoming,* and the world's only seven-master, the all-steel *Thomas W. Lawson.* Bath Iron Works, the only shipyard still active here, built more destroyers during World War II than the Japanese Navy. It still sends cargo carriers and frigates down the ways.

The town that launched a thousand ships has been rejuvenated with an imaginative downtown restoration project. Restaurants, craft

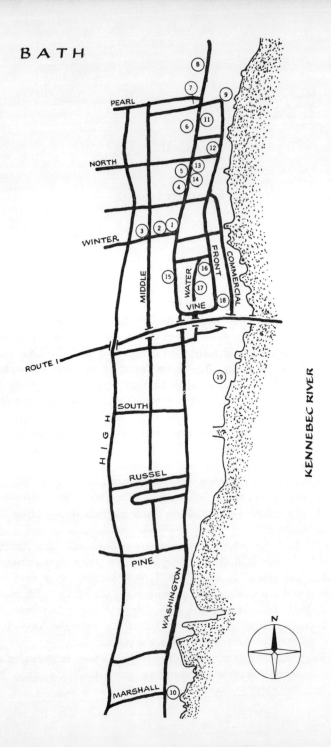

BATH

PEARL

NORTH

WINTER

ROUTE I

SOUTH

RUSSEL

PINE

MARSHALL

HIGH

MIDDLE

WATER

VINE

FRONT

COMMERCIAL

WASHINGTON

KENNEBEC RIVER

N

shops, and art galleries have transformed waterfront business blocks and warehouses into prime real estate. A historic district along Washington Street reflects Bath's prosperous maritime heritage with its handsome nineteenth-century shipbuilders' mansions and stately churches.

The **Winter Street Center** (1) is emblematic of this community's commitment to preserve its past. A Bath landmark since 1843, this Gothic Revival church with its massive four-stage steeple was saved from demolition in 1971 and is now part of the Bath Marine Museum. Inside are exhibits on seafaring, shipworkers' life, and regional maritime history, and more than two hundred model ships, including *Virginia. Open daily end of May–end of Oct.; Sun. Nov.—mid-May.*

A gracefully sculptured fountain by William Zorach entitled "Spirit of the Sea" graces a pond bordered by lawns and tall elms in a park across from Washington Street.

The Greek Revival parsonage of the **United Church of Christ** (2) was built in 1848 by William Larrabee, who also constructed navy gunboats during the Civil War. The nearby 1843 **Church of New Jerusalem** (3) is an imposing Greek Revival temple used by the Swedenborgian congregation.

A stroll down Washington Street passes the impressive Ionic portico of the 1845 **McLellan House** (4), a home once graced by no fewer than five grand pianos. The **Captain John Richardson House** (5), a Carpenter Gothic cottage completed in 1850, had an unusual influence on its occupants: Only sons have been born to families residing there. (Effects on passersby have not been recorded.) This quaint residence has board-and-batten siding and steep gables decorated with eaves called "barge boards."

The brick **Patton House** (6) is one of several lavish Italianate Bath homes designed by Francis Fassett. Small windows under the eaves, peculiar to local Italianate residences, are rare elsewhere. More Mediterranean influences on another **Patton house** (7), this one built in 1858, include graceful porch arches, Palladian windows, and handsome granite steps.

Shipbuilder **Stephen Larrabee** (8) thought his business success should be reflected in a grander residence. In 1852 he commissioned designer Francis Fassett to add an Italianate wing to a simple structure built about 1790. The house was later occupied by the Newell family, including father Peter and son John, who both became presidents of the Bath Iron Works.

The shipbuilding skills honed by artisans in the yards of Larrabee and other maritime magnates are showcased at the **Apprenticeshop** (9), part of the Bath Marine Museum. Its riverside setting gives the construction of traditional Maine craft an appropriately rustic atmosphere. *Open daily end of May–end of Oct.*

The fifty-foot launch *Sasanoa* takes museum visitors for a scenic cruise on the Kennebec, past the modern boat-building of the Bath Iron Works to the **Percy and Small Shipyard** (10), the only surviving yard where wooden sailing vessels were once built. Founded in 1896 and closed in 1930, its restored buildings are now part of the marine museum. The 1884 *Seguin,* the last wooden steam tugboat in the nation, is docked here. Indoor exhibits show period machinery and tools, and fifteen small craft once active off the Maine coast. *Open daily end of May–end of Oct.*

Once the New England coast was dotted with yards like this, modest

Percy and Small Shipyard

affairs with three or four barn-sized buildings for storage and rigging. From these humble origins came some of the grandest sailing ships to grace the waves. In 1909 *Wyoming,* the greatest of all schooners, was launched here. This six-master was 330 feet long and required a fourteen-man crew. This ship could transport two hundred railroad cars' worth of coal on week-long voyages from New England to Chesapeake Bay. *Cora F. Cressey,* launched in 1902, was another grand lady from the Percy and Small yard. Her bow was forty feet above the waterline to compensate for a shallow draft. Nicknamed "Queen of the Atlantic Seaboard," this vessel never knew a wave to break over her bow.

A nearby **colonial home** (11) with a massive central chimney is one of Bath's few buildings from that era (most were destroyed during the French and Indian War). This 1769 home reflects Bath's affluence during its shipbuilding heyday. Maritime tycoons often built ostentatious additions to humble cottages, which then became back ells. During winter lulls in construction, shipwrights decorated their residences with ornate carvings, such as the Gothic gingerbread trim added to this home.

The 1827 **Captain John Patten House** (12), a handsome Federal dwelling with an intricate portico, is named for a member of the family that owned the largest merchant fleet in the United States in the 1830s. The packet ships and schooners of Bath's great shipbuilding families—the Pattens, Sewalls, and Houghtons—transported cotton from southern ports to England and Europe, and returned with manufactured goods. From the War of 1812 to the Civil War, Bath's greatest shipbuilding era, brigs and schooners took lumber and fish to southern American ports, and sailed back to Maine laden with rum, molasses, and sugar from the West Indies.

The thirty-two-room **Sewall House** (13), a Georgian mansion built in 1844, is named for the owners of the only American fleet of steel sailing ships, constructed in the 1890s. Now part of the marine museum, the house's displays tell the story of southern Maine shipbuilding. Featuring the nineteenth-century age of sail, many models, paintings, photographs, dioramas, and related displays explain Bath's contribution to the industry. One exhibit area is an imaginative children's room with items labeled "Please Touch." *Open daily end of May–end of Oct; Sun. Nov.–mid-May.*

Next door the Italianate **Captain William Drummond House** (14)

Sewall House

was constructed by another Bath shipbuilder to include the town's first inside toilet. Carved wreaths around third-story windows and Corinthian columns at the entrance show Greek Revival influences.

The tour leaves the Washington Street historic area and passes the **Performing Arts Center at Bath (15)**, where concerts, film festivals, and theatrical productions are held in an 1846 Gothic structure nicknamed the Chocolate Church (its dark brown paint imitates sandstone). Local papers, radio stations, and posters list the current events at the center.

The **Downtown Restoration Project (16)** returned Water, Center, and Front streets to their nineteenth-century appearance with old-fashioned streetlamps, brick sidewalks, and park benches. Crafts and farm produce are sold here at an open-air market every Saturday.

An 1803 bell in the **Old Town Hall (17)** rings four times daily and

for special occasions such as Independence Day. A Fourth of July celebration in 1839 at the town hall included forty toasts to diverse subjects, ranging from "the heroes and sages of the Revolution," to "old
maids and bachelors who, like the baseless fabric of a vision, leave not
a wreck behind."

Past the **Old Custom House** (18) where Bath's first schooner was
launched in 1734, and south of Route 1, summer visitors can tour the
huge **Bath Iron Works** (19), last in a long line of storied Bath shipyards. Launchings are open to the public.

Towering above the yard, and in fact dominating the entire region,
is the four-hundred-foot-high Bath Iron Works crane. (At Yuletide
the town's Christmas tree atop the crane can be seen for thirty miles.)
More than 1,200 tons of steel were used in its construction. The crane
can lift ship sections weighing as much as 220 tons, yet it can be operated by one person.

Bath Iron Works

Peapods, Pinkies, and Skiffs—
Maine's Traditional Craft

The chunking of an adze on oaken timbers and the fresh, sharp smell of newly cut wood greet visitors to the Apprenticeshop, where boats are once again being built with Maine's time-honored methods.

The shop itself is constructed of driftwood and well-aged beams and planks salvaged from old buildings along the coast. A catwalk on one side affords an overhead view of the work in progress. Apprentices can be seen using traditional skills, tools, and materials to build classic Maine boats: dories, pinkies, skiffs, peapods, and Muscongus Bay sloops. One early project was the construction of wooden batteaux, commissioned for a reenactment of Benedict Arnold's 1775 attack on Quebec.

Hallowell

Maine's Attic

Visitors to Hallowell may not be able to buy anything new on Water Street, but they can purchase a nineteenth-century rocking horse, a grandfather clock, or perhaps even a Governor Winthrop desk. Hallowell is one of the few cities in the United States whose main street is lined almost exclusively with antique shops, a distinction that has earned this community of 2,800 the nickname "antique capital of Maine."

No one is certain why Hallowell has become such a renowned repository of the past, but its picturesque location only enhances its fame. The city's graceful church spires pierce a canopy of green along a broad bend in the Kennebec River; a steep hill dotted with well-preserved vintage homes overlooks a compact business district whose main thoroughfare, Water Street, has early commercial buildings that now contain thriving antique shops.

Hallowell grew accustomed to prosperity during the nineteenth century. A forest of schooner masts towered above wharves bustling with longshoremen unloading molasses and rum from the West Indies, and packing Kennebec River ice in sawdust to cool mint juleps in the southern states and gin and tonics in Great Britain. Teamsters guided straining oxen hauling hundred-ton slabs of gray granite quarried north of town for shipment around the world.

When these industries became obsolete, Hallowell declined, and by the 1950s it was a typically depressed one-street city. That faded thoroughfare and the entire community were infused with new life when peddling the past became profitable. Now visitors come from all over to search for treasures in more than twenty shops delightfully cluttered with everything from rare primitive paintings to exquisitely eccentric brooches.

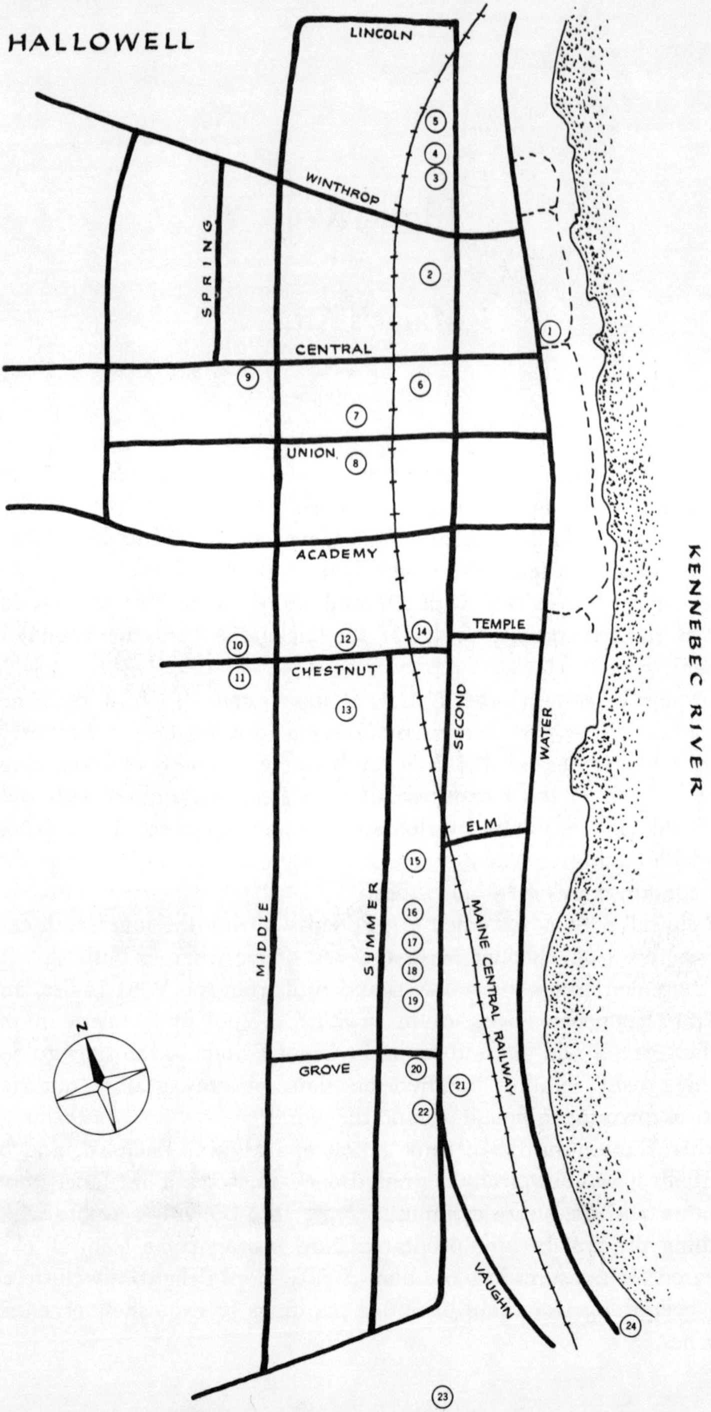
HALLOWELL
LINCOLN
WINTHROP
SPRING
CENTRAL
UNION
ACADEMY
TEMPLE
CHESTNUT
SECOND
WATER
ELM
MIDDLE
SUMMER
MAINE CENTRAL RAILWAY
GROVE
VAUGHN
KENNEBEC RIVER
N
1
2
3
4
5
6
7
8
9
10
11
12
13
14
15
16
17
18
19
20
21
22
23
24

Water Street antique shops

Many stores have specialties, and dealers help shoppers find their exotic requests elsewhere. Cooperation rather than competition makes this a relaxed and appealing place to browse or buy. Earthly Delights offers "cactus and succulents" while McLean's Antiques sells "doll houses and related miniatures." Stamp collectors flock to Howard's, while musicians track down early dulcimers at the Stephen Lapidus store.

When window shopping palls (or the car is filled with antiques), venture beyond Water Street to explore Hallowell's other attractions. Characteristic of the town's imaginative restoration is **Kennebec Row** (1), a block of five identical attached dwellings constructed in the early 1800s. When renovations are completed, it will house shops and offices.

A fire lane behind the stores on Water Street doubles as a riverside path that passes a community flower garden at the foot of Central Street. Benches and picnic tables are scattered amid lawns and shrubs, and the trail leads to a public landing at the end of Temple Street. (Day-long cruises to the ocean and back are favored by local boaters.)

Luminaries such as James K. Polk, Daniel Webster, and Ralph Waldo Emerson were entertained at the **Worster House** (2), an 1833 Georgian hostelry that now contains apartments.

A nearby row of early dwellings includes the 1825 brick-and-wood **Masters House** (3), the early nineteenth-century **Perley House** (4) with its sleek Ionic columns, and the c. 1800 **Agry House** (5), enhanced by an imposing entrance.

Founded in 1842, the **Hubbard Free Library** (6) is now housed in an 1894 Gothic structure of native granite. It contains the Hallowell Collection of early documents and photographs, and a 1602 Bible printed in Geneva, Switzerland. *Open daily except holidays.*

A traditional white spire graces the 1824 **First Baptist Church** (7), originally built as a Unitarian Society meetinghouse.

The outstanding **St. Matthew's Episcopal Church** (8) was built in 1860 from a design by Richard Upjohn, an architect who advocated the use of Gothic Revival style in America. Decorated with a stained-glass window depicting the birth of Christ, this board-and-batten structure is a favorite subject for art students from nearby Colby College. This ecclesiastical corner of town also includes the 1826 **Cox Memorial United Methodist Church** (9), named for the first Methodist missionary in Africa. A stained-glass window depicts Melville B. Cox preaching to an African tribesman. The missionary died in Liberia' in 1833.

The Greek Revival **Cooper-Sanborn House** (**10**) caused a sensation when it was built in 1850 for Captain Henry Cooper. Delicately fluted Ionic columns frame the portico of this classic mansion, formerly the Highlawn Nursing Home and once the most outstanding residence in town.

Spacious halls, high studded ceilings, and a circular staircase grace the elegant **Benjamin Wells House** (**11**), built in 1820 for a druggist noted for his temperance and nautical sentiments (his dining room was a replica captain's cabin paneled with cypress).

Before old furniture became antiques, Hallowell was known as the "granite city" for the high-quality gray stone quarried west of Winthrop Street. Memorials in Hallowell granite include the Maine capitol in Augusta, the Stonewall Jackson monument in New Orleans, and the 105-foot-tall Yorktown monument in Virginia. The New York capitol in Albany accounted for the output of one Hallowell quarry for twenty-one years.

A downhill stroll along Chestnut Street passes the **Tenney House** (**12**), a colonial clapboard mansion built in 1815 by publisher Ezekiel Goodale, and the 1810 **Rufus Page House** (**13**), which has an immense front door topped by a leaded-glass fanlight.

The 127-foot-tall landmark steeple of the **Old Congregational Church** (**14**) leads visitors to Second Street. The first church on this site was built in 1796; the present granite structure was dedicated in 1885.

A series of handsome buildings outside of Hallowell's historic district exemplify the richness of the city's architecture. Just beyond the 1878 **Sacred Heart Catholic Church** (**15**) are the **Beeman-Carr House** (**16**), built about 1800 with a cellar storage hole for rum kegs, and the narrow **Steeves-Currier House** (**17**), built in the early 1830s and still illuminated by the original windows.

The c. 1838 **Howard House** (**18**) was once the residence of the great-grandson of a commander of Fort Western. (This 1754 bastion has been restored in downtown Augusta.)

Charles Vaughan, a leading citizen in the 1800s who built a prodigious brewery, a distillery, and a flour mill, donated land for Hallowell's first cemetery on a site now occupied by the **Watts House** (**19**), built about 1820. The few bodies that had been interred here were transferred to a graveyard laid out on Hinkley's Plain north of town on Water Street.

The **DeWitt Smith House** (**20**), a beautiful home built about 1833

Steeves-Currier House (*left*) **and Beeman-Carr House**

by lawyer John Otis, boasts a massive central hall and double parlors with twin fireplaces. The **Moores House** (21), an 1840 dwelling perched on a riverbank terrace, affords views of the swift Kennebec. Named for an Indian god, this river flows 164 miles from Moosehead Lake, Maine's largest, through rugged timberland flecked with lakes and ponds. Near Hallowell it eases past rolling countryside dotted with dairy farms, then joins the ocean thirty miles south of the city. The Kennebec, along with its major tributary the Androscoggin, drains more than half of Maine.

At the end of Second Street beyond the 1795 **Parson Gillet House** (22) is the **Vaughan Homestead** (23), a Federal dwelling built in 1794 for Benjamin Vaughan, a grandson and heir of town founder Dr. Benjamin Hallowell. Vaughan and his brother Charles were political refugees from England who not only implanted their version of continental culture on their adopted Down East community but also imported, grafted, and propagated apple trees at the state's first commercial nursery. Exports of the tart fruit and cider established Hallowell as the nineteenth-century apple capital of Maine, and proved that fruit trees could thrive in the state's harsh climate.

Wooden signs in a scenic riverbank lookout identify part of the fateful **Benedict Arnold Trail (24).** In November 1775 Arnold, a former horse trader, druggist, and bookseller, led 1,100 troops from Virginia, Pennsylvania, and New Hampshire through northern Maine and down the Chaudière River in an attempt to capture Quebec City.

Their timing was poor. Swamps, forests, and cold claimed half of Arnold's men and most of the food and weapons. Starving survivors ate grease and chewed boiled moccasins. The troops reached Quebec December 31 and were promptly repulsed; Arnold was shot in the leg. But they continued to lay siege to the town until spring when 10,000 British reinforcements sent the general and his men back to the United States.

This historic spot affords a view of a broad bend in the Kennebec known as "the hook." The lovely city nestled along its steep banks looks like a tintype from the past, but Hallowell is not a museum piece. Its energetic citizens work and reside amid a living heritage.

A Down-East Dessert Spiked with Spice

Each spring the farms near Hallowell are alight with apple trees in bloom. It was here in the 1820s that America's first commercial orchard was planted. Descendants of early farmers still enjoy an old-fashioned dessert called apple pandowdy.

The dish, also known as apple cobbler, has many versions. Most use molasses, a West Indian import that figured in many early recipes, and spices carried by New England seamen returning from China and Indonesia.

Peel 6 tart cooking apples, core and slice thinly. Place the apples in a buttered eight-by-ten-inch pan, and cover them with a mixture of 1½ cups light molasses, 1 teaspoon each nutmeg and cinnamon, and ½ teaspoon each ground cloves and ginger. Top this mixture with the pastry for a 1-crust pie, and bake for 1 hour at 350° F.

Serve warm, with the crust down and the apple mixture on top, accompanied by heavy cream.

Wiscasset

A Castle, Two Derelicts, and a House of Wonders

Visitors to Wiscasset's **Waterfront Park** (1) can see the abandoned schooners *Hesper* and *Luther Little,* stuck like beached whales in the Sheepscot River's mud since 1932. They are forlorn reminders of Wiscasset's days as a thriving port; pleasure craft anchored at a nearby yacht club reflect the town's transition to a charming port of call for tourists.

The nineteenth century was Wiscasset's most prosperous. Its year-round harbor, fourteen miles from the sea and one of Maine's deepest, made it a favorite berth for great sailing ships. An adventurous soul could cross the half-mile-wide harbor by leaping from deck to deck; one wharf was nearly two football fields long. Today, only rows of ancient pilings remain. Sea captains and shipping tycoons, wealthy and sophisticated from their travels, built many of Wiscasset's fine homes. Ship carpenters added their nautical embellishments during the winter when shipyards were closed.

The 1870 **Customs House** (2) served as Wiscasset's post office after the town's foreign trade declined. A survivor of two great nineteenth-century fires that leveled the waterfront, it now houses a boutique with one of Maine's finest selections of toys. *Open Mon.–Sat.*

The **Pumpkin House** (3), built in 1807 and named for its distinctive color, had the town's only marble fireplaces of its day. A circular staircase rises from a broad foyer.

"You can move any house in town with eight yokes of oxen and a hogshead of rum," goes an old Wiscasset saw. The **Elmes House** (4), built in 1825 beside the village green, verified this saying when it was moved to its present location in 1845.

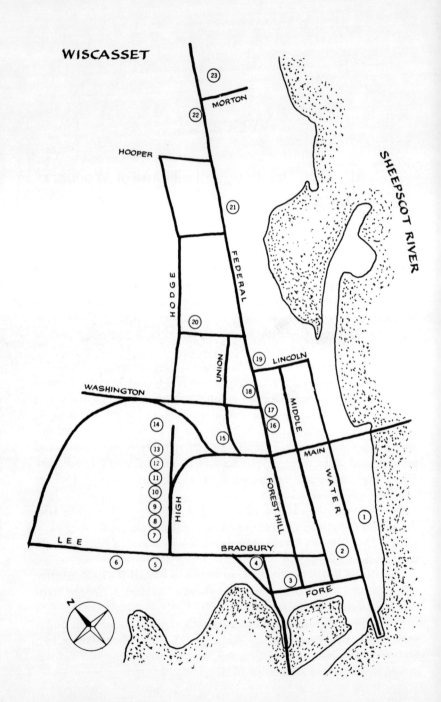

WISCASSET

SHEEPSCOT RIVER

MORTON

HOOPER

HODGE

FEDERAL

UNION

LINCOLN

WASHINGTON

MIDDLE

MAIN

HIGH

FOREST HILL

WATER

LEE

BRADBURY

FORE

N

Hesper and *Luther*

Castle Tucker (5), named for its resemblance to a mansion in Dunbar, Scotland, has a commanding view of Wiscasset harbor from Windmill Hill. Built in 1807 by Judge Silas Lee, this round-winged structure has original Victorian furnishings and an unusual flying staircase. Judge Lee, a county chief justice and a congressman, spent his fortune to build this lavish residence for his wife, Tempe. After Lee's death, a series of odd tenants and the building's romantic appearance—and perhaps something else—fostered its reputation as a haunted house. An unsuperstitious shipowner named Captain Richard

Tucker bought it in 1858 and added its portico two years later. *Open Mon.–Sat. July–Aug.*

Woodcarver's art embellishes the **Samuel Lane Page House** (6), built in 1837. Its portico has grapevine tracery topped by a dove to imitate iron grillwork of the Victorian era. Edbury Hatch of Newcastle, the last of the nineteenth-century carvers of ships' figureheads, created this delicate masterpiece after work ran out in the shipyards.

An aristocratic gathering of gracious mansions rims hillside High Street. The 1811 **Major Abiel Wood House** (7) is a fine example of Federal architecture. Its interior has elaborate woodwork and high ceilings. The 1834 **Captain Tucker House** (8) has a walk-in dining room closet built to hold the china Tucker brought back from his frequent voyages to France. The 1805 **Joseph T. Wood House** (9) was sold soon after its completion to one Major Moses Carleton for one hundred puncheons of rum (a puncheon is an eighty-four-gallon cask). Joseph Wood later sold the rum for a more conventional $12,000.

The 1844 **Patrick Lennox House** (10) is named for the organizer of a syndicate formed to purchase the whaling ship *Wiscasset* in 1833. A whale-tooth carving of the vessel, one of Maine's few whalers, served as a model for a weather vane atop the Municipal Building at Route 1 and Gardiner Road.

The 1852 **Musical Wonder House** (11) is a museum displaying more than two hundred years of mechanical musical instruments. "Musical automata" include a nineteenth-century mechanical pipe organ, an 1812 Swiss music box, performing French musical dolls, player pianos, and spring-operated "talking machines." A boutique in this refurnished sea captain's home sells vintage sheet music and music boxes and rolls. Guided tours feature demonstrations of instruments. *Open daily June–mid-Sept.*

One of Maine's most beautiful homes was built on High Street in 1792 by **Judge Silas Lee** (12). This graceful two-story frame house, backed by formal gardens, has original woodwork and Chinese wallpaper.

The bell of the **Congregational Church** (13) was made from the remains of a Paul Revere bell that was destroyed along with an earlier Congregational church in a 1907 fire. The church's organ dates from 1827.

On the crest of the prettiest green in Maine is the **Lincoln County Courthouse** (14), whose chambers often echoed with Daniel

Congregational Church (*foreground*) **and Lincoln County Court-house**

Webster's oration. Completed in 1824 by master builder Tileston Cushing of Bath, it is the oldest continuously used courthouse in Maine. *Open Mon.–Fri. except holidays.*

Seven fireplaces heat the three-story **Marean House (15).** This

1795 dwelling was later renovated into a fine example of Federal architecture.

A lovely sunken flower garden at the corner of Main and Federal streets softens the crumbling stone foundations of a long-since demolished tavern.

Captain William Nickels spent a fortune in 1807 to build his great retirement mansion on Main Street. In those days, when a carpenter earned a dollar a day, that came to about $14,000. Like many great residences built along the New England coast by retired sea captains, the **Nickels-Sortwell House** (16) is a Federal structure which reflects the influence of Bulfinch, McIntire, and Benjamin—outstanding architects of the period. These men established a simplified American variation of English Georgian architecture. The shady, welcoming approach to the house includes "one of the most beautiful New England doorways," according to early photographer Samuel Chamberlain. It is enhanced by a portico, given additional character by a slight sag and Corinthian columns; a terrace railing adds a final touch of distinction.

Nickels-Sortwell House

The mansion is also noted for its fireplaces and woodwork; carving in the front hall took two years to complete. Here a circular staircase, decorated with rope molding, rises to an oval skylight that floods the room with light. A parlor has simple furnishings with styles ranging from a late eighteenth-century mahogany clock (these tall timepieces were the most expensive furniture in colonial days) to the rolling contours of a graceful Empire sofa. This refurnished mansion now houses the Society for the Preservation of New England Antiquities, which maintains about sixty of the region's historic homes. *Open Tues.–Sun. June–end of Oct.*

The **Lincoln County Fire Museum** (**17**) has displays of antique fire-fighting equipment such as the town's 1803 hand pump. America's first voluntary fire-fighting organization was established here in 1801. Equipment was supplied and maintained by the firemen themselves: two leather buckets, two canvas sacks, and a "bed key" to unlock jointed four-poster beds. The Wiscasset Fire Society was also a charity and a social club "to promote the interest, happiness and prosperity of [its members]," a role it still maintains. *Open by appointment through the Lincoln County Museum and Old Jail.*

Beyond the 1763 **Kingsbury House** (**18**), the oldest two-story dwelling in town, is the **Old Burying Ground** (**19**), also known as the Ancient Cemetery. This peaceful resting place, surrounded by a picket fence and commanding a view of the bay, was laid out in 1735. The earliest tombstone is that of Joshua Pool, who drowned when his canoe capsized in the Sheepscot River in 1739. An obelisk with a windy Latin epitaph honors Samuel Sewall (d. 1814), chief justice of the Commonwealth of Massachusetts. The simpler and more moving epitaph of Thomas Woodman (d. 1796) reads:

> *In foreign climes, alas! resigns his breath,*
> *His friends far from him in the hour of death.*

The **Maine Art Gallery** (**20**), housed in the 1807 Old Academy, has summer exhibitions of painting and sculpture by the state's foremost artists. *Open daily June–mid-Sept.; Sat. and Sun. mid-Sept.–May.*

Along Federal Street are several noteworthy houses including the **Octagon House** (**21**), built in 1855 and one of Maine's few remaining eight-sided structures, and the **Damon House** (**22**), which dates from 1805.

The **Old Lincoln County Jail** (23), completed in 1811 and used until 1954, was the first penitentiary in what is now Maine. The forty-man prison was constructed of huge granite blocks quarried near the mouth of the Sheepscot River. The jailor's house, added in 1839, now contains the Lincoln County Museum. There are changing displays and a tool exhibit. Prisoners' graffiti is featured in the jail. *Open daily June–mid-Sept.*

Old Lincoln County Jail

Grunt, Anyone?

Nothing can match the taste of wild blueberries. Their low bushes cover much of Maine's barren ground, especially northeast of Wiscasset, where harvesting the crop is a major industry. The tart taste of the small wild berries—and the satisfaction of foraging for your own dessert—makes them far superior to the sweet cultivated variety.

Despite its unappetizing name, blueberry grunt has long been a favorite New England dish. To make it, prepare a smooth batter of 1 cup flour, 2 teaspoons baking powder, ¼ teaspoon salt, and ½ cup light cream. Stew 2 cups cleaned berries for about 1 minute in 1 cup water and ½ cup sugar. Then drop the batter into the blueberries by the tablespoonful, spacing the dumplings an inch apart. Lower the heat, cover, and simmer for 20 minutes. When a toothpick stuck into a dumpling comes out clean, the pudding is done.

Serve hot, with cream or whipped cream on the side.

Camden/Rockport

Tonic Air, Windjammers, and André the Seal

During a 1912 summer's end party at Camden's **Whitehall Inn** (1), a shy guest named Edna St. Vincent Millay won first prize for best costume. She recited one of her poems on request, and so impressed a vacationing professor from Cincinnati that he insisted she return next evening to recite another one of her works. Edna complied with "Renascence," which describes a scene from atop nearby **Mount Battie** (2):

> *All I could see from where I stood*
> *Was three long mountains and a wood;*
> *I turned and looked the other way,*
> *And saw three islands in a bay . . .*
> *Over these things I could not see;*
> *These were the things that bounded me . . .*

Nestled by a snug harbor rimmed with hills, Camden has retained the beauty that graced the borders of young Millay's life. Antique shops and art galleries line quiet streets abloom with flowers.

In Victorian times this "jewel of the Penobscot" was favored for its "tonic air, salubrious climate, and healthful waters." Today, Camden still offers splendid natural beauty and diversions seldom found in communities this size, such as a theater group, a chamber music ensemble, a summer art gallery, and specialty shops noted for their silver and knit goods.

The Whitehall Inn is renowned not only for its gracious accommodations but also as the place where poet Millay's talent was first discovered. In the parlor a corner bookcase is stocked with some of

CAMDEN / ROCKPORT

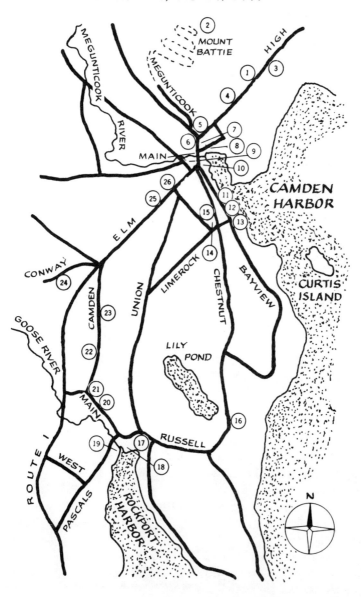

Millay's books, photographs of the poet, an unpublished manuscript, and a facsimile of the original draft of "Renascence." The innkeeper has compiled a scrapbook of pictures and articles about Millay. From the veranda visitors can appreciate the inspiration she derived from Penobscot Bay, with its spruce-tufted islands scalloped with lacy foam.

A short distance up the hill from the Whitehall Inn looms **Norumbega (3)**. This stone-and-oak castle was built about 1886 by Joseph B. Stearns, inventor of the duplex system of telegraph.

A stroll down wooded High Street passes several venerable dwellings, including the 1798 **Dr. Joseph Huse House (4)**. It once belonged to a physician who practiced here for fifty years, as did his nephew Dr. Jonathan Huse, whose 1820 dwelling is next door.

Walkers keen to share Millay's vantage (and prepared for a vigorous climb) can follow a one-mile switchback trail at the end of Megunticook Street up 1,300-foot Mount Battie. A plaque atop a

Victory Chimes

viewing tower at the summit honors Millay, and commands panoramas of Camden's quiet beauty: graceful windjammers scudding out to the island-dotted bay, lobster boats bobbing in the snug harbor, and at dusk the sun easing behind the rounded, blue Camden Hills.

The 1895 **Holly M. Bean House** (5) on Monument Square is named for a shipbuilder who launched more than fifty vessels here, including America's first six-masted ship, the 2,970-ton *George W. Wells.*

The **Micah Hobbs House** (6), part of which dates from about 1780, boasted the town's first running water. Hobbs and his brother tapped a spring on Mount Battie and went to the well no more.

Tranquil in its lovely harborside park, the **Camden Public Library** (7) offers quiet repose amid timeless volumes, as well as paintings, model ships, and Millay memorabilia. *Open daily except holidays.* Behind the library is the **Amphitheater** (8), a shady oasis with cut

granite seats where outdoor plays, concerts, and special events are
held. The **Suffolk Gallery** (9) facing the village green specializes in
European paintings and eighteenth-century English pottery and furniture. *Open Mon.–Sat.*

The town's great windjammers anchor at the **Camden Public Landing** (10). The fleet includes the 137-foot *Roseway,* Maine's tall ship
in the Bicentennial "Operation Sail," and *Adventure,* featured in
the film *Captains Courageous.* The ships weigh anchor Monday morning about ten o'clock for six-day cruises among the islands and bays of
Maine. Vacationers eager for blue-water thrills can haul the sheets,
learn how to shoot the stars, explore remote anchorages in "hundred-
harbored Maine," eat lobster at quiet rocky coves, or just relax.

Cocktails on deck, then dinner in the boiler room is *de rigueur* on
board *John Wanamaker,* a retired tugboat converted into a quaint
dockside restaurant.

The Megunticook River thunders into the harbor in a cooling waterfall near the public landing. A beach along Bayview Street has a
jungle gym for children and picnic benches on grassy slopes extending
down to the water. Waterfront culture thrives on Bayview Street. The
Brott Gallery (11) features works by Maine artists. *Open Mon.–Sat.*
Next door **Perspectives** (12) exhibits and sells pottery, leatherwork,
clothing, and jewelry by the state's craftsmen. *Open Mon.–Sat. mid-
June–Dec.* **Thar She Blows** (13) houses antique marine artifacts, including binnacles, sea chests, telescopes, ship models, and decorative
rope work fashioned by bored sailors. *Open daily May–Oct.; by appointment Nov.–Apr.*

The 1800 **Jacob's House** (14) once stood on a 143-acre farm. The
site of the farm's lime quarries is today's Union Street.

Some scenes from the movie *Peyton Place* were filmed at **Thayer-
croft** (15), an 1821 home built by Jonathan Thayer, a judge and
"gentleman of distinction." (Whitehall Inn also had a bit part in the
movie.)

Ambitious walkers hike a pastoral 2½ miles over a wooded hill on
Chestnut Street to Camden's twin city of Rockport, an attractive
fishing village and summer resort. Belted Galloway cattle graze in
meadows here, and at dusk the twitters and trills of foraging birds
echo in darkening roadside glades.

The rambling 1795 **Daniel Barrett House** (16) stands beside a pasture and the Lily Pond, with its carpet of fragrant blossoms. At the
turn of the century "Lily Pond Ice" was known as far south as Flor-

ida. A few enterprising Rockporters made a fortune cutting about 50,000 tons of ice each winter for twenty-five cents a ton and selling it dockside a mile away for four dollars a ton.

The **Old Firehouse** (17) has had many uses—from fire station to livery stable to town offices—but its present role as a gallery for well-known Maine artists seems to best complement its scenic harborside setting. *Open daily June–mid-Sept.*

The Rockport Garden Club sponsors a July open-house tour to view horticultural accomplishments at local estates. The club's members have such green thumbs that even Rockport and Camden streetlamps sprout flowers. A resident brought back the idea from Lymington, England, in the 1920s. A blacksmith made wire baskets, which the club still fills with geraniums, petunias, and ivies. The garden club also restored the **Rockport Town Hall and Opera House** (18), now a theater and concert hall. Recitals are held Thursday evenings in July and August. Concerts and plays are occasionally presented in summer at Mary Lea Park, a wide swath of grass and trees between the opera house and the harbor.

Like the abandoned fireplaces of some titan, **lime kilns** (19) crumble near the mouth of the Goose River. Nearby is the Rockport marina, summer home of André the seal. For almost twenty years this plump denizen of Rockport's harbor has migrated south in autumn to his cushy quarters at Boston's New England Aquarium. But for the warm season he always swims back here, where he performs daily at 4 P.M. in return for piscine rewards. A statue of André in Mary Lea Park was erected by the seal's admirers.

A stroll uphill along Rockport's Main Street passes the 1840 **John Pascal House** (20), named for a master shipbuilder who launched more than sixty ships. A widow's walk graces the roof.

Carved pineapples over the front door of the Victorian **Treat House** (21) signify more than the handiwork of a moonlighting ship carpenter dreaming of warmer ports. This tropical fruit meant a hearty welcome awaited within.

A walk up Camden Street features the **Eben Thorndike Homestead** (22), once the home of a descendant of Rockport's first settler, and the Federal **Tyler-Carleton Mansion** (23), built about 1800. Just before the War of 1812, sails stripped from a vessel that had violated the Embargo Act were stored in its cellar.

A side trip along Conway Road is a step into the past. Surrounded by grounds landscaped with maples, oaks, apple trees, lilacs, and weeping willows, the 1780 **Old Conway House** (24) provides a rustic home for the Camden-Rockport Historical Society. This Cape Cod-style farmhouse with its hand-hewn beams fastened with treenails (or "trunnels"—wooden pegs), brick oven, and fanlight over the front door is a testament to the skill of colonial carpenters. An adja-

Old Conway House

cent barn contains a refurnished schoolroom, a nineteenth-century fire engine named *Molineaux*, and a locomotive that once hauled lime from nearby quarries to Rockport's kilns. A blacksmith shop is fully equipped (except for the spreading chestnut tree). Tools include a scarred and worn ox lifter used to hoist the beasts for shoeing. In the Mary Meeker Cramer Museum here are ship models, nautical items, an extensive costume collection, and many documents, including a copy of Camden's first town map (1795). *Open Mon.–Fri. July–mid-Sept.* Trails in a nearby sixty-six-acre nature park wander through woods and flower-dotted fields.

A stately fourteen-room Victorian mansion now houses the **Gallery Shop of Camden (25),** which specializes in stained and blown glass, dollhouse miniatures, and ethnic clothing. In summer, crafts are displayed in an adjacent barn. *Open Mon.–Sat.*

The white spire of the 1834 **Congregational Church (26)** beckons walkers back down the hill and into Camden—a gesture that belies the town's sometimes stormy relationship with the clergy. Camden was indicted in 1794 and fined two pounds under a Massachusetts law for failing to support a minister. The following year the town was forced to turn to itinerant preachers for spiritual sustenance. The citizens lured their first minister in 1805 with a $500 salary. At ordination ceremonies one John Norton of Lincolnville "made an unnatural fool of himself by imbibing to excess and while endeavoring to accomplish the feat of a glutton, swallowed a piece of unmasticated meat and choked to death."

Nearby is the Conway Boulder, which honors Camden's Civil War hero. In 1861 Union Army quartermaster William Conway refused a Confederate demand to lower the flag at a naval yard in Pensacola, Florida. He was imprisoned for his patriotism.

When Conway's shipmate visited Camden in 1905, he was distressed to find no reminders of his friend's heroism. A stirring celebration the following year included seven battleships, five destroyers, and a parade attended by 10,000. Sixty horses hauled this thirty-ton boulder from a nearby hill to its present location. A plaque on the boulder reminds Camden of its valiant native son.

A Magic Circle of Flame

Kilns at the mouth of the Goose River are reminders that Rockport was once one of the nation's largest producers of lime, a valuable fertilizer and building mortar. The Capitol in Washington is held together with Rockport lime.

Kilns were usually twenty-foot-high fieldstone furnaces built into a hillside with a hearth opening near the base covered by a massive iron door. An arch of limestone blocks was built in the kiln, leaving air

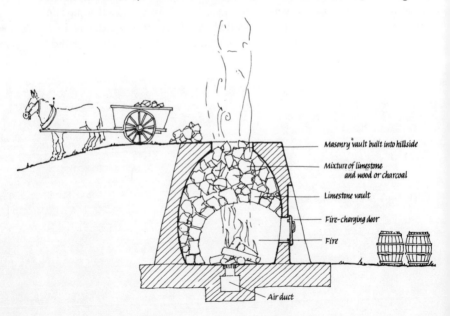

Masonry vault built into hillside

Mixture of limestone and wood or charcoal

Limestone vault

Fire-charging door

Fire

Air duct

space for a wood fire below. Above the arch was a mixture of lime-stone chunks and wood or charcoal, which was ignited along with the fire. "All these innumerable blocks and fragments of marble," wrote Hawthorne in 1852, mistaking limestone for marble, "were red-hot and vividly on fire, sending up great spouts of blue flame, which quivered aloft and danced madly, as within a magic circle. . . ."

The limer tended this miniature purgatory for a week, preventing the fire from dying or becoming too hot and melting the limestone into slag. The right temperature would turn limestone into a fine powder which sifted through to the base of the kiln.

When the mixture burned itself out, the powder was packed in casks for shipment aboard "limers." These coastal schooners had to be leakproof since a chemical reaction between lime and water could ignite the ship. Rockport Harbor shelters the charred remains of limers sunk by a fiery cancer in their holds.

Bangor

Bangor Cultivates the Devil's Half-Acre

Bangor was like "a star on the edge of night," wrote Henry David Thoreau in 1846 on his visit to the Maine woods. The town must have seemed celestial only by comparison to the surrounding "howling wilderness." In the next decade 2½ million acres of forest were opened up in central Maine, and New England's last frontier turned Bangor into the rowdiest, busiest lumber port on earth.

The boom lasted as long as the tall timber. For thirty years Bangor shipped as much as 150 million board feet a year. Lumberjacks descended on this tough, swaggering town in spring at the end of logging season for drinking, wenching, and fighting with blue-water sailors in a part of town once called the Devil's Half-Acre.

On Exchange Street two enterprising women rented a house and hung a shingle to advertise their services: "Gentlemen's Washing Taken In." The gentlemen taken to these cleaners, however, paid for services more lascivious than laundering. Perhaps the most famous Bangor brothel was Fan Jones's Skyblue House on Harlow Street. Its chimney was a beacon painted bright blue twice a year to attract loggers from the forest and sailors from the sea.

Today Maine's third largest city (pop. 33,000) is the reverse of that rambunctious age. Lumber barons built gracious mansions and brought Bangor a reputation as the state's cultural capital.

The town's many parks, including a verdant fringe of trees and grass along Kenduskeag Stream, enhance this bustling, cosmopolitan center on the broad Penobscot River. A hillside grove in **Davenport Park (1)** enfolds a bronze monument and eagle honoring the battleship *Maine* and servicemen killed in the Spanish-American War. On the wedge-

BANGOR

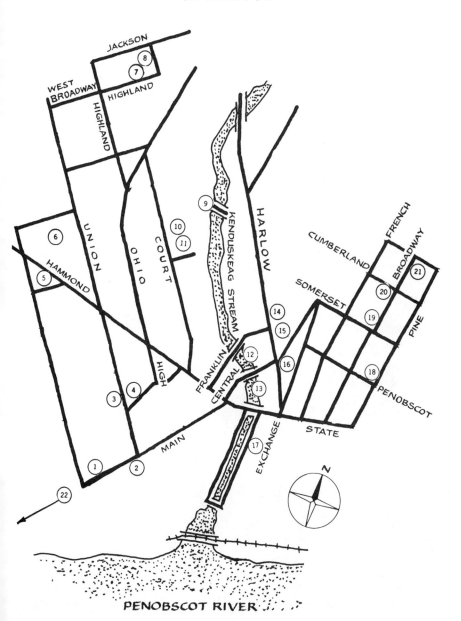

shaped granite base, which resembles a ship's prow, are the original shield and scroll recovered from *Maine*'s wreckage after it was blown up in Havana harbor.

Architect Charles G. Bryant, who designed **Bangor House** (2), also met an unfortunate end: He was scalped in Texas. One of his hotel's first functions after its grand opening in 1834 was a dinner for Daniel Webster, then New England's favorite candidate for President. Like most Maine hotels, this hostelry used the "Bangor Plan" during Prohibition: Owners paid standard fines twice a year and the police ignored violations. The hotel is now an apartment building.

The English Regency **Isaac Farrar Mansion** (3) was built in 1843 by a wealthy lumberman. Bricks were shipped from England, roof slates from Bangor in Wales, and mahogany for the dining room from Santo Domingo. Formerly a law school and music conservatory, it is now owned by the YWCA. *Open daily.*

The rival mansion that businessman Thomas A. Hill built a year later is now the Grand Army Memorial Home, which houses the **Bangor Historical Society–Penobscot Heritage Museum** (4). Among 20,000 items displayed in this Greek Revival residence are portraits by

Bangor Theological Seminary

Jeremiah Hardy, a nineteen-foot Penobscot Indian canoe used in lumber drives, a collection of lumbering tools, and a cannon from the Penobscot Expedition during the Revolutionary War. *Open Tues.–Fri.*

The **Hannibal Hamlin House** (5) was bought in 1851 by Lincoln's first Vice-president. Now the Bangor Theological Seminary's presidential residence, the house has two black marble fireplaces, ceiling-to-floor drawing room windows with paneled shutters, and ornately carved doors. *Open by prearrangement.*

Graced by a well-treed campus, the **Bangor Theological Seminary** (6) was founded in 1814 as the Maine Charity School for underprivileged children. There are prearranged tours.

A walk up the gentle, shaded slopes of Thomas Hill, via West Broadway with its outstanding post-Civil War mansions, passes the lavish 1857 Italianate **Joseph Low House** (7) and **The Standpipe** (8), a cylindrical wooden structure that rises above the treetops like a squat parapet. It was erected in 1898 by a sawmill owner named Ashley B. Tower to conceal a water tower and preserve the neighborhood's beauty; instead it dominates the skyline.

Maine's longest covered bridge (212 feet) now spans Kenduskeag Stream down the hill from **Coe Park** (9). Built in 1881 and slated for demolition in 1961, the Morse Bridge was moved here from Valley Avenue. The Bangor Bridge, constructed in the 1840s and long since demolished, dwarfed this structure. A 742-footer that spanned the Penobscot River, it had portals with flared tops, reflecting that era's craze for Egyptian architecture. Maine bridges were used for more than traffic: Lumbermen on projecting piers kept logs moving to prevent jams. Bridges were also excellent viewing platforms to watch huge logs glide by.

The Greek Revival **Nathaniel Hatch House** (10) affords more fine views of the Kenduskeag Valley from a knoll. This 1830 brick home with pillared front and rear porticoes is now Kenduskeag Terrace, a housing project for the elderly. The nearby 1858 **William Blake Mansion** (11) was built in Second Empire style for a wealthy Bangor merchant.

Norumbega Parkway (12), a peaceful spot for resting weary feet or picnicking along Kenduskeag Stream, takes its name either from Spanish ("country of the Northmen") or an Indian dialect ("still waters between falls"). A war memorial designed by Charles E. Tefft of Brewer depicts a woman with palm fronds in one hand and light in the other.

Farther downstream is **Kenduskeag Mall** (13), a continuation of

The Standpipe

the parkway's lawns and leafy glades. There is less confusion over this name, an Indian word for "eel-catching place." A statue in this pedestrian mall by Tefft honors Hannibal Hamlin, and a bronze plaque on a boulder commemorates Samuel de Champlain's landing here in 1604.

Near the boulder are two cannons, one recovered from Havana harbor after the Spanish-American War, the other from the 1779 Penobscot Expedition, a disastrous excursion seldom mentioned in history books. A fleet of twenty-three vessels and 1,000 troops sailed from Boston to recapture British-held Castine at the mouth of the Penobscot. The American contingent, which included General Peleg Wadsworth (Longfellow's grandfather) and Lieutenant Colonel Paul Revere, was

Morse Bridge, Coe Park

routed by four British vessels, and without firing a shot they scuttled their fleet to avoid capture.

About ten ships reached Bangor, where they were blown up near the mouth of Kenduskeag Stream; they still lie at the bottom of the harbor. Lieutenant Colonel Revere, on his return to Boston, was arrested for cowardice, but was found innocent of the charges.

More than 400,000 volumes are in the imposing 1915 brick-and-marble **Bangor Public Library** (14), founded in 1883. Its art collection features paintings by Jeremiah Hardy and a bronze bust of Hannibal Hamlin. Local artists' works are often exhibited. *Open daily except holidays.* The nearby **Pierce Memorial** (15) is a vigorous testament to the city's logging heritage. This bronze monument by Tefft depicts three rivermen breaking up a log jam.

Stone blocks used in construction of the classical **Bangor City Hall** (16) were on a train bound for Richmond, Virginia, when word of Bangor's disastrous 1911 fire reached the contractor who had bought them. He sent the blocks north to help rebuild the city.

Central Street, which spans Kenduskeag Stream, seems a peaceable downtown area, but in 1937 it was the scene of a gun battle between the FBI and the Brady Gang. The G-men were tipped off by the proprietor of Dakin's Sporting Goods Store on Broad Street when these midwestern hoodlums tried to buy weapons. Leader Al Brady and his cohort Clarence Shaffer were killed. James Dalhover was captured in the store and returned to Indiana, where he was tried for murder and electrocuted.

Bangor's past and present come to life at the **Merrill Bank** (17) in a twenty-three-by-seven-foot mural by Hall Groat of New York. This monumental work depicts local landmarks, many of them on this tour: the Isaac Farrar House, The Standpipe, and Bangor House, and others that have succumbed to fire or the wrecker's ball. *Open Mon.–Sat.*

The **Edward Kent–Jonas Cutting House** (18), a splendid Greek Revival residence, was named for two law partners. Kent was Bangor's mayor (1836–37) and Maine's governor (1838–39 and 1840–42). Jonas Cutting was a state supreme court justice (1854–75).

The tour leaves downtown and ascends Broadway on wooded Thomas Hill to a quiet neighborhood. A four-block area here with elegant early homes has been declared a historic district. Some of the more outstanding residences include the 1802 **Daniel B. Hinckley Home** (19), built in late Federal style, and the 1866 **P. A. Strickland House** (20), a 2½-story Victorian dwelling with mansard roofs. Charles Bulfinch designed the **Smith Boutelle House** (21) and Presidents McKinley and Garfield graced its small balcony as guests. Doric columns and intricate carvings enhance this neighborhood showpiece.

The Roistering, Perilous Life of a Lumberjack

A thirty-one-foot-high statue of Paul Bunyan in **Bass Park** (22) *at the end of Main Street recalls Bangor's days as the lumber capital of the world. The city issues a birth certificate that "proves" the mythical lumberman was born here.*

Real-life lumberjacks were less impressive, according to an 1889 ac-

count: "*They do not appear robust; many of them are pale, hollow-cheeked, and with sunken chests. . . .*"

Not surprising, considering the dangers and deprivations of the Maine woods. Bunked in crude, windowless log cabins, lumberjacks felled trees all winter with twelve-pound axes, removed bark, and dragged logs to riverbanks with horses or oxen.

In spring river drivers guided log booms—most 300 by 60 feet, others a half-mile long—down the Penobscot to Bangor. Gruesome memorials to drowned or mangled log jockeys (also known as "bubble cuffers") can still be found in remote areas: boots nailed to a tree above an otherwise unmarked grave.

If they survived winter and spring breakup, lumberjacks descended on Bangor in "a roistering plague" to blow their wages in orgies of excess. Brawling lumbermen seldom used guns or knives: They kicked. Scars left on tavern ceilings by their hob-nailed boots were called shantyman's smallpox.

Bar Harbor

A Summer Carnival of Tin Lizzies
and Clothesline Art

Clinging to the rocky northeast shore of Mount Desert Island, Bar Harbor has been a summer retreat ever since Abnaki Indians paddled here to feast on abundant berries, fish, and lobster.

Samuel de Champlain coasted the largest of Maine's 2,000 islands in 1604 and named it L'Isle des Monts-Deserts (Isle of Bare Mountains), which locals now pronounce as though it followed dinner.

Artists of the Hudson River School came here in the 1840s to capture on canvas the island's realm of rock and fog. Outdoorsy Boston intellectuals and clergymen, who reveled in spartan regimes and rugged hiking, followed in the 1860s. They boarded at local homes where fish was served three times a day, seven days a week. ("It stimulates and adds to the brain," noted one great thinker.)

Such monotonous fare would not do for barons of industry and finance like A. Atwater Kent, Joseph Pulitzer, and George V. Vanderbilt, who built ostentatious "cottages" the following decade. Interested in neither seascapes nor hiking, strand nor summit, they rusticated in grand residences that defined American opulence and excess in that gay, glittering era. "With no income tax," wrote one historian, "a plethora of servants, and eggs twenty cents a dozen, joy could be unrestrained."

Although that gaudy life-style ended with World War I and income tax, it took a natural disaster to destroy most of the grand cottages. In October 1947 the island was "so dry it could have patched hell two times over." A windswept forest fire wiped out a third of the 220 estates, and burned over much of the 11,000 scenic acres that John D. Rockefeller had donated for Acadia National Park.

BAR HARBOR

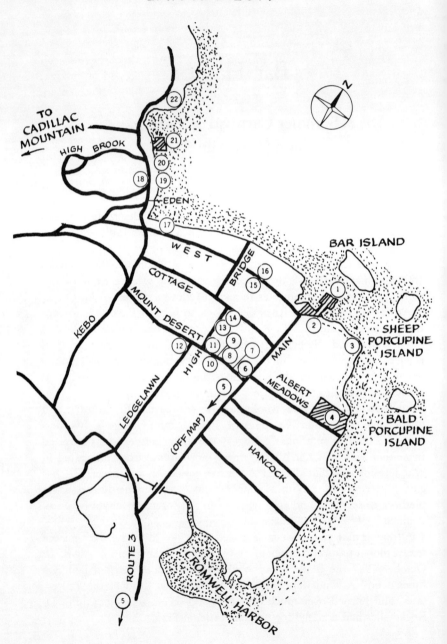

Motels have arisen from the ruins, and the forest is green again. To-day's visitors are not quite as well heeled as those glamorous Gatsbys of old, but their love of backpacking and cookouts seems more appropriate to this setting than yachting and black-tie banquets.

"Now there's a more sophisticated tourist," says a doctor who's been a summer resident most of his life. "They're interested in hiking, climbing, the sort of thing that brought people to Bar Harbor before the wealthy came."

The town is now a side trip for campers whose destination is the magical beauty of nearby Acadia National Park. Many visitors are attracted by galas such as the Antique Auto Show in the third week of June, when Stanley Steamers and Model T's sputter and chug through the streets before retreating to the athletic field just south of town for various competitions.

Others more inclined to the strains of string quartets than the symphony of Tin Lizzies patronize concerts at various locales during an August music festival. Still more quiet pursuits beckon down secluded lanes and side streets which yield delightful discoveries: a cluttered antique shop, a hushed old cemetery, or a rustic summer cottage.

In summer activity is centered at the **town pier** (1), with its souvenir shop and information booth. Anglers can land harbor pollock and

Town pier

mackerel here in late July; lobster can be purchased with less effort. Boats leave the pier several times a day for cruises along the rock-bound coast offering views of the great estates perched on tumbled cliffs overlooking Frenchman Bay. Other vessels can be chartered by landlubbers anxious to land a trophy fish, even if it's just a cod.

A Fourth of July parade includes more antique cars, marching bands, and colorful floats; and sometimes fireworks at the pier cap the day's festivities.

A trail from **Agamont Park (2)**, with its fountain, flower beds, and hawthorn trees leads to the Shore Path, a strand-skirting walk past large estates. The trail winds behind the **Bar Harbor Motor Inn (3)**, once the Mount Desert Reading Room. Barons of industry and finance gathered at this exclusive club to gamble, drink port, exchange business tips, and keep an eye on their sleek yachts anchored offshore.

Beyond the inn, the trail skirts Balance Rock, a glacial erratic

Shore Path

poised precariously on the shore, passes elegant summer homes, and threads clumps of birch and pine. Rocks cleft with wild purple asters provide perches for gulls; at low tide tiny tidal pools teem with crustaceans darting between fingers of seaweed. Offshore can be seen the four Porcupine Islands—Sheep, Burnt, Long, and Bald.

The trail can also be entered at **Grant Park** (4), below Albert Meadows; several other paths between here and the motor inn lead back into town.

The world's largest mammalian genetics research laboratory is a strenuous two-mile walk on Route 3, but at least most of it is on sidewalk. Those who have made the trek agree that **Jackson Laboratory** (5) is well worth a visit. Mice help scientists there unravel the mystery of hereditary and other diseases. Precisely controlled inbreeding over hundreds of generations has produced mice with leukemia, diabetes, and mammary cancer; researchers study them to help solve today's incurable diseases. A million "Jax" mice are distributed each year to researchers around the world. The center offers one-hour programs with a speaker and a film about the institute. *Tues., Wed., Fri. at 3:00 mid-June–mid-Sept.*

In summer the **village Green** (6) resounds to the stentorian strains of the town band Monday and Thursday at 8 P.M. Local artists put their work "on the line" here during the Clothesline Art Exhibit in July. Drawings, etchings, and watercolors brighten clotheslines and snow fences during the unusual exhibition. A craft show is also held on the Green in August.

This part of Mount Desert Street has an ecclesiastical tranquillity enhanced by the 1887 **Congregational Church** (7), built of native pink granite. Next door a more enduring calm permeates the small, orderly **Town Cemetery** (8), dominated by a Civil War monument. The burying ground is liberally salted with the graves of sea captains, including Captain James Hamor whose stone bears a bas-relief depicting a shipwreck in stormy seas.

A July fair and luncheon enliven the pink granite **St. Saviour's Episcopal Church** (9), an 1879 cruciform structure with Tiffany stained-glass windows.

The charming and informal atmosphere of the Bar Harbor Historical Museum in the basement of **Jesup Memorial Library** (10) is enhanced by Windsor chairs flanking a snug fireplace. Over the mantel is a painting of Hulls Cove, the first settlement hereabouts (1768). The museum's extensive photograph collection recaptures the nostalgia of Bar Harbor's grand cottages, steamboats, and early hotels. *Open Mon.–Fri. afternoons mid-June–mid-Sept.*

In 1900 retired Boston publisher Lewis Roberts built a cottage called **Thornhedge** (11), now an elegant inn. Many rooms in the cheery yellow hostelry contain their original furniture. The nearby granite **Holy Redeemer Catholic Church** (12) hosts a fair and auction in August.

At the **Masonic Lodge** (13) the smell of fresh flapjacks quickens appetites in August during the Blueberry Pancake Breakfast.

A lovely piazza surrounds **Central House** (14), built in 1887 and once owned by Washington *Post* publisher John McLean (his son later brought the Hope diamond). The dwelling is now an inn. **Manor House Inn** (15), in another summer cottage, has turn-of-the-century decor that captures the era's gracious living style.

String concerts are held at the **Bar Harbor Club** (16) during the August music festival. At low tide visitors can walk from the end of Bridge Street here about two hundred yards offshore to Bar Island. It's a fine spot for picnics, but watch out for the tides. "People do get stranded there," notes a cheery information booth attendant, "but sometimes intentionally."

Fieldstone fences and shady driveways along West Street hint at gracious homes set back among the trees. The **Maine Sea Coast Mission** (17) is housed in a 1913 Georgian estate once owned by a Campbell Soup heir. Mariner-minister Rev. Stanley Haskell administers an offshore parish "from Kittery to Calais," bringing spiritual and material aid to islanders via the sixty-five-foot *Sunbeam IV*. Also known as "God's Tugboat," the vessel is berthed at nearby Northeast Harbor when Rev. Haskell isn't dropping in on a Sunday to bring church services to an island without a pastor.

The **Cleftstone Inn** (18) is housed in a historic mansion furnished with period pieces and works of art from around the world.

A former Oblate Seminary with a splendid location on the rocky shore of Frenchman Bay now houses the **College of the Atlantic** (19), a coeducational school founded in 1969. The Turrets, a summer home built by J. J. Emery of Cincinnati after the plans of a French castle, is being restored as offices and a dormitory. Open to the public are poetry readings, lectures, films, and galleries with woodcuts, sculpture, paintings, and original Audubon prints. *Open daily.*

Seven magnificently landscaped acres overlooking the ocean surround the mansion of Sir Harry Oakes, a drifter and prospector who eventually became a millionaire. Oakes made his fortune at a northern Ontario gold mine, and owned a thirty-seven-room residence in Niagara Falls in addition to this Bar Harbor summer home. Oakes moved to the Bahamas in the mid-1930s to avoid taxes, and in 1943 he was found murdered in his Nassau home. His son-in-law was charged with the killing, but was acquitted, and the case was never solved. Today, Oakes's estate is a hostelry called **Atlantic Oakes-by-the-Sea (20).**

Luxurious Wingwood House once stood on the site of the present-day **Novia Scotia Ferry terminal (21).** Mr. and Mrs. E. T. Stotesbury's palatial "cottage" included forty servants' rooms, twenty-eight bathrooms (her own had solid gold fixtures), and a dining room decorated in eighteenth-century English style. The house was rebuilt twice at a total cost of $1 million before it was torn down.

Patterned after an Italian villa, **Sonogee Mansion (22)** echoes the wealth and grandeur once associated with this summer resort. Built in 1903, this forty-room mansion is now a nursing home. Its opulent interior once included a solid marble staircase and hand-painted French wallpaper. One of its owners was A. Atwater Kent, the radio magnate of the 1920s.

Broiled or Boiled, a Gourmet's Delight

Lobsters were once so abundant in Maine's coastal waters that they were used for codfish bait, or even garden fertilizer. Only the poor would deign to dine on seafood that sold for two cents a pound. Today's high prices are the unfortunate result of a dwindling supply and a demand—or craving—that has made lobster a succulent luxury.

Maine fishermen harvest a third of the lobsters eaten in North America. Cold offshore waters provide an ideal habitat for the crustaceans. They are caught in baited traps made of wooden laths and net, and stored alive underwater in enclosures called pounds until ready to be sent to market. Minimum size is one pound; at this weight a lobster is about five years old.

Wily lobsters that manage to escape the boiling pot can grow to massive size. The biggest on record, a forty-two-pound monster, is displayed in the Boston Museum of Natural History.

How to cook and eat a lobster

Look for the liveliest one when you choose a lobster from a tank. The 1–1¼-pounder, called a chicken lobster, is the most desirable size.

To cook lobster, first boil a deep pot of seawater, or heavily salted water. Grip the lobster by the back and plunge it headfirst into the water. Cover and let simmer 12–15 minutes for a 1-pound lobster, adding a minute for each additional ¼ pound.

After the lobster cools slightly, there's more work to do. Turn it shell side down, and split the underside from head to tail. Remove the dark intestinal vein that runs down the back, and the small white sac that is the stomach. Leave the "tomalley"—the green liver—located in the head; it's considered by many to be a delicacy.

Crack the claws with a hammer or nutcracker, and break the rest of the body with your hands. The rest is easy: dip lobster meat in melted butter, and enjoy.

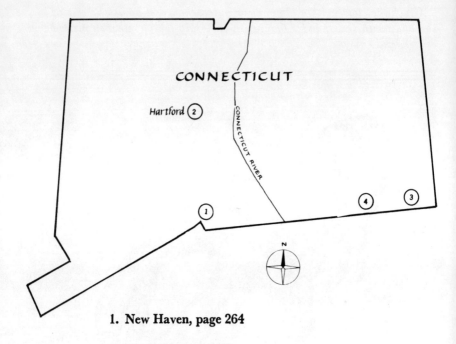

CONNECTICUT

Connecticut is a state of mind as well as of rounded hills and shingled steeples rising above town commons. Adriaen Block, in 1614, was the first to sail into the Connecticut River, that waterway that splits Connecticut and Massachusetts and separates Vermont and New Hampshire. It was the river by which Connecticut's first settlers, coming from Massachusetts in 1663, founded Hartford, and went so far as to write a Constitution. These ancestors of today's Yankees—taciturn, inventive, stubbornly independent—hacked their livelihood from the equally stubborn New England wilderness. Their farms and villages not only survived but prospered. Eventually, dairy products, poultry, and tobacco were overshadowed by aircraft engines, silverware, machinery, submarines, and forty-five insurance companies. Despite this change, a sense of antiquity and quiet charm lingers throughout Connecticut. Mellowed brick, weathered stone, and the subtle echoes of three centuries of American history enchant and entice the visitor.

New Haven

From the Tables Down at Mory's . . .

New Haven's Green (1), a registered National Historic Landmark, is the center of nine squares laid out in the summer of 1638 by surveyor John Brockett. The city plan, based on ancient Roman and British fortifications of the same pattern, made New Haven the first planned city in America.

The symmetry of the nine squares has remained unchanged since the colony was established in 1638, and the Green has remained the focal point of New Haven's religious, social, political, and economic development. Starting as a cow pasture and burial ground, the Green then became the site of the first statehouse in 1763, although cows continued to graze there for another fifty-eight years. Nathan Hale raced and wrestled here while a student at Yale. Sinners were held in pillories and stocks, and criminals incarcerated in a jail here. Some 3,000 invading British and Hessian troops encamped on the Green on July 5 and 6, 1779. Today the Green is the site of a Summer Festival and symphony concerts, and a magnet for kite-flyers, picnickers, and Frisbee-throwers.

The three churches on the Green were all erected in a fit of ecumenicalism between 1812 and 1815. **United Congregational Church** (2), or North Church, is a classic example of Federalist architecture whose design, like that of neighboring Center Church, was derived from St. Martin's-in-the-Fields in London. **Center Church** (3), which traces its origin to 1638, is a masterpiece of Georgian architecture. The British allowed structural timbers for the massive brick building to be floated through their blockade during the War of 1812. It has an ornate roof balustrade decorated with urns, an elaborate pediment carv-

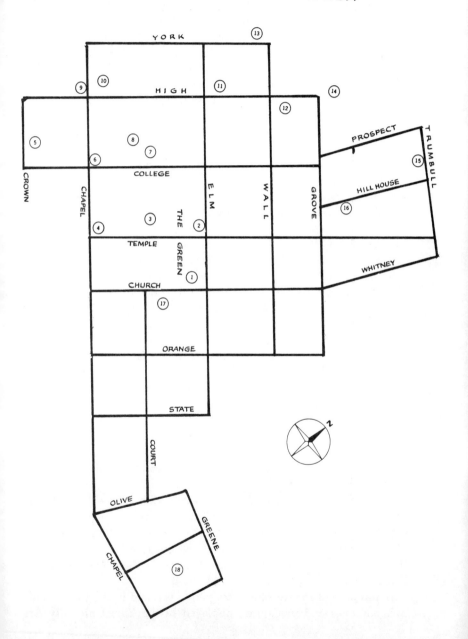

NEW HAVEN

ing, and a superb spire. Inside, a Tiffany window depicts a scene of the colony's founding. In the crypt below is the resting place of 130 seventeenth- and eighteenth-century townsfolk, including Margaret Mansfield Arnold, Benedict Arnold's first wife. **Trinity Episcopal Church** (4) was designed by Ithiel Town and completed in 1815. The tower, the long, pointed Tiffany stained-glass window, and the Aeolian-Skinner organ are among its distinctive features. The Choir of Men and Boys of Trinity Church is well known for its concerts and recordings.

Louis' Lunch (5), of "Whiffinpoof Song" fame, is also the birthplace of a great American invention. Owned by three generations of the Lassen family, the restaurant is said to be the place where the hamburger originated. *Open daily.*

At the corner of Chapel and College streets was once located **Beers Taverne** (6), where Captain Benedict Arnold demanded and received the keys to the powder house from the town selectmen. Arnold was commander of the Second Company, Governor's Guard, one of the first units to volunteer for action at Lexington. Arnold operated a shop across from the Green on Chapel Street, and the sign which hung over his establishment has been reerected in its original location.

The William Lyon Phelps Gate, the curved archway on College Street, marks the entry of the **Old Campus** (7), where Yale was established in 1709. The university's Visitor's Information Office is located here; guided tours of the campus are available when the college is in session.

Connecticut Hall (8), a registered National Landmark, is the oldest building on the Yale campus, and one of the oldest in New Haven. It was completed in 1752; the fourth floor and gambrel roof were added later. Nathan Hale, whose statue stands outside, studied and lived in this building during his years at Yale. He left New Haven in 1776, never to return. It also housed Noah Webster and William Howard Taft.

The last major work of architect Louis Kahn, Yale's **Center for British Art** (9) is a striking contrast with surrounding Georgian buildings. The gallery contains the finest collection outside England of British paintings, prints, drawings, sculpture, and rare books dating from the sixteenth through nineteenth centuries, and includes works by Gainsborough, Hogarth, Turner, and Stubbs.

A chronicle of the Revolutionary period is found in the John Trumbull paintings and miniatures, displayed in the **Yale University Art**

Gallery (10). Other outstanding collections include Italian Renaissance paintings, pre-Columbian art, and African sculpture. Among the best-known works are Van Gogh's "Night Café," sculpture by Henry Moore, and excavations from Dura-Europas, a former Roman outpost in the Syrian Desert. *Open Tues.–Sun.*

Sterling Memorial Library (11), fourth largest in the United States, houses approximately 3.5 million books and periodicals, and presents displays of important papers, writings, and books. Opened in 1931, it was designed by architect James Gamble Rogers. North along High Street is **Beinecke Rare Book and Manuscript Library** (12), an elegant structure combining granite, bronze, glass, and thin, translucent marble walls through which glows an amber light that changes with the sun. A Gutenberg Bible, James Audubon's original bird prints, medieval manuscripts, and the letters of Mark Twain, Jack London, Ernest Hemingway, and Gertrude Stein are among the most prominent items in this collection.

A short detour down Wall Street leads to **Mory's** (13), the famed private club, which has occupied the modest Federal-style house at 306 York since 1912. Farther north is **Grove Street Cemetery** (14), a small, parklike retreat on the edge of the Yale campus. In September 1796 the cemetery was laid out, lots were sold, and where appropriate, donated to the city (for the poor and for deceased strangers), to Yale, and for "People of Color." Within three years, business sagged, despite the lowering of gravestone prices from five to three dollars. In the years that followed, however, Grove Street Cemetery became a New Haven institution. It has a handsome, restrained appearance, no doubt influenced by the no-nonsense theology of neighboring Yale. A chart posted inside the gate locates the graves of such distinguished persons as Timothy Dwight, Eli Whitney, Noah Webster, Charles Goodyear, and Lyman Beecher, a liberal revivalist and the father of Henry Ward Beecher and Harriet Beecher Stowe.

Charles Dickens described Hillhouse Avenue, east of Grove Street, as "the most beautiful street in America" when he visited New Haven in 1846. Hillhouse Avenue contains six buildings which bear the acorn plaque of the New Haven Preservation Trust, and one, the 1849 **J. Dwight Dana House** (15), is a registered National Landmark. The street also includes the residency of the president and secretary of Yale University, and the **Yale Collection of Musical Instruments** (16), more than eight hundred instruments dating from 1550 to 1850. Regular concerts are performed here.

Back at the Green, New Haven's **City Hall (17)** is a superb example of Victorian Gothic Revival architecture. The building's facade and bell tower have been completely restored, and a major reconstruction of the interior is under way. Here is yet another reminder of Captain Benedict Arnold's early patriotism: a plaque on the front of City Hall commemorates Arnold's leadership of the New Haven militia in 1775.

City Hall

A slow recovery from economic recession in the early 1900s plunged many of New Haven's neighborhoods into dilapidation. **Wooster Square (18)** was set aside in 1825 during a period of prosperity for this small, close-knit community. It was named after General David Wooster, a local Revolutionary War hero. The square was soon ringed with mansions overlooking a bustling harbor; an oval path ran around it, and hay was raised on it for its upkeep. A century later, it was surrounded by slums. In the 1960s a major urban-renewal effort led to the restoration of remaining old houses and fences. Today the entire area is designated a Historic District, administered by a mayoral commission.

Cassidento House

The original promoters of Wooster Square had an almost clean slate with which to work, and the "development" that resulted was one of New England's finest examples of planned urbanization. Houses were built in facing pairs across the green, and large square masses weighted the corners to give the area a classical effect. Much of that effect is now gone, and visitors must stretch their imagination to visualize the square's former air of cool serenity. At one time the harbor was visible from the foot of Brewery Street, nearby, framed by two Greek Revival mansions that flanked the entrance of the square like gateposts. Hughes Place, at the other end of the square, gave a similar vista to the north, where once a gracefully spired church stood. The finishing touch to this symmetry was an iron fence that encircled an oval path (the ground was leveled and sown with hay—thrifty residents used the profits for upkeep).

A number of interesting architectural features are evident along Wooster Square's Chapel and Greene streets. Residences such as the Cassidento House and Number 541 Chapel are conspicuous examples of the discipline the square imposed on the individual owners. Number 541, for example, on a critical corner lot, had to conform and balance with other corner houses, and a side elevation was designed which acts as a facade. A carved parapet surrounded the roof, and a Doric porch faced Chapel Street. Like most of the early houses of the square, the building is still painted white.

Another nineteenth-century survivor, albeit in a much altered state, is the old Wooster Square Congregational Church, erected in 1855. The building has burned twice, the steeple blown down once. Built by a group of Congregationalists who went bankrupt, it was acquired by the Baptists in 1856 and by the Catholics (who still hold services there) in 1899. An almost completely new design was used in reconstruction after the first fire, in 1874. A second remodeling following the second fire in 1904 created the eclectic Italian Renaissance building seen today. The three front windows survived the fire and the remodeler and date from 1874. Only the side walls and tall arched windows preserve the original structure.

The smaller streets that grew up around Wooster Square between 1835 and 1875—Greene, St. John, Lyon, William—carried on its general tone but on far less lavish scales. Like the main square, they represent a prosperous, stylish New Haven of another century.

Hartford

Roller-coaster Fortunes and Connecticut Yankees

In 1636 Thomas Hooker left Cambridge, Massachusetts, with a band of discontented families and walked to what is now Hartford. Since then, the city has seen more demographic, economic, and even geographic changes than any other in Connecticut. After three centuries of boom and decline, soaring growth and painful urbanization, Hartford today is an eye-opening community that thrives on the changeable tide of city life.

The city's history unfolds at the **Old State House (1)**, the first of many New England public buildings designed by Boston architect Charles Bulfinch. Completed in 1796, the cupola was added in 1826—two years after Lafayette was entertained here. The building served as the State Capitol until 1879 and then as Hartford City Hall until 1915. Exhibits include a collection of early American Indian artifacts. *Open daily.*

Henry Hobson Richardson built **Cheney House (2)** of Connecticut brownstone in 1877. Originally a multi-use building, each of the ground-floor arches marked the storefront for a separate business. On the upper floors were elegant apartments used by the Cheney family—wealthy silk product manufacturers—when visiting Hartford from their home in Manchester. The building is being restored to its former glory.

The most obvious feature of **Christ Church (3)** is its tall spire, created, supposedly, to move the congregation to "heavenly thoughts." The structure was one of the first Gothic churches in the New World; its design is a montage of medieval English churches and cathedrals.

The twelve-acre urban-renewal complex of **Constitution Plaza (4)**

HARTFORD

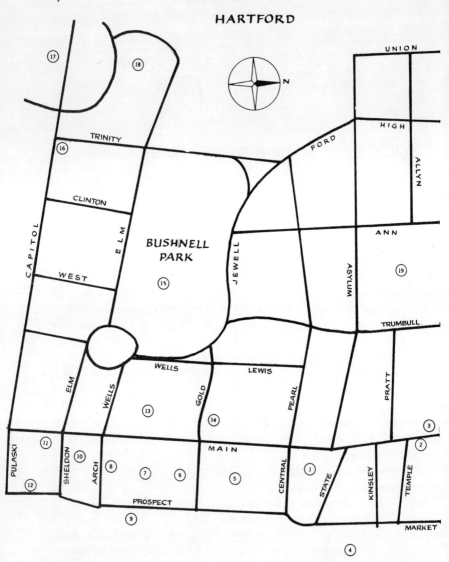

comprises eight modern office and commercial buildings of glass and concrete, intermingled with raised walkways and landscaped plazas. Replacing what used to be a run-down neighborhood, the Plaza is a unique urban park. The fountain was designed not to splash— even when the Plaza wind blows. Inside the Connecticut Bank and

Old State House

Trust building, a giant Alexander Calder mobile graces the commercial banking room. The Plaza's two-sided building—the only one in the world—houses the Phoenix Mutual Life Insurance Company, one of forty-five insurance companies in the city. (When the Phoenix was founded in 1851, it was their policy to insure only teetotalers.)

The **Traveler's Insurance Company** (5) completely financed the construction of Constitution Plaza (one of their office buildings is on the south end of the promenade). In the lobby is the largest tapestry in the world woven from a single thread. Beyond the Plaza is the Traveler's Tower, the highest point in the city. The company's first customer was Colonel James Bolter, who in 1863 had his life insured for $5,000 for a trip from the post office to his home. His premium? Two cents. The Traveler's Tower is also the site of Sanford's Tavern—the scene of the famous Charter Oak incident. To ensure the independence of Connecticut from the sinister James II in 1687, Captain Joseph Wadsworth took the charter and squirreled it away in a tree. Sir Edmund Andros, the King's lackey, was able to take over the colony for two years but never the charter. The original document is still intact and can be seen at the State Library. The oak died years ago, but its descendant still stands on the grounds of Center Church. *Open Mon.–Fri.*

En route to the Wadsworth Atheneum, strollers pass a notorious symbol of artistic controversy, the Stone Field Sculpture, installed in August 1977. The thirty-six glacial boulders, weighing from 1,000 pounds to 11 tons, are the work of New York sculptor Carl Andre. To commemorate its fiftieth anniversary, the Hartford Foundation for Public Giving commissioned the work for $87,000.

Art of a more traditional nature, in magnificent variety, is displayed at the **Wadsworth Atheneum** (6), one of the finest but least-known museums in America. In 1841, when Hartford was a small town of 14,000, Daniel Wadsworth interested a group of citizens in founding the first public art gallery in America and donated property for the site. The museum opened in 1844 with a modest display of eighty-two objects, the most impressive of which were paintings by John Trumbull. National prominence came to the museum in 1917 when J. P. Morgan (who was born in Hartford) presented it with exquisite Greek and Roman bronzes and eighteenth-century porcelain. Nearly ten years later the Wallace Nutting Collection of Furniture of the Pilgrim Century was donated. The Atheneum began to expand under the leadership of A. Everett Austin, a man of eclectic taste and strong will. Before seventeenth-century Baroque painting was highly regarded, Austin bought works by Caravaggio, Poussin, Murillo, and Lorrain. He acquired Italian Renaissance and nineteenth-century French paintings, and added to the already impressive American works by Hopper, Shahn, Peale, Copley, and West. In recent years the Atheneum has maintained its forward-looking reputation by acquiring works by such contemporary artists as Andrew Wyeth, Calder, Pollock, and Rauschenburg. Some 160 permanent and visiting exhibits acquaint visitors with fine art, period costumes, firearms, furniture, and a "tactile gallery" that invites touching. *Open daily.*

The most famous inhabitant of **Burr Mall** (7), nestled between the Atheneum and the Municipal Building, is Calder's "Stegosaurus," which he designed for the city in 1971. The ornate **Municipal Building** (8) has been the seat of city government since 1914. The staircase leading from Burr Mall takes visitors onto the frosted glass ceiling of the bottom level. The glass gallery which forms the roof of the building provides a feeling of soaring spaciousness. Though the **Hartford Times** (9) closed its doors in 1976, plaques on the outside of the

Wadsworth Atheneum

160-year-old structure record historical events that took place here. The interesting facade was brought to Hartford from an old church in New York.

The Hartford **Public Library** (10) is west of the Municipal Building on Main Street. Private for its first fifty-eight years, the library turned public in 1893. The present building was completed in 1957; its notable Hartford Collection includes books by local authors and works about the city. The library spans a highway which in turn is built over the Park River—a submerged waterway that used to flood parts of the city before it was rerouted underground. The river empties into the Connecticut at Dutch Point—so named for a trading post that occupied the mouth in 1623. The English took over the site, and so enraged the Dutch that they called the pilferers "Jankes," slang for pirates. The term evolved into "Yankee," and the phrase "Connecticut Yankee' was coined. *Open daily.*

Old Center Church

The **Butler-McCook Homestead** (11) is the present home of the Antiquarian and Landmark Societies, Inc., of Connecticut. It was built in 1782 and first occupied by Dr. Daniel Butler. At the rear of the house is a garden which overlooks the **Amos Bull Home** (12), built in 1788. Bull, a colorful merchant, choirmaster, and teacher, moved into the house with wife number three (of five) and set up a grammar school. Today it houses the Connecticut Historical Commission. *Open daily mid-May–mid-Oct.*

Bushnell Tower (13), across from the Municipal Building, was built in 1969 and designed by I. M. Pei. Mirrored in its gold walls is the white steeple of **Center Church** (14), site of the ratification of the U. S. Constitution by Connecticut. Nestled quietly beside Center Church is the Ancient Burying Ground, a temporary resting ground for visitors and a permanent one for some of Hartford's most prominent citizens. Among several fascinating last lines is this verse epitaph for Samuel Stone (d. 1663) :

> *Errors corrupt by sinnewous dispute*
> *He did oppugne, and clearly them confute:*
> *Above all things, he Christ his Lord prefer'd*
> *Hartford! thy richest jewel's here interd.*

Across Jewell Street is **Bushnell Park** (15), until 1853 an inhabited junkyard, now a registered national landmark containing five hundred trees of 150 varieties. The park's design was influenced by Frederick Law Olmsted, a Hartford resident and the designer of New York's Central Park. The park is also home for the Bushnell Park Carousel, one of the last true carousels in existence. The ride is made up of forty-eight hand-carved and brightly painted horses and two "lovers' chariots." Music is provided by a refurbished Wurlitzer Band Organ and riders are given the chance to catch the elusive brass ring. Rising over Trinity Street, which bisects the park, is the Civil War Memorial Arch.

Bushnell Memorial Hall (16), located at Trinity and Capitol, is a 2,728-seat auditorium given to the city by descendants of the Reverend Dr. Horace Bushnell. The interior of the brick-and-limestone hall is richly decorated in Art Deco—a fashion popular when the hall was built in the 1930s.

The Italian Renaissance **Connecticut State Library** (17) is the repository of state archives, books, and manuscripts pertaining to Connecticut history. The original Royal Oak Charter and the Colt

Bushnell Memorial Auditorium

company's firearms collection are also displayed here. A full-length portrait of George Washington by Stuart hangs in Memorial Hall. The State Supreme Court occupies the west wing of the building.

A great golden dome rises above the Connecticut **State Capitol** (18), a marble-and-granite edifice erected in 1878. Bas-reliefs and statues of historic scenes and figures adorn the exterior. Of special interest are the legislative chambers and the Hall of Flags. *Open Mon.–Fri.*

The largest complex in the downtown business district is the Hartford **Civic Center** (19), a megastructure which includes 70,000 square feet of exhibition/assembly space, an enclosed mall and connecting hotel. Plans are under way for a new coliseum seating 16,000 —despite its concern for the past, Hartford thrives on progress.

Mystic Seaport

Mirror of a Maritime Past

The smell of fresh paint and Stockholm tar, the ring of the caulker's mallet, and the echo of voices from aloft as sails are bent on are the smells and sounds of Mystic Seaport, a mirror of New England's maritime past. In the seventeenth century, Mystic-built ships developed a lucrative West Indies trade; in the early 1800s, when sealing became profitable, they sailed to Cape Horn. They plied whaling waters several decades later, and made for California during the Gold Rush. Mystic shipyards built transports for the Union Army during the Civil War, and from the 1860s to the 1890s, large, sleek racing yachts. Mystic Seaport opened in 1929, a small collection of maritime memorabilia housed in an old textile mill. Today it is a forty-acre museum masquerading as a bustling riverside port of the 1800s. *Open daily April–Nov.*

Of all the exhibits at Mystic Seaport, the most treasured is the wooden whaleship **Charles W. Morgan** (1). Built in 1841 at the yard of Jethro and Zachariah Hillman in New Bedford, she has outlived all others of her kind. Her maiden voyage lasted three years and took her around the Horn to the whaling grounds of the Pacific. Her crew did battle with whales wherever they found them—pursuing their prey in puny rowboats on "Nantucket sleigh rides," foaming over the deep behind some frantic sperm whale. The old *Morgan* was whaling at sea until 1921, the last known wooden whaler in the world. The huge try-pots used for converting blubber into whale oil are forward; below are the cramped quarters in which her officers and men lived during those long months. The captain's wife sometimes managed to fit into this constricted space, too, and the starboard cabin is fitted with the

MYSTIC SEAPORT

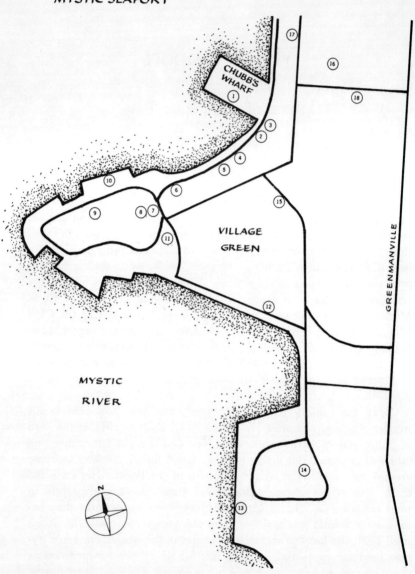

gimbaled swinging berth ordered by Captain Tom Landers in 1864
as a luxury for his seagoing wife. At Mystic, the *Morgan* has been
given new life; however, her future depends on continual preservation.
In 1968 it was decided to restore her to the rig of a topsail bark, which
she carried from the early 1880s to the end of her whaling career

(*Morgan* is capable of carrying 13,000 square feet of sail). Her hull has also been repainted to appear as she was during most of her last eighty years.

The barrel was an essential element in life both at sea and ashore. Thus the **cooper** (2) was indispensable to port life. Casks intended for spirits, molasses, whale oil, or other liquids had to be tight, and he was held responsible for leakage as well as accuracy of measurement. The building in which the working exhibit is housed, once a barn on the Thomas Greenman property, has been modified to include typical features of a cooperage, including double doors and an overhead loft for storage.

Opened in 1833, the **Mystic Bank** (3) was the first in the community. The heart of Mystic was then at the head of the river in what is now Old Mystic. Donated to the museum in 1948, the bank was dismantled stone by stone and reconstructed on its present site. Only the portico at the entrance is a reproduction. The Shipping Office on the second floor contains furniture and records of a typical nineteenth-century office.

The **Mystic Press** (4)—set up to resemble a newspaper and printing shop of the late 1800s—contains the tools and technology of the journeyman printer's trade. From shops such as these, with their Wells and Washington presses, platen job presses, and Cranston cylinder press, came the almanacs, newspapers, books, and handbills so important to community life.

A last refuge of a dying art, the Mystic **Shipcarver's Shop** (5) displays an important collection of figureheads, nameboards, eagles, and other carvings. Most carvers of the last century might be compared with the stonemasons and sculptors of medieval times; both were anonymous craftsmen who worked without formal training and won little acclaim.

The **Shipsmith Shop** (6) once stood at the head of Merrill's Wharf in New Bedford. The building is the only known marine ironwork shop to have survived from the last century. The smithy made fittings for the *Morgan* more than a century ago. Today the great hearth heats most of the ironware used in restoring Seaport ships and shops.

Stocking supplies for both men and vessels, the **Ship Chandlery** (7) was the supermarket of its day. Contracting for provisions at the chandlery was the responsibility of the ship's "husband," a man authorized by the owners to arrange repairs, freight, towage, and the hiring of officers and crew. Lack of shipboard refrigeration discouraged variety, but chandlers offered salt fish and meat, hardtack, molasses,

Buckingham House

potatoes, onions and other winter vegetables, spices, and flour. Hard goods ranged from needles and beeswax to lanterns, buoys, logs, and inkstands.

Charles Mallory came to Mystic as a sailmaker in 1816; by midcentury he was one of the state's most prosperous shipowners. The **Mallory Sail Loft (8)**, originally located downriver, was moved here by barge in 1951. Until the 1870s, when blueprints which included the sail area were supplied, the sailmaker was his own patternmaker. Sail outlines were chalked on the floor of the loft; in order to have uninterrupted work space, the potbellied stove was hung from the ceiling. Sailmaking tools displayed · here bear such intriguing names as "palms," "fids," and "commanders."

The 250-foot-long **Plymouth Cordage Company Ropewalk (9)** was built by its founder, Bourne Spooner, in 1824, and operated until 1947. Sinews of a sailing ship, manila yarns were fed from bobbins into a collector plate. Rolling machines then twisted the strands into rope for rigging.

The veteran training ship **Joseph Conrad (10)** sailed under three flags before mooring permanently at Mystic in 1947. Built in Copenhagen in 1882 and named *Georg Stage* as a memorial to the young son of shipowner Frederik Stage, the 103-foot vessel was designed to accommodate eighty boys in training for the Danish merchant service. Alan Villiers took her, under the British flag and renamed *Joseph Conrad,* on a 58,000-mile voyage around the world which lasted more than two years. After a brief stint as an American training ship, *Conrad* was transferred to Mystic Seaport. Today she is a floating dormitory for visiting student groups as well as an exhibit, although she goes to sea no longer.

A ship model is much like its full-size counterpart, and the **Model Restoration Shop (11)** looks after maintenance and construction of the Seaport's valuable miniatures.

Sabino (12) is the last of the coal-fired, steam-powered passen-

Mystic boat builders

Charles W. Morgan

ger ferries. Built in 1908 in East Boothbay, Maine, she spent most of her career ferrying passengers and cargo along the northern coast. *Sabino* is operated on the Mystic River during the warmer months on regularly scheduled runs. A cruise on the steamer, her seventy-five-horsepower engine fired and signal bells clanging, is an enjoyable flashback to the early 1900s.

Near *Sabino*'s berth is the **Henry B. duPont Preservation Shipyard (13)**, a working exhibit unique in the United States. Here visitors can observe painstaking restoration work on vessels that range from whaleboats to *Morgan* itself. Buildings in the facility include the one-hundred-foot-long main shop, the lumber storage shed, and the paint shop. A major project currently under way is restoration of the ninety-two-foot keel assembly from the whaleship **Thames (14)**, set up on blocks in a shed near the shipyard gates. Built twenty-three years before *Morgan*, she ended her career as a breakwater in Sag Harbor, New York, after being condemned in 1838.

The exhibit in the **Children's Museum (15)**, "Children Who Went to Sea," tells of the many children who lived aboard sailing ships during the last half of the nineteenth century, when captains often took their families to sea. A typical child's bunk can be climbed into and is fitted out with a porthole looking out on the sea. The dolls, dollhouses, toys, and games are all reproductions of actual toys described by men and women who went to sea as children.

North of Chubb's Wharf and *Charles W. Morgan* are several specialized exhibits ranging from an outstanding collection of **ship's figureheads (16)** to the restored cabin of the square-rigger **Benjamin F. Packard (17)**. The **Seaport Planetarium (18)** demonstrates the importance of astronomy to navigation and holds evening classes in navigation, meteorology, and astronomy.

In all, Mystic Seaport's exhaustive—and exhausting—inventory of maritime history includes more than sixty buildings and two hundred vessels. In each of them is the clean scent of salt air, tar, and hemp and—impressionable visitors claim—the ghost of that oily smell savored by generations of whalemen.

Scrimshaw and Scrimshanders

For almost a century, many of America's 20,000 whalemen spent most of their leisure hours aboard ship carving whalebone and teeth—scrimshaw. In their isolation they developed a unique American folk art.

A coarse file was used to rough-finish the bone or tooth, a finer file to work it down, then a piece of sandpaper or sharkskin to smooth it. A sail needle served to inscribe intricate designs of ships, whales, land scenes, or portraits of loved ones. India ink was worked into the striations by the "scrimshander," then palmed smooth. Often a tooth was soaked in brine to give the ivory an orange richness. Holes were drilled with gimlets made of nails, and countersinking for inlay of mother-of-pearl was scraped out with a knife. Finishing was done with wood ashes, and polishing with the palm of the hand.

New London

Yankee Seaport Reborn

When the long jibs of returning whaleships jutted over New London's Water and Bank streets, top-hatted owners rushed down to count the heavy casks being rolled onto the wharf. Womenfolk, dressed in Sunday best, would show off three-year-old children their returning husbands had never seen; here and there other wives would realize that they were widows, their children fatherless.

The scene was the same at Nantucket, Edgartown, New Bedford, or any of the other Yankee ports where the whaleships and their precious cargoes meant livelihoods and fortunes. Oil boiled from blubber was used in lamps and as a lubricant. Spermaceti, bailed from the heads of sperm whales, went into candles. Ambergris, an odd material found in sick sperms, was prized for making perfume. Whalebone, not really bone but horny, toothlike strips which filled the mouths of the toothless right and bowhead whales, was cut into stays for corsets, collars, skirt hoops, and umbrellas. A host of dockside traders flourished with the whaling industry. Sailmakers, sparmakers, ropemakers, riggers, coopers, ironworkers, toolmakers, and chandlers all felt a proprietorship in the sea and its greatest animal.

New London's **Whale Oil Row** (1) is a conspicuous reminder of the town's whaling days. A row of four great Greek Revival mansions, designed in 1830 by architect Ezra Chappell, line a section of Huntington Street. The sixteen massive columns (four per house) are attributed to John Bishon, one of New London's busiest builders, who also made the columns for the Huntington Street Baptist Church. Whale oil and conspicuous consumption built these houses for prosperous whaling-ship owners. Apparently none minded the curious rubber-

NEW LONDON

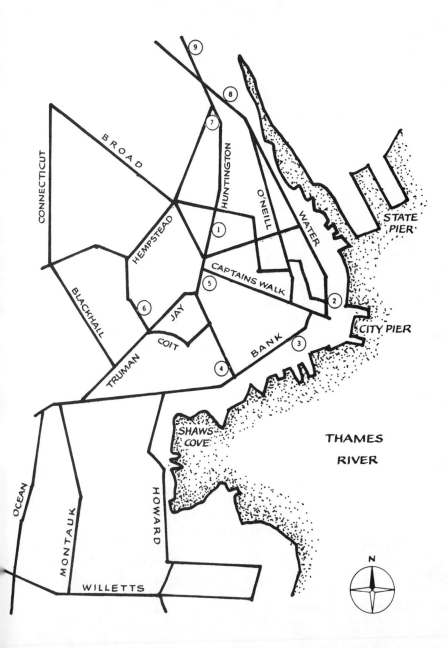

New London Lighthouse

stamp similarity of the four massive edifices. Number Three Whale Oil Row now houses the Tale of the Whale Museum. The nucleus of the museum consists of the personal collection of its founder, Carl H. Wies, and includes a fully rigged whaleboat once used on *Charles W. Morgan* out of Mystic, harpoons and fleshing knives, lances, scrimshaw, and ship's logs. *Open Tues.–Sun.*

The end of New London's whaling era was signaled by the construction, in 1887, of **Union Station** (2). The building replaced a smaller facility destroyed by fire in 1883. The railway stop was designed by architect Henry Robson Richardson. Notable features include the vaulted ceiling and elaborate brickwork.

New London's **Custom House** (3) was raised in 1833 and is made of granite from nearby quarries. Robert Mills, its designer, is also known for the Washington Monument. The front door of the Custom House was once part of the frigate U.S.S. *Constitution*. (During repairs to the vessel, some of her timbers were reserved for special public works projects.)

Connecticut's Naval Office during the Revolution was located at the home of **Captain Nathaniel Shaw** (4) and his son, Nathaniel Shaw, Jr., the latter who served as naval agent. The elder Shaw, who came from London in 1722, soon became a shipmaster and owner. In 1756 a shipload of Acadians, expelled from Nova Scotia by the British, reached the port and Shaw aided them by engaging thirty-five to quarry stone from his land and build his house. When Benedict Arnold burned New London in 1781, fires were set in the building, but it was saved by neighbors. Despite several additions and alterations, the Shaw House was still in family hands into the twentieth century; it is now a museum displaying maritime art and artifacts, and a room once occupied by General George Washington. *Open Tues.–Sat.*

Philemon Hall, one of New London's most prosperous whale-oil merchants, donated the **Public Library** (5) to the town in 1892. Henry Hobson Richardson is credited with the building's design, although actual construction was supervised by his successors.

Hempsted House (6) is one of only a few remaining seventeenth-century buildings in Connecticut, and the only existing house in New London to have survived the razing of the city by Benedict Arnold. The west part of the house dates to 1678; the eastern wing was added in 1728. The diary of Joshua Hempsted II was used as a guide in restoring the house, resulting in an accurate reproduction of the life-style of a well-to-do eighteenth-century New England family. Displays in-

Joshua Hempsted House

clude pewter and brass, wooden ware, cupboards and chests, early
Carver chairs, handspun and woven fabrics, and a primitive baby
walker. *Open Tues.–Sat. mid-May–mid-Oct.*

An abandoned air hangs about the **Ancient Burying Ground** (7)
between Huntington and Hempstead streets. Among an excellent
collection of seventeenth- and eighteenth-century stones is a large, flat
red marker inscribed "An epitaph on Captaine Richard Lord deceased
May 17 1662 aetatis suae 51," followed by several lines of interesting
verse, including:

> *The bright starre of our cavallrie lyes here*
> *Unto the State a counsellour full deare . . .*

Another fascinating epitaph is that of Captain Adam Shapley, "who
bravely gave his Life for his Country a fatal Wound at Fort Griswold
Sept. 6th 1781 caused his Death."

> *Shapley, thy deed reverse*
> *the Common doom*
> *and make thy name*
> *immortal in a tomb*

Other distinguished men buried here include Curdon Saltonstall (d. 1724), a colonial governor of Connecticut, and "A boy patriot of the American Revolution," Johnathan Brooks (1768–1848). North of the burying ground, in the shadow of Interstate 95, is the **Olde Town Mill** (8), the oldest in America still capable of grinding corn.

Of unusual charm and distinction, the **Deshon-Allyn House** (9), located on the grounds of the Lyman-Allyn Museum, was built in 1829 by Captain Dabiel Deshon, a prosperous whaling master. The exterior is of massive granite, the corners edged with finished stone quoins. Beneath the eaves a heavy, carved cornice is carried around the building. The mullions (strips of wood that divide the window-panes) are carved and ornamented with lead palmettes. The same treatment is applied to a beautiful Palladian window above the front door. Four square rooms, each with fireplace, flank the central hall and are finished as in 1829 with pieces from the Lyman-Allyn Museum. On permanent display in the museum building are collections of Egyptian, Greek, and Roman artifacts, Renaissance art, and European paintings, furniture, silver, and decorative arts. Also on display is the Lydia S. Baratz Collection of Doll Houses and Furniture, Dolls and Toys, most dating from the last century. *Open Tues.–Sun.*

"A Dead Whale or a Stove Boat"

The taking of the world's largest living creature was grueling work. Only the whaler's captain might get rich; the crew had to settle for the excitement and danger of the chase. When a whale was sighted, the whaleboats were lowered. Four crewmen, facing aft, plied pulling oars while the harpooner took his place at the bow oar. At point-blank range the harpooner would sink his sharp iron firmly into place and, if there was time, set another harpoon. Fastened to one end was about 1,800 feet of manila line, coiled in a wooden tub so that it would play out without jamming. If the whale chose to run, the whalemen were in for a wild "Nantucket sleigh ride" until they could draw close enough for the kill. Occasionally a wounded whale would stove, or wreck, a whaleboat—hence the whaleman's motto, "a dead whale or a stove boat." Finally, the tired whale was dispatched with a sharp killing lance. Ahead was the dirty work of fleshing the carcass and rendering the oil, and weeks of boredom before another whale was sighted.

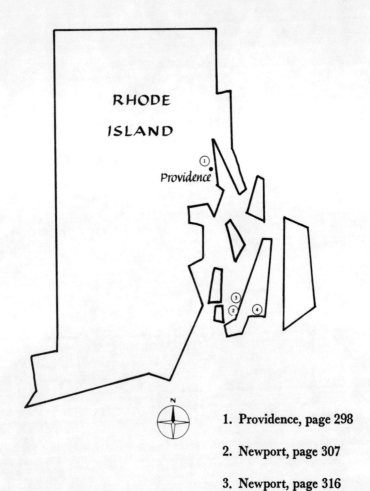

RHODE

ISLAND

Providence

RHODE ISLAND

The State of Rhode Island and Providence Plantations—America's smallest in area and longest in name—has three times the population of Alaska, the largest in area, yet still preserves winding lanes, neat farms, and empty beaches. Vast industry contrasts with elegant resorts, and colonial landmarks with atomic submarines. The state, chartered as a "lively experiment . . . in religious concernments," sets a lively pace in commerce and arts.

Its swift streams and skilled people helped father America's Industrial Revolution, and its factories still produce an amazing amount and variety of goods. Another revolution, America's War of Independence, also had roots here, for Rhode Island drew blood in several skirmishes long before the Boston Tea Party. Its citizens were the first to declare their independence—on May 4, 1776—two months ahead of the rest of the colonies.

The Atlantic gave Rhode Island its early settlers, fed them, and today draws tourists to its harbors and beaches. Evidence of the forces of wind and wave is everywhere. Coastlines carved by tides are as varied as the directions they face. Quiet coves and inlets backed by gently rolling fields, jagged cliffs, and white beaches provide beauty that never repeats itself along the entire coastline.

Providence

Religious Haven, Urban Museum

Seeking a haven for "persons distressed of conscience," Roger Williams
in 1636 founded Providence, Rhode Island's earliest settlement. A century and a half later, at the outbreak of the Revolution, Providence
had grown from a scattering of first settlers struggling to survive, into a
thriving town of 4,000. There was a brisk and profitable trade with the
West Indies and with other colonies. Shipbuilders, distillers, and
weavers prospered. Fourth-generation Yankees enjoyed the good life:
a substantial home, handsome furniture, books, and a little learning.
Congregational and Episcopal churches and a Quaker meetinghouse
had been founded, and Rhode Island College, now Brown University,
had been moved from Warren in 1770.

The Western, or Weybosset, Shore was a swampy peninsula dotted
with small houses, shops, and farms. When the War of 1812 weakened
the foreign trade, many Providence merchants sold their ships and
invested in mills. Fortunes were made and lost quickly, and the prosperous built solid brick mansions on the West Side. Westminster and
Weybosset streets became fashionable addresses. Commercial growth
boomed after the Civil War. Manufacturing had expanded rapidly
with war production, and Rhode Island continued to industrialize and
urbanize. Downtown Providence grew thick with offices, warehouses,
and industries. Around it sprung up new neighborhoods to house the
clerks, mechanics, and seamstresses. By the turn of the century,
Providence had become a true commercial, civic, and cultural center.
Today the city's buildings, many of which were the biggest and best of
their time, provide a compelling record of urban New England.

Until 1846, the area covered by Exchange Place and **City Hall (1)**

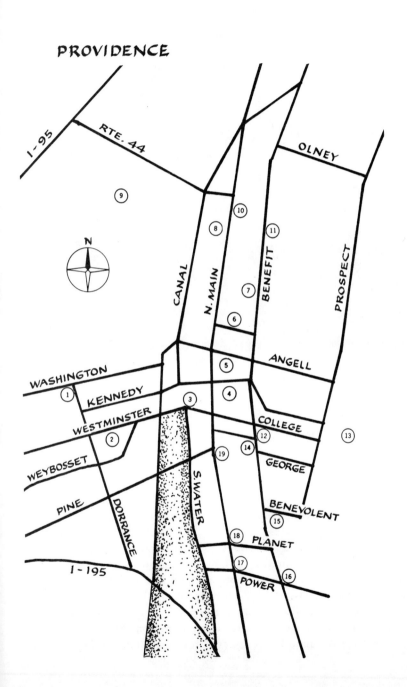

PROVIDENCE

Providence City Hall

was the Great Salt Cove. That year the Providence and Worcester Railway filled in much of the cove for freight yards and a passenger station (now gone). The dignified granite edifice of City Hall was raised in 1878. Designed in the "General Grant" (mansard Victorian) style, it reflected the pomp and plushness of city government in a time of prosperity and optimism. The character of the period is most evident in the City Council Chamber and Alderman's Chamber, both on the third floor: oak wainscoting, columns, and furniture; carved ceilings; tiled floors; etched and stained glass; and gilded wallpaper.

Another elegant reminder of nineteenth-century prosperity is the **Arcade** (2), the first enclosed shopping mall in the United States, and an architectural treasure. The construction of the three-tiered Greek Revival building in 1828 initiated downtown growth. Its granite columns, among the largest in the country, were dragged by fifteen yoke of oxen from the Bare Ledge Quarry in nearby Johnson. Beneath the once-rose-colored skylights are rhythmic cast-iron staircases and balustrades.

The Arcade eclipsed an earlier architectural focal point, **Market House** (3), erected in 1770. This is where Weybosset farmers brought their produce to sell to the East Side households, and later served as the first city hall. The second floor was at various times a banquet hall, barracks for French soldiers, and mayor's office. One of the markers on the building records the height of water in the "great gale of 1815" when ships were swept over the square. This mark was surpassed in 1938 when a hurricane brought floodwaters that reached a depth of 13 feet 8½ inches at Market House, and all downtown Providence wallowed in seawater. Today a dam and floodgates across the Providence River protect the city.

Founded in 1877, Rhode Island School of Design's **Museum of Art** (4) is noted for its collections of classical art, nineteenth-century French and American paintings, European decorative arts, and Oriental costumes. The exhibits are arranged as far as possible in chronological order so that visitors can proceed from the arts of ancient Egypt through galleries devoted to Greece and Rome, to those of the Middle Ages, Renaissance, and the arts of today. The permanent collection includes such works as Picasso's "Les Soupeurs," Degas' "Standing Dancer," and the bronze "Study for the Statue of Balzac," by Rodin. An integral part of the museum is Pendleton House, a replica of an early nineteenth-century Georgian dwelling. The house contains the Charles L. Pendleton Collection of American Furniture and Decorative Arts. One room on the ground floor is devoted to the arts of Rhode Island and includes examples of the work of cabinetmakers Job Townsend and John Goddard.

The first Baptist church in this country was founded in 1638 by the great champion of religious freedom, Roger Williams; it is one of the two oldest churches in Rhode Island. An excellent example of eighteenth-century Georgian architecture, the present **First Baptist Church building** (5) was dedicated in 1775, "midway between the battles of Lexington and Bunker Hill." It was designed by Joseph Brown, second of four brothers who played a leading part in the economic and civic life of the period. The impressive steeple towers 185 feet above the city; Brown borrowed the design from an English pattern book. The interior is carefully preserved in its colonial form, including a crystal chandelier first lighted in 1792. In the steeple hangs a bell with the inscription:

First Baptist Church

For freedom of conscience the town was first planted;
Persuasion, not force, was used by the people;
This church is the oldest, and has not recanted,
Enjoying and granting bell, temple and steeple.

Erected in 1769, the **Brick School House** (6) served both as school and as public forum for heated town meetings. It was the temporary home of Brown University in 1770; thirty years later it became the first public school in Providence. The building is now the headquarters of the Providence Preservation Society.

A block farther along Main Street stands the **Old State House** (7), meeting place of the General Assembly from 1762 until 1900. It now houses the Sixth District Court. The early brick building, completed in 1762, has brownstone trim, a hip roof, and a tower belfry that was added in 1851. On May 4, 1776, the Assembly passed an act here proclaiming Rhode Island to be the first free republic in the New World. Of the sixty delegates there were only six dissenting votes. Later, the hall was the site of much social life, and Washington, Lafayette, and Adams were entertained here in grand style. Across the Parade a number of eighteenth-century houses suggest the style of colonial Providence.

Roger Williams Spring (8) is enshrined in a small park bounded by North Main and Canal streets. By a Proprietors' Grant of 1721, "liberty is reserved for the inhabitants to fetch water at this spring forever." Across the street a plaque indicates the approximate location of Williams' house.

Rhode Island's **State Capitol** (9) is one of the most beautiful in the country. Built of white Georgia marble in the early 1900s, it has the second largest marble dome in the world (only St. Peter's in Rome is larger). Chiseled above an entrance is a sentence from the Royal Charter of 1663, granted by King Charles II, which stated one purpose of the colony: "To hold forth a lively experiment that a most flourishing civil state may stand and best be maintained with full liberty in religious concernments." High above is Independent Man, a statue 235 feet above the ground on a huge lantern atop the capitol. The statue originally proposed to represent Roger Williams. When the statue was commissioned in 1899, no one could discover what Williams looked like, so the figure became the Independent Man, symbol of Rhode Island's concern for personal freedom. In the state reception room hangs a full-length portrait of Washington by Rhode Island artist Gilbert Stuart. The original parchment charter granted by Charles II is enshrined in the Senate Lobby.

The Mother Church of the Episcopal Diocese of Rhode Island, the **Cathedral of St. John** (10) was built in 1810 to replace an earlier church dating from 1722. The present church's style was influenced by the old Hollis Street Church in Boston, designed by Charles Bulfinch.

St. John's burial ground, with stones from the early eighteenth century, contains graves of many of Rhode Island's builders and shapers, and is open to visitors by way of the parish house beside the cathedral.

Benefit Street, Providence's second road, was built in the 1750s for the "common benefit" of people who wanted a street farther from the river. Today the old houses of Benefit Street, saved from the wrecker's ball, constitute one of the loveliest neighborhoods in New England. Designed by John Holden Greene, who planned many of the Benefit Street homes, the 1810 **Sullivan Dorr House** (11) has a three-story central section between two two-story wings. Thomas W. Dorr, Sullivan's son, led the Dorr Rebellion for universal manhood suffrage in 1842. The main house is elaborately decorated with neoclassical and Gothic carved wood trim, and is connected to the outbuildings in an L-shape to conform to the steep hillside site.

Across the street is a row of houses characteristic of those built during post-Revolutionary prosperity. They are Georgian in style, with gabled roofs, central chimneys, and symmetrical facades. Farther south along Benefit Street is a harmonious collection of homes, from Colonial to Greek Revival to Italianate Victorian. On the corner of College Street is the Providence **Athenaeum** (12), founded in 1836. The ivy-draped building is in the form of a Greek Doric temple in antis. In the library alcoves was conducted the literary courtship of Edgar Allan Poe and Sarah Helen Whitman. A library copy of the December 1847 *American Review* contains an anonymous poem, "Ulalume," below which Poe wrote his signature. The library owns paintings ascribed to Van Dyke and Reynolds, and "The Hours," a miniature by Edward G. Malbone. *Open Mon.–Fri.*

East of Benefit Street and the heart of the College Hill District, **Brown University** (13) is the seventh oldest of America's colleges and the first to endorse complete religious freedom. University Hall, the original "college edifice," is a design borrowed from Princeton's Nassau Hall. This building served as a barracks and a hospital for French and American forces during the Revolution and is a National Historic Landmark. A special event is "The Illumination," which takes place on Independence Day, Christmas, and other special occasions. Lighted candles are placed in the windows of the darkened building, producing a striking effect. The tradition began when George Washington received an honorary degree here in 1790.

The university's John Hay Library contains one of the finest collections of Abraham Lincoln's books and manuscripts; a nearly complete

Benefit Street homes

collection of the writings of John Hay, who served as Lincoln's secretary; and the Harris Collection of American Poetry and Drama. The John Carter Brown Library's collection of Americana printed during the colonial period is perhaps the country's finest, and an outstanding Chinese collection is housed in the John D. Rockefeller, Jr., Library.

As would be expected of a building designed by architect Philip Johnson, the Albert and Vera List Art Building, dedicated in 1971, is modern and functional. Outside are cantilevered sun screens and a jagged roof line; inside is the university's art department and the David Winston Bell Gallery. The Annmary Brown Memorial comprises a mausoleum, art museum, and library. The Hawkins Collection of Incunabula, one of the world's most extensive, is of particular interest to book fanciers. Student guided tours of the campus leave from the Corliss-Bracket House, corner Prospect and Angell streets, several times daily from September to December.

Farther along Benefit Street is the **Stephen Hopkins House (14),** whose owner was ten times governor of the Colony of Rhode Island, member of the Continental Congress, and a signer of the Declaration of Independence. "My hand trembles but my heart does not," he said as he inscribed his name with palsied hand. The original part of the house dates from 1707; Hopkins built the Georgian addition in 1743. George Washington was a guest here on two occasions. Elegant period furniture and an eighteenth-century garden complement the house.

One of the largest bells ever cast in the foundry of Paul Revere and Sons still peals from the steeple of the Federal-style **First Unitarian Church** (15). Although organized in 1720 as the First Congregational Church, the present building was not completed until 1816. Four huge columns support the pediment of the portico, and great two-story windows enhance the interior light. The delicate carving and decoration on the ceiling are in Adamesque style popular at the time. *Open daily.*

Wealthy merchant and city father John Brown built his impressive **Georgian mansion** (16) in 1786. An unusual exhibit here is his chariot, constructed in Philadelphia in 1782 and believed to be the oldest carriage made in America. The building, now the home of the Rhode Island Historical Society, contains a fine collection of Rhode Island furniture, paintings, silver, and pewter. *Open Tues.–Sun.*

At the corner of Power Street is the **Talma Theater** (17), a brick building with portico, erected as a church in 1833. During the Civil War it served as a theater for amateur companies, and in 1915 became the home of the Providence Boys' Club.

Nearby is the site of **Sabin Tavern** (18), built about 1763 and a depot for the first stagecoach line to Boston. A tablet on the present building records how a group of patriots met to plan an attack on the British revenue cutter *Gaspee*. On June 9, 1772, the packet *Hannah* lured *Gaspee* into shoal water. Merchants threatened by oppressive tax laws rowed to the scene in small boats, burned *Gaspee,* and wounded her skipper.

The **Joseph Brown House** (19), like many other residences of the time, was thrown open to Rochambeau's officers when the French were encamped in Providence. "One of those gallant fellows," it is reported, "rode his spirited charger up the flight of steps" and into the long hall. On the ground once stood a great pear tree, the fruit of which Washington himself is supposed to have savored.

Newport—Downtown

Along the "Thaymes,"
Gabled Roofs and Offhand Grace

Newport is a city with class, where repairers of yachts outnumber repairers of shoes, and a Rolls-Royce can careen down Bellevue Avenue wearing, with offhand grace, a bumper sticker that reads, "Eat More Possum." There is a layering of time and style here that makes Newport the most interesting summer city in America. It is a place that has not been offended by tall buildings that cut the landscape away from its citizens. Newport remains a city for people, where doorways are open and people poke their heads out to say hello to other people walking by, or just to smell the sea.

The **Colony House** (1), at the head of Washington Square, may well be America's real Independence Hall. It was here that the Rhode Island legislature foreswore its allegiance to George III on May 4, 1776, thus making Rhode Island the first independent republic in the Americas. Built thirty-four years earlier, the structure is one of the few remaining pre-Revolutionary brick buildings in Newport. During the war, George Washington met here with French General Rochambeau to plan the final defeat of Cornwallis at Yorktown. In the Governor's Council Chamber hangs a full-length portrait of Washington. *Open Mon.–Sat.*

Erected a century before the Revolution, the **Wanton-Lyman-Hazard House** (2) is often overlooked by residents and visitors alike. The interior is furnished in the style of the seventeenth and eighteenth centuries, and many of the linens, curtains, and counterpanes were created on traditional looms, also on display.

The founder and first pastor of the **United Baptist Church** (3) was Dr. John Clarke, who obtained from King Charles II Rhode Island's

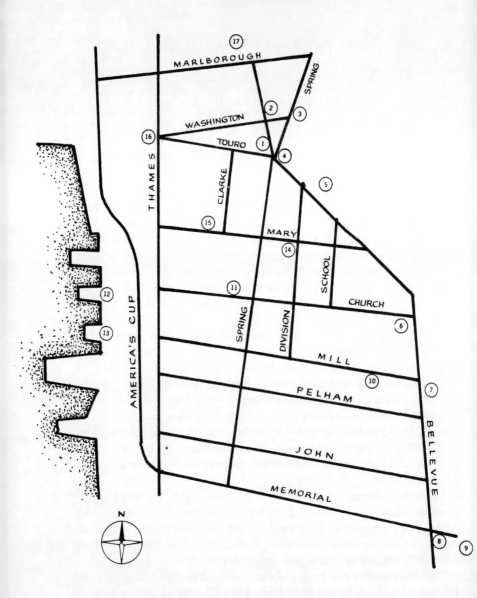

NEWPORT –
DOWNTOWN

Colony House

Royal Charter in 1663. The charter set down, for the first time in any commonwealth in the world, the principle of "full liberty in religious concernments." It is credited with influencing Thomas Jefferson in the writing of the Declaration of Independence. The church has a small historical room featuring old portraits, communion services, and antique furniture.

An architectural gem, the **Touro Synagogue** (4) is the oldest in the United States, and its interior is considered by many to be the most beautiful. Built in 1763, it was declared a National Historic Site in 1943. The synagogue was designed by Peter Harrison, the most noted American architect of the mid-eighteenth century, and is still in active use. The church was founded by Portuguese Jews, and the service still follows the Sephardic or Spanish-Portuguese Orthodox ritual.

Newport's **Historical Society building** (5) was erected as the Seventh-Day Baptist Meeting House. A charming architectural feature is the half-wineglass pulpit. The building houses a Junior Museum and a Marine Museum displaying Rhode Island silver and pewter, historic

Touro Synagogue

documents, and original copies of the Newport *Mercury,* America's oldest newspaper still in publication. *Open Tues.–Sun.*

Redwood Library (6), too, is the oldest building of its kind still in use. It was built in the time of George Washington, whose bronze statue by French sculptor Jean Antoine Houdon stands before the main entrance. The classical design of the country's first architect, Peter Harrison, distinguishes the library, now private. Among its patrons were Gilbert Stuart (whose painting career began in Newport), William and Henry James, and Edith Wharton.

With its year-round succession of art exhibits, musical events, and lectures, the **Art Association of Newport (7),** on landscaped grounds on Bellevue Avenue, fills an important place in the city's cultural life. The main building was designed by Richard Morris Hunt for John N. A. Griswold in 1862–63, drawing his inspiration from the half-timbered buildings of Europe. It preceded the great, classical mansions of the Cliff Walk, which brought Hunt his greatest fame. *Open Tues.–Sun.*

The **Newport Casino (8)** encompasses the International Tennis Hall of Fame and the Tennis Museum. Lawn games, tennis and racket courts, and bowling alleys once made this the most complete resort in

Redwood Library

America. Beyond the semicircular piazza is a long stretch of ground, the site of the USLTA Men's Championship Tournaments from 1881 to 1914.

One Casino Terrace, the **Newport Automobile Museum** (9), has the largest collection of antique and classic cars in New England. All are in running condition, ranging from a showroom-condition Ford Model A to a sleek 1967 Aston Martin coupé, identical to the one driven by James Bond in the movie *Goldfinger*. A new addition is a collection of World War II military vehicles. *Open daily May–Sept.*

The most controversial building in America, the **Old Stone Mill** (10) has been variously attributed to Vikings, Indians, the Portuguese, and early farmers. Despite exhaustive research, no one knows exactly when it was built. Best guesses place it somewhere between 1100 and 1650, although recent thinking suggests it was built as a windmill by Governor Benedict Arnold. Still, the peculiar architecture, along with the suit of armor found farther up the coast and immortalized in Longfellow's "The Skeleton in Armor," has convinced many locals that the Vikings were responsible. Sitting in one of Newport's prettiest parks, the tower is well worth a visit.

Old Stone Mill

The lovely Georgian frame **Trinity Church** (11) was built in 1726 for the first Anglican parish in Rhode Island. Considered one of America's outstanding colonial churches, the building was designed by Richard Monday and was modeled after the London churches of Christopher Wren. It is noted for its delicate wooden spire topped with a gold bishop's miter. The triple-decked wineglass pulpit is unusual. In the small cemetery beside the building is the grave of Admiral de Ternay, who arrived with Rochambeau to join the Revolution, but died here of fever.

Berthed at Sayer's Wharf off Thames Street (Newporters pronounce it "Thaymes") is the reconstructed British frigate **H.M.S. Rose**

Trinity Church

(12). *Rose* is a faithful copy of the original ship sent to Newport in 1774 to put an end to colonial smuggling. The twenty-four-gun ship blocked Newport Harbor, spurring the Congress to found the first Continental Navy. *Rose* left Newport and was sunk three years later off Georgia. The new *Rose* was built in Nova Scotia in 1969, using the

H.M.S. *Rose*

original plans and some of the original timber. Inside the 170-foot ship are the well-furnished captain's cabins, nine-pounders that are still fired on special occasions, and the cramped belowdecks area where the crew lived.

Farther down the harbor front, the sloop **Providence** (13) is a sixty-seven-foot replica of the first American warship. The original

Providence was christened *Katy* and launched about 1768 by wealthy merchant John Brown. Used briefly for whaling, the twelve-gun sloop was taken into the Rhode Island Navy in 1775 and fired the first American naval cannon shots. Trapped in Penobscot Bay, she was burned and sunk to avoid capture. Visitors may board at dockside when the ship is berthed in Newport.

At Mary and Division streets, the **Lucas-Johnson House** (14) dates back to the early 1700s and was the home of a French Huguenot settler. During the Stamp Act riots of 1765, the property was saved from damage when its owner agreed to resign as Newport stamp master. French forces in Newport occupied the house during the Revolution and Commodore Oliver Hazard Perry lived there afterward.

The **Vernon House** (15) was Count Rochambeau's headquarters at Newport during the Revolution, and his meeting place with General Washington. Its classic rusticated exterior has been attributed to Peter Harrison. The fine stairs retain the ramped rails and twisted balusters of an earlier day and were set at the back of the broad central hall behind a low dividing arch sprung from brackets.

Business was good in eighteenth-century Newport, and in 1753 proprietors along Long Wharf voted that "Liberty be granted the applicants to erect a market house where the upper watch house now stands." Some twenty years later the **Brick Market** (16) was completed in English-academic style. The main floor was used as a market and watchhouse, the second and third floors were let for shops and offices. During the late 1700s artist Alexander Placide rented an upper floor for a theater and painted a seascape with ships, which can still be seen today, directly onto the plaster of the east wall.

White Horse Tavern (17), three centuries old, is thought to be the oldest in America. It once served as the stage for fiery political rhetoric and, when Newport was the colonial capital, as the meeting place of the Rhode Island legislature. One story goes that the politicians were so unhappy with the White Horse's cuisine that they had a new eatery, the Colony House, built within walking distance. *Open daily.*

Newport—the Cliff Walk

Playground of the Very Rich

A former French ambassador referred to them as "horrors," perhaps forgetting Versailles. "Summer cottages" the millionaires called the pleasure palaces they raised from the Gay Nineties to the Roaring Twenties, when Newport was a symbol of the glamorous, conspicuous good life.

Most of the royal names of Amercia were here: Vanderbilt, Widener, Duke, Astor, Mills. No matter that a family might spend no more than a month here each summer, each cottage had to be more

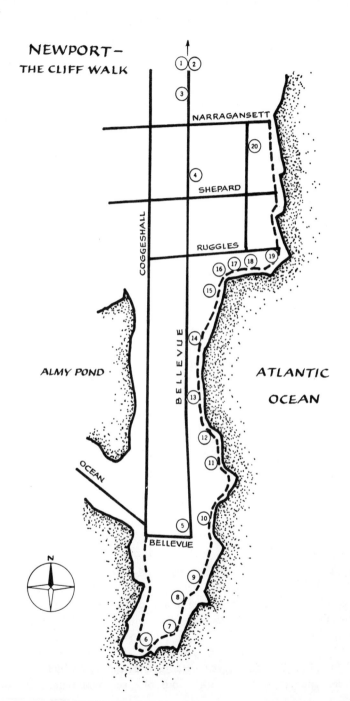

NEWPORT–
THE CLIFF WALK

NARRAGANSETT

SHEPARD

COGGESHALL

RUGGLES

BELLEVUE

ALMY POND

ATLANTIC

OCEAN

OCEAN

BELLEVUE

N

opulent than the next. Mrs. Stuyvesant Fish had two ballrooms in her palatial home. Art collector Forsythe Wickes had a Newport home and his wife had one, too—next door. Newporters say that at Belcourt Castle, Oliver Hazard Perry Belmont's home, the horses not only had three sets of tack (for morning, afternoon, and evening) but, like their master, slept under linen. Robert Goelet, admonished by his pastor for upholstering his pew in gold plush, snapped, "I was born in gold plush, I live in gold plush, and I intend to die in gold plush!"

James Gordon Bennett, editor of the New York *Herald* and son of its founder, was expelled from the Reading Room when a guest of his rode a horse through that staid establishment. He retaliated by hiring McKim, Mead and White and building a club of his own—the **Newport Casino** (1). The shingled casino was the site of the first national tennis championship, in 1881. Now a bit weather-beaten, the building houses the National Lawn Tennis Hall of Fame. The casino stands at one end of fashionable Bellevue Avenue near the Cliff Walk, a spectacular promenade through the playground of the very rich.

This right-of-way was first marked by fishermen as early as 1640, and the citizens of Newport have exercised the right ever since. In the last century, when the mansions were built, their owners objected to such intrusions by strangers. But whenever a fence went up, it was just as quickly torn down, and the offending householder taken to court for obstructing the public way. Since then the owners have contented themselves with surrounding their properties with meticulously trimmed hedges.

Most of the path is paved, but in places skirts precipitous cliffs and should be followed with care. On Sunday afternoons hundreds of strollers enliven a scene that has changed little in a century: white triangles of sails and lobster-pot buoys bobbing in Newport harbor, with the fairy-tale skyline of the great homes rising on the landward side.

Possibly the oldest mansion along the "Gold Coast" is **Kingscote** (2), a rather modest dwelling compared with the marble castles that followed it. Built in 1839 for George Noble Jones of Savannah, it houses a priceless collection of porcelain and paintings donated by later owner William Henry King, a merchant of the China trade. The building's interior is rich with parquet floors, Tiffany glass, and dark wood ceilings. *Open daily May–Oct.*

The Elms (3), an elegant French-style mansion which stands in a garden shaded by thirty-eight kinds of trees, was scheduled for the

The Elms

View from the Elms's terrace

wrecker's ball when the Newport Preservation Society raised money for its purchase in 1962. Its original furnishings had been auctioned off for $486,000, but Newporters refurnished it with precious antiques. Today it stands as lavishly appointed as ever. The grounds include bronze and marble statues, fountains, and formal sunken gardens. The mansion was built in 1901 for coal magnate Edward J. Berwind, and for years Mrs. Berwind entertained at gala balls. Now, on summer Saturday nights, the house again gleams with lights, and soft music accompanies visitors through the stately rooms. *Open daily May–Oct.*

Considered one of the finest Victorian homes in America, **Château-sur-Mer** (4) was raised in 1852 by William S. Wetmore and remodeled twenty years later by Richard Hunt, who added the first French ballroom in the city. Many of the furnishings are original, including a collection of Rose Medallion and Rose Mandarin china sets. On the second floor is a delightful collection of Victorian toys and dollhouses. Near the library was a billiard room for George Peabody Wetmore, governor and senator, but when he died his spinster daughters had the pool table removed and the cue racks turned into coatracks. *Open daily May–Oct.*

Architect Richard Hunt built **Belcourt Castle** (5) for Oliver Hazard Perry Belmont in 1891, based on plans from a Louis XIII hunting lodge he saw in France. Now owned by the Horace B. Tinney family,

Belcourt Castle

it houses their collection of furniture, paintings, rugs, armor, and other works of art from thirty-two countries. The sixty rooms are each done in a different period of French, Italian, or English design. Within them is said to be the largest private collection of stained glass in America. Perhaps the most striking single display is a twenty-three-karat gold Royal Coronation Coach, decorated with oil paintings and weighing four tons. *Open daily May–Oct.*

Famous names and bits of Americana abound in these mansions. Sprawled on putting-green lawns is **The Waves (6)**, the spectacular home of John Russell Pope, the architect who designed the Jefferson Memorial, the National Gallery, and the National Archives Building. Doris Duke's **Rough Point (7)** is surrounded by barbed wire and patrolled by barking mastiffs. **Rock Cliff (8)**, dating from 1869, was the residence of longtime defender of the America's Cup, Harold S. Vanderbilt. Next door, **Ocean View (9)** was erected in 1866 for financier Ogden Mills. Architect Horace Trumbauer designed **Miramar (10)** for the Wideners of Philadelphia. **Beaulieu (11)**, with its fine mansard roof, is the former home of master capitalist John Jacob Astor, and later Cornelius Vanderbilt II.

In late afternoon, sun streams through the windows of William K. Vanderbilt's **Marble House (12)**, strikes fire from the heavy beveled-glass doors and mirrors, reflects off gold walls, and glows from red, yellow, and white marble. The dining room, with mottled pink walls and Corinthian pilasters, is furnished with solid bronze chairs. Footmen to move such chairs were essential at formal affairs, and Vanderbilt supplied them, liveried in maroon coats, gilt garters, and patent-leather shoes. One of the few cottages to display its original furnishings, Marble House was completed in 1892. It was here that Mrs. O. H. P. Belmont (the former Mrs. Vanderbilt) threw Newport's most memorable party—ten courses in which the hundred "guests" were dogs in various forms of fancy dress. The dogs dined on such *haute cuisine* as stewed liver and rice, and shredded dog biscuits. *Open daily May–Oct.*

Beechwood (13), another of the cottages open to the public, was owned by Mrs. William Astor. It, too, had an ornate ballroom with intricately painted angels on the ceiling and a spectacular view of the ocean. While the interior was being completed in 1852, a small army of Italian craftsmen camped in the cavernous basement. *Open daily May–Oct.*

A rare newcomer to the Cliff Walk is **Sea Cliff (14)**. Only twenty-five years old, it is the work of architect Frederic Rhinelander King, who also designed Newport's Trinity Church Parish House. Beyond is **Rosecliffe** (15). Of gleaming terra cotta, it is a copy of the Grand Trianon in Versailles and has the largest ballroom in Newport. Skirting the cliffs, the trail passes the sizable Queen Anne cottage of **Honeysuckle Lodge** (16); **Midcliff** (17), now a girls' school; and **Angelsea** (18), a rambling cottage crowned with a vast slate roof.

Soon the finest of the Cliff Walk mansions comes into view. William Vanderbilt made a good try with Marble House, but his brother Cornelius dwarfed even that multimillion-dollar achievement with **The Breakers** (19), a palace in Renaissance style and one of the most ornate houses on the continent. The Breakers is overpowering: a mazelike conglomeration of limestone from Caen, marble in a dozen hues, wrought iron, massive chandeliers, alabaster, antique tapestries, stained glass, huge rugs, ornate fireplaces, and tooled and gilded leather "wallpaper." The Great Hall soars to a ceiling with a painted sky forty-five feet above the floor. Nearby, the huge dining room also has a distant ceiling, devoted to a painting of the Aurora at Dawn. Two crystal chandeliers, fitted for both gas and electricity, illuminate twelve alabaster columns, above which rest life-size goddesses and nymphs. The table, fully extended, seats thirty-four. Clearly, this was no room for a quick snack, so the family had another dining room, with pale green antique paneling, for everyday use. The carriage house and stable has a major collection of horse-drawn coaches and buggies, and a tunnel leading to the coal cellar will accommodate a wagon and full team. *Open daily May–Oct.*

Ochre Court (20), the main building of Salve Regina College, was built in 1890 by Ogden Goelet, a wealthy New York real estate developer. The superb ironwork first seen at the entrance gates is continued inside the house. A solid marble table, supported by a carved figure of Atlas, dominates the interior. Other rooms open to the public contain fine period furniture and paintings, and there is a beautiful medieval stained-glass window above the landing of the grand staircase. Outside, the grounds sweep down to the Cliff Walk and a beautiful view of the ocean. Ochre Court, like most of Newport's cottages, has gracefully survived as a reminder of the extravagance of a bygone era.

Newport—the Point

"Yankee Georgetown":
Rhode Island Renaissance

The Point is that part of Newport north of Long Wharf and west of Thames Street, running along the inner harbor. Until 1725 it was a placid, rural area with a sprinkling of houses lining the Upper Thames. Then a prominent Quaker family, the Eastons, bought up most of the area and began selling off lots. The first to move in were ship's carpenters. They were joined by members of the Townsend and Goddard families, cabinetmakers famous for their fine furniture. The next group of residents were sea captains who found the Point convenient to Washington Street docks. By 1821, there were twenty-one sea captains living on Bridge Street alone. Over the years many of these eighteenth- and nineteenth-century homes fell into disrepair, but are now being reborn as new residents salvage and restore this "Yankee Georgetown." Many of the homes are not open to the public except for an occasional house tour sponsored by the Point Association, Operation Clapboard, or Christmas-in-Newport.

Recently restored, the **Quaker Meeting House (1)** dates from 1699 and is the oldest in America. It is the site of the New England Yearly Meeting of the Society of Friends. An outstanding example of late seventeenth-century architecture, the meetinghouse contains models and architectural exhibits. *Open daily.*

At 44 Thames is the **Job Bennett House (2)**, owned by a Tory who was forced to flee Newport when his allegiance was discovered. Bennett placed a mark on the large chimney that identified him as a Tory to the British in the harbor but which couldn't be seen by prying neighbors. The roof is a fine example of the gable-on-hip style.

Also on Thames Street, the **John Stevens House (3)** was built in

NEWPORT –
THE POINT

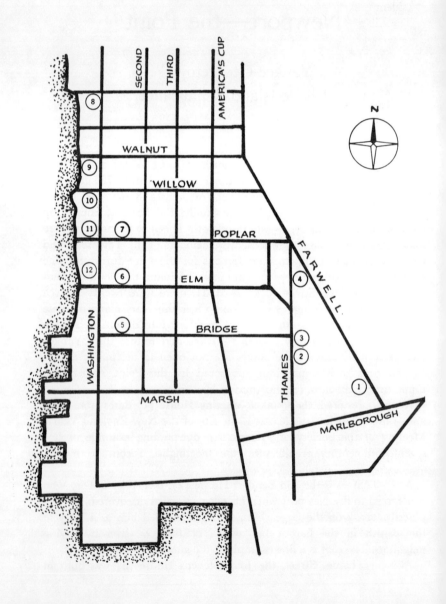

1709 by the noted stonecarver, who had his shop across the street. It was enlarged in 1750 as Stevens' business prospered. When President Kennedy was killed in 1963, John Howard Benson, a later owner of the shop, was commissioned to carve the memorial to the late President in Arlington Cemetery.

The **Liberty Tree** (4) that stands in a tiny city park at the corner of Thames and Farwell streets is the fourth-generation tree to bear that name. The original was planted to symbolize opposition to the Stamp Act. The British cut down the tree when they occupied the city in 1776, but it was replanted when they left several years later. The present tree was planted and rededicated in 1897.

Pitt's Head Tavern (5) was built before 1726 as an end-chimney half-a-house on Charles Street. The present large, gambrel-roofed building was doubled in size before 1765 but framing for the massive chimney, fireplaces, and the stairway belong to an earlier period. Sold for the third time in 1765, the building soon displayed the "Sign of the Right Honorable William Pitt's Head" and became one of Newport's most popular drinking establishments.

Built around 1719, the **Sheffield-Huntington House** (6) has a tremendous fireplace with bake oven and pewter cupboard above. There are four paneled fireplace walls inside, and eight fireplaces altogether.

John Tripp House

In the main hall is a mural painted in 1969 by primitivist Eveline Roberge, who still maintains a studio in Newport.

The large, handsome **Dennis House** (7) was probably built around 1740 by William Grafton. The pineapple doorway, a symbol of welcome, dates to the days of the clipper ships, when captains back from the South Seas placed pineapples outside their homes to invite neighbors in to share that tropical delicacy.

Painted red, the charming two-story **John Tripp House** (8) dates from the early eighteenth century and has a stone end chimney with an ornamental beehive oven. It was purchased by the city for one dollar from Providence, then carted board by board and stone by stone to its present location.

The **Sanford-Covell House** (9) is one of the few Victorian homes on the Point. The Covell family occupied the house for three generations since purchasing it in 1895; it was donated to the Society for the Preservation of New England Antiquities in 1972. Designed by William Ralph Emerson, it is a forerunner of Newport's resort archi-

Hunter House

tecture. Interior walls are frescoed in multicolor Classical style and the house has a dramatic three-story staircase.

The **Thomas Robinson House** (10) has the distinction of having belonged to one family for more than two hundred years. The oldest part of the residence dates from 1725. In 1760 Quaker Tom Robinson bought the house and built an addition, converting the former two-story building into the large, gambrel-roofed house of today. Only a few minor changes have been made since then.

The large, three-story gambrel at 62 Washington Street is the **Captain John Warren House** (11), built about 1736. Among its design features are double steps, a central fanlight door, and wrought-iron railings. Originally a two-story house, it was enlarged around 1774 by Captain Warren to a central hall house with two interior chimneys, a typical design favored by affluent eighteenth-century New Englanders.

Nearby, the **Hunter House** (12) is considered one of the ten best examples of Colonial architecture in America. The house, with its furniture treasures, is a National Historic Landmark and is open to the public. The residence was built in 1748 by Jonathan Nicols, later deputy governor of Rhode Island; later tenants included Governor Joseph Wanton, Jr., and William Hunter, U.S. senator and ambassador to Brazil. It also served as headquarters for Admiral de Ternay, commander of the French naval force stationed here during the Revolution. Beautifully restored by the Preservation Society of Newport County, the house contains a priceless collection of furniture by the Point's own Goddard and Townsend families. *Open daily.*

Boating's World Series

As J. P. Morgan said, "If you have to ask what it costs to run a yacht, you can't afford one." Those were the days when sportsmen raced in vessels piled high with billowing canvas and weighed down with the trappings of the good life. That spirit is nurtured by today's America's Cup races, yachting's premier contest of men and boats.

Bitterness often haunted the Cup races. The Earl of Dunraven, who challenged twice in the 1890s, howled about unruly spectator boats, suspected Yankee trickery in waterline measurements of Defender, and refused to withdraw after fouling her. In contrast was the endearing demeanor of Sir Thomas Lipton, the tea king, to whom an English lady once suggested that the Americans "put something in the water over there which makes you lose."

"I completely agree with you, madam," he replied. "It's a better boat."

Today's races match high-performance—and highly expensive—twelve-meter sloops. Columbia, first of these modern boats, marked a trend to less lavish Cup races—and their resumption after a twenty-year pause. Owned by a syndicate, she sailed to victory over Britain's Sceptre in 1958 with an amateur crew in one of the event's most memorable series. Under new rules adopted in 1956, minimum waterlines were reduced from sixty-five to forty-four feet, and challengers need no longer "proceed under sail, on their own bottoms, to wherever the contest is to take place."

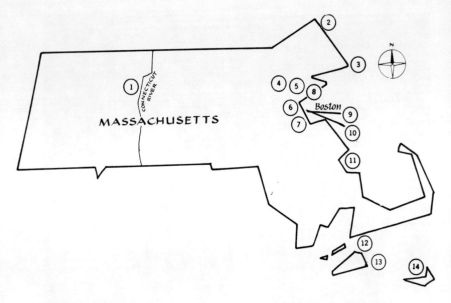

MASSACHUSETTS

South and seaward from the rest of New England lies the bulge of lowland from which islands trail off and the arm of Cape Cod curves toward the Atlantic. It was here that the Pilgrims first made land, and here that New England began.

From its first struggling coastal colonies, Massachusetts bred a free and independent people. The fires of the American Revolution were kindled here, and the town meeting, the basic democratic institution, still governs many communities. Brilliant rebels, writers, painters, philosophers, judges, teachers, and three Presidents have come from this state.

Industry and commerce are as much a part of Massachusetts as the salt marshes of Cape Cod and cranberry bogs of Plymouth. Drab factory towns of the last century are being reborn as affluent suburbs.

Massachusetts has mountains, ocean beaches, summer resorts as old as the Republic, and a variety of metropolitan culture. It has more historic places in a smaller area, more picturesque cities and towns, and more of a sense of America's past than any other state in the Union.

Deerfield

A Frontier Outpost Flourishes

An hour before dawn on February 29, 1704, Deerfield's town sentry shivered and dozed, unaware of nearly 350 stealthy figures crossing the fields outside the village. There was no warning that morning—only a sudden awakening to a terrible death. Indians, led by French-Canadians, burst in on sleeping families and stabbed them in their beds. Elsewhere the attackers waited for the flames to drive their victims out. When the massacre was over, more than half of Deerfield's settlers had been killed or taken prisoner.

Deerfield was the last outpost on New England's frontier when it was settled in 1669. Devastated twice, by the 1704 massacre and the earlier Bloody Brook Massacre of 1675, its resettlement brought agricultural prosperity and a determination never to forget its past. Though the town's fortunes have waxed and waned for three centuries, its historic traditions have never faltered. History buffs and schoolboys still read about the massacre; some visitors come here just to see the site. Others are brought by Deerfield Academy, the town's distinguished preparatory school. And lately have come new crowds: summer campers and winter skiers bound for the Vermont hills, antique collectors and shunpikers roaming the Connecticut River Valley, and autumn-color connoisseurs driving the popular Mohawk Trail. The village lures them all—in growing numbers each year—without benefit of advertising or even a chamber of commerce. The visitors find simply "The Street," a mile-long lane of elms and maples bordered by three centuries of carefully preserved American history. Those houses managed by Historic Deerfield are open Monday through Saturday 9:30–4:30, and Sunday 1:00–4:30. Most charge modest admissions.

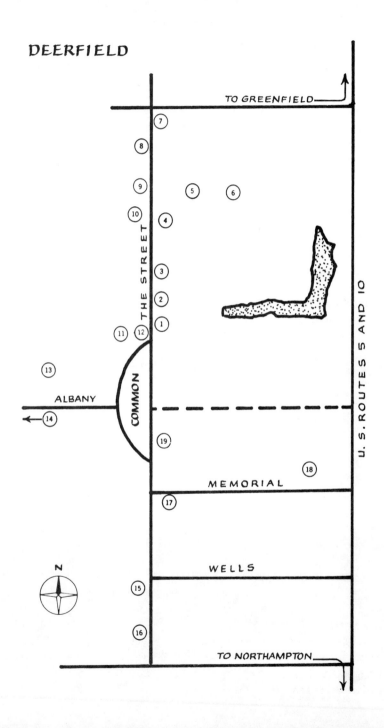

Built in Charlemont, Massachusetts, when it was still a French and Indian War outpost, the **Hall Tavern** (1) is now a visitor orientation center. The tavern once served travelers journeying along the Mohawk Trail between Boston and the Hudson Valley. A seven-room museum displays outstanding New England country furniture, pewter, treen, textiles, miniature furniture, and a stenciled ballroom. At one time in its register could be seen the names of Ralph Waldo Emerson, Henry Thoreau, and other noted guests.

In 1793 one traveler, Rev. William Bentley of Salem, noted in his diary that Joseph Stebbins was the "richest farmer in Hampshire County and began his industry in Shoe making, Tanning, etc." The Stebbins family was well-to-do by Yankee standards, and this wealth is reflected in the **Asa Stebbins House** (2). An aura of elegance pervades this handsome brick home, completed in the 1790s. Portraits by Stuart and Greenwood are displayed with Hepplewhite and Sheraton furniture plus ceramics, glassware, and a number of fine rugs. Hand-painted wall decorations can be seen in the pantry and dining room, and the south parlor has a beautifully molded plaster ceiling.

Allen House

Deerfield's **Liberty Pole** (3) stands near the Stebbins House. During the hectic days of indecision before the Revolution, it was a custom in many New England towns to erect such poles as rallying points for patriot activities. The original pole was brought into town on July 28, 1774, but malicious Tories sawed the pole in half the night before it was to be raised. Undeterred, youthful Whigs erected another in front of a store then owned by David Field. In recognition of Pearl Harbor Day, the present Liberty Pole was erected in 1946 on the site of the original. From its mast flies the Taunton Flag, the British ensign with the words "Liberty and Union" inscribed across its lower field.

The wooden-frame saltbox **Allen House** (4), with its feather-edge paneling, was the home of Historic Deerfield's founders, Mr. and Mrs. Harry N. Flynt, and displays their collection of rare Boston and Connecticut Valley furniture, needlework, and household accessories.

The **Parker and Russell Silver Shop** (5), a modest Deerfield farmhouse, contains a country parlor of the Federal period, a silversmith's workshop, a number of clocks, and an outstanding collection of American and English silver, with examples by Revere, Dummer, Coney, Myers, and others.

A handsome Victorian barn is the setting for the **Helen Geier Flynt Fabric Hall** (6), and its displays of American, English, and European needlework, textiles, and costumes of the seventeenth, eighteenth, and nineteenth centuries. Most notable are the New England crewel embroidery spreads, most of which date from the 1700s.

Asa Stebbins built the brick **Wright House** (7) for his son, Asa, Jr., in 1824. There is an excellent loan collection of mostly Federal-period furniture with pieces by Phyfe, Sheraton, and Frothingham, and early China Trade tea sets.

The home of Deerfield's Tory minister during the Revolution, **Ashley House** (8) was later moved from its foundations and used as a tobacco barn for seventy-five years. The Reverend Ashley stubbornly supported the King, even though for years his parish refused to pay him his salary or furnish him with firewood. On the Sunday afternoon after the Battle of Bunker Hill, they even blocked his way to his own church. Painstakingly restored to its original site and appearance, it shows the comfortable life of a New England minister in the late 1700s. The front parlor is considered to be one of the finest eighteenth-century rooms in America.

Owned for two centuries by the Sheldon family, the 1743 **Sheldon-Hawks House** (9) contains the original paneling and a rear staircase

Flame Stitch pocketbook

with a double approach; a sewing room exhibits period dresses and fabrics.

In 1698 Ensign John Sheldon built the largest and most impressive house in the village. Mindful of the constant threat of Indian attack, he placed it within a stockade made of oak and yellow pine filled with brick. On the morning of the 1704 massacre, his was the last house to fall, as the stoutly spiked door finally gave way to the blows of tomahawks. The house was set aflame, but Ensign Sheldon managed to escape, later making three trips to Canada to rescue Deerfield captives. The existing, central-chimney **Indian House** (10) is a repro-

Wright House

duction. The original door, with a hole chopped through by a tomahawk, is displayed in Memorial Hall.

The modern **U. S. Post Office** (11) reflects the distinctive architecture of the Third Meetinghouse of Deerfield, which served the village between 1696 and 1728. Next door, the nondenominational **First Church of Deerfield** (12), known as the "Brick Church" to distinguish it from the "White Church" across the street, has held services since 1824. Its windows are recessed in narrow round-top arches, and the facade has three doors.

West of the Civil War monument are the mellowed brick buildings of **Deerfield Academy** (13), whose motto is "Be Worthy of Your Heritage." Founded in 1797, the institution flourished, then waned, until Frank L. Boyden took over as headmaster in 1902 and brought it to premier rank among college preparatory schools. It offers a four-year curriculum to boys aged thirteen to eighteen.

Also on Albany Road is Deerfield's **Old Burying Ground** (14), famous for its beauty, preservation, and interesting stones. Near the south side of the cemetery, forty-eight men, women, and children—all victims of the French and Indian raid of 1704—share a common grave beneath a grassy knoll. Near the west side stands the oldest stone in the graveyard, marking the final resting place of the first town clerk, Joseph Barnard, who met death in an earlier Indian attack in 1695. Several epitaphs bear words of warning for the living:

> *Listen to me ye Mortal men Beware*
> *That you engage no more in Direful*
> *War, By means of War my soul from*
> *Earth is fled, my Body loged, in*
> *Mansions of the Dead.*

The **Dwight Barnard House** (15), built by a wealthy merchant in 1725, had become a tenement in 1950 when it was carefully dismantled and moved to Deerfield. Its unusual kitchen includes the comforts of a living room, and distinctive grained paneling can be seen in the south bedroom. Another room is furnished as an eighteenth-century doctor's office.

Moved seven times around the village of Deerfield, the **Wilson Printing Shop** (16) has been a grocery, book bindery, and residence. The 1816 frame structure houses a working hand press and printed material of the last two centuries.

The style and furnishings of the elegant **Wells-Thorn House** (17) bring the visitor from the seventeenth-century frontier to the urbanity of the Federal period. The central part of the restored clapboard residence was built about 1717 by Ebeneezer Wells, a farmer and tavern keeper, who added the front section some thirty-five years later. A lawyer's office of about 1800 has been fitted out and contains several belongings of Caleb Strong, an early governor of Massachusetts.

The earliest of the connecting brick structures of **Memorial Hall** (18) was designed by Benjamin Asher in 1797 for Deerfield Academy, founded the same year. The extensive collection includes Indian artifacts, early American furniture, metalware, tools, tavern signs, and musical instruments. A replica of a colonial kitchen, installed in 1880, is believed to be one of the oldest period-room reproductions in the country.

Its position on the Town Common made the **Frary House** (19) a choice location for the Frary family in pioneer days and a profitable tavern for the Barnards later on. Parts of this frame house are of undetermined age, but most of it was built in the mid-eighteenth century. Stormy Whig meetings were held here during the Revolution, and

Wilson Printing Office

Benedict Arnold is said to have stopped by on his way to join Ethan Allen's attack on Fort Ticonderoga in 1775. An elegant ballroom, country furniture, pewter, ceramics, and weaving equipment reflect the interests of Miss Alice C. Baker, who restored the house in 1890. The house, and Deerfield itself, owes a debt to New Englanders who filled attics with furniture, papers, and mementos of their forebears.

Newburyport

New England's Pompeii Recalls Its Golden Age

The late author John P. Marquand suggested that Newburyport, with its array of eighteenth- and nineteenth-century buildings, is a kind of New England Pompeii, buried intact under the ash of an eruptive change in New England's economy. At the time of the Revolution, only New York, Philadelphia, and Boston were larger. Shipbuilding, fishing, and foreign trade brought a golden age to the town between 1783 and the War of 1812. This new wealth generated a tremendous amount of building—magnificent houses, churches, and public offices. New streets were surveyed, a turnpike between Boston and Newburyport was constructed, and the first chain suspension bridge in the country spanned the Merrimack River.

The glow of prosperity was short-lived, however, due to a series of crippling events. Jefferson's Embargo and the War of 1812 damaged foreign trade, and a tragic fire in 1811 razed sixteen acres of the business district and wharves. Although the town began rebuilding almost before the ashes had cooled, and shipbuilding again flourished by mid-century, Newburyport never fully recovered her former preeminence. The Federal period buildings, which still line city streets, are an eloquent reminder of Newburyport's brief blaze of glory.

Patrick Tracy built the mansion that now serves as the **Public Library** (1) in 1771 for his son Nathaniel, who sent out the first privateer used by the Colonies during the War of Independence. During those war years, he made and lost a fortune of more than $4 million, a staggering sum in those days. Among the many famous guests entertained here were George Washington, John Quincy Adams, Lafayette, Benedict Arnold, and Aaron Burr. Displayed inside are several marine

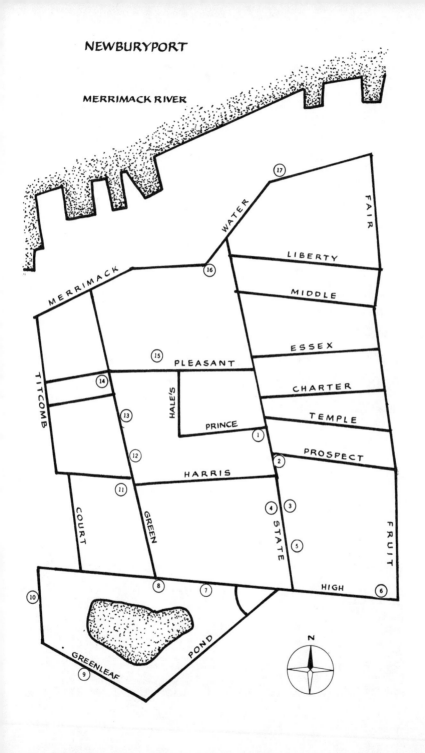

paintings and a model of *Dreadnaught,* the famous clipper ship built in Newburyport.

Across the street is the **Institute for Savings** (2), one of the most important formal Victorian buildings in town. Built in 1872, it has elaborate classical details ranging from large rectangular cornerstones (called quoins) to Corinthian pillars supporting an elegant balustrade.

Dalton House (3), completed in 1746, is a typical Georgian mansion of the mid-eighteenth century. This architectural style, named after the line of kings who came to the throne in 1714, is dressier than the simple, functional earlier period houses. Rustication—the use of wood to imitate cut stone—gives the front of the building a feeling of solidity. An early resident was Tristam Dalton, senator to the first United States Congress from Massachusetts.

An interesting contrast to Dalton House is the 1800 **Carter-Tilton House** (4) across the street. During the Federal period, when this residence was built, architecture became lighter, more delicate, and more restrained. The small, toothlike blocks along the lower edge of the cornice are called, appropriately, dentils.

The **Titcomb-Raymond-Healy House** (5), c. 1808, is similar but simpler in design. An arched window graces the center of the second floor. Down State Street are a variety of interesting iron and picket fences.

Historic High Street, dating from the 1600s, runs between Atkinson Common, Newburyport, and Newbury, where it is known as High Road. Outstanding examples of early American architecture can be seen along its entire length. For many years the center of Newburyport's high society was High Street's **Cushing House** (6). Built about 1808 for a local sea captain, the Federal house was sold a decade later to John Cushing, the father of statesman Caleb Cushing. Though Caleb won his fame in Washington, Canton, and Madrid, one of his most important deeds was accomplished in the dining room of this Newburyport home. In 1852 he sat down with the senator from Mississippi, Jefferson Davis, and settled upon Franklin Pierce as the candidate for President on the Democratic ticket. Successful, President Pierce made Cushing his Attorney General. In 1956 the home was given by the Cushing heirs to the Historical Society and is now open to the public. On the walls hangs a priceless collection of paintings by local and itinerant artists. Furniture, silver, glass, clocks, china, paperweights, needlework, and other works of Yankee craftsmen and artists are displayed, along with many of their tools. The charming gardens

High Street mansion

contain many plants more than one hundred years old, and a nineteenth-century summerhouse.

Bartlett Mall (7), the broad promenade on the eastern side of Frog Pond, was laid out in 1800. At one time the area contained a rope walk—a long, narrow, shedlike building for winding cordage which rigged Newburyport ships.

The **Superior Courthouse (8)**, beyond the Chamber of Commerce Information Booth, was designed in 1805 by Charles Bulfinch, who left his elegant imprint on the statehouses in Boston and Hartford. The front of the building was remodeled in 1853, but the rear retains the original features: The first-floor windows have recessed arches, and the second-floor windows have keystone lintels typical of Bulfinch.

Superior Courthouse

The most famous gravestone in Newburyport is found at the top of the **Old Hill Burying Ground (9)**. The large, handsome stone of Mrs. Mary McHard is etched with the memorable epitaph: ". . . suddenly summoned to the Skies & snatched from the eager embraces of her friends, (and the throbbing hearts of her disconsolate family confessed their fairest prospects of sublunary bliss were in one moment dashed) by swallowing a Pea at her own table, whence in a few hours she sweetly breathed her soul away into her SAVIOUR'S arms, on the 18th day of March A.D. 1780. . . ." The epitaph then subsides into verse. Here, too, is buried Lord Timothy Dexter, who was elevated to the peerage by local wags and was all too happy to accept the title. He built a splendid mansion on High Street and filled it with statues of the world's greatest men (including himself). A book he published in 1802, *A Pickle for the Knowing Ones,* was marked by a complete lack of punctuation. A subsequent edition contained a page of commas and periods with the instruction that readers "pepper and salt it as they please."

The **Old Jail** (10), at the north end of the Mall, sits behind a high spiked stone wall. It was built in 1824 with huge blocks of granite hauled from Rockport by oxen. The complex consists of the jail, the warden's residence (now a private home), a folk art gallery in what was once the jail's kitchen, and a cobbled courtyard complete with stocks and cannon.

Number **16 Harris Street** (11) is an attractive example of the many simple Greek Revival houses built in Newburyport between 1830 and 1850. After the War of 1812, money was harder to come by, and many people abandoned the more pretentious Federal-style mansions, which were expensive to heat and maintain.

John Quincy Adams courted Mary Frazier in the 1790 **Frazier-Greenleaf House** (12) while studying law with the Newburyport jurist Theophilus Parsons in the late 1780s. Miss Frazier rejected Adams' suit, however, because her family and friends felt that his prospects were "none too good."

The **Bradbury-Spalding House** (13) gambrel roof and five windows across the front are typical of late eighteenth-century Georgian style. The doorway is like a miniature classical temple, with pillars supporting a triangular pediment. The house was built after 1786 by Theophilus Bradbury, a member of Congress during Washington's administration and a justice of the Massachusetts Supreme Court in 1797. Another distinguished owner was Wallace Nutting, the well-known authority on antiques.

The small park at the corner of Green and Pleasant streets is **Brown Square** (14). The square was laid out in 1802 by merchant Moses Brown, who imported molasses for the local rum distilleries at his wharves at the foot of Green Street. He had planned to build a block of brick stores and houses, which were never finished. The wall of the adjacent Garrison Inn was "red-tailed"—ready for the addition that was never built. The statue in the center of Brown Square is of

Inn Street

William Lloyd Garrison, the "Great Emancipator," who was born in Newburyport in 1805.

Architect Samuel McIntyre said that the steeple of the **Church of the First Religious Society of Newburyport (Unitarian) (15)** "rivals anything in New England." The main door is highlighted by a delicate fanlight; above is a Palladian window. The two side doors are framed by Doric pilasters.

Market Square (16) has always been a center of activity for the town. Even before 1635, a spot near the river's edge called Watts Cellar was used by fishermen to store their catch. A meetinghouse was built here in 1725, but was torn down in 1801. The land was then laid out as a marketplace for farm produce, and artisans began setting up shops here. The rows of brick commercial buildings which now occupy the site are unique in that they were all built at one time, after the Great Fire of 1811. This was one of the country's earliest attempts at urban renewal.

Robert Mills, who designed the U. S. Treasury Building and the Washington Monument, was especially proud of the fireproof quality of his designs. This undoubtedly played a part in his being chosen to design the new **Custom House** (17) after the old one had burned to the ground in the Great Fire. The building is Greek Revival in design, with a massive Doric entry porch. The large, rough-hewn gray granite blocks enhance the feeling of solidity. Vessels registered here from far-off ports with Madeira wine, Bilbao silk, Irish linen, gunpowder from Rotterdam, and cargoes of molasses, sugar, coffee, and bales of cotton from the West Indies.

Gloucester

Gloucester Trusts in the Sea

Gloucester has always looked to the sea. It was a town with a job to do
—wresting a harvest from Georges Bank off Massachusetts and the
Grand Banks of Newfoundland. Summer and winter the fishermen
took whatever the Atlantic served in the way of fog, ice, and gales.
Sudden storms might drown scores of dorymen. But they were as
tough as their ships—these hard-nosed Yankees who filled the holds
of their sleek schooners with cod, mackerel, and halibut, then raced
home, topsails set, the captain sniffing for the smell of Cape Ann.
Gloucester has managed to preserve a fair slice of this maritime
heritage within its buildings, parks, and museums. Though progress
has intruded and much has changed in this port community, many of
its streets retain the quiet and contained grace of an earlier time.

Atop a hillside park sits the three-story **Fitz Hugh Lane House (1)**,
made of granite blocks in 1849. The lower floors were the residence of
Gloucester native Fitz Hugh Lane, one of America's finest marine artists. Because of its solid construction, the house also served for a time
as a jail, and for that reason is often called the Old Stone Jug. A
collection of Lane's paintings is in the Cape Ann Historical Association
on Pleasant Street.

In June 1975 Gloucester's newest **park (2)** was dedicated to
Solomon Jacobs, a renowned Gloucester schoonerman known as the
"King of the Mackerel Killers." Sol could smell mackerel under the
keel of his boat, it was claimed, and many of his rivals believed it—one
trip from Georges Bank in the early 1900s netted him 197,000 pounds
of codfish. The park, a window on the waterfront, and the Lane
House Park are attempts to provide public space on the inner harbor.

GLOUCESTER

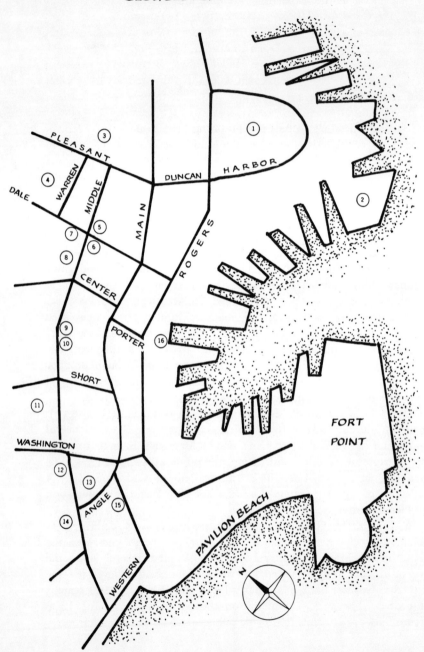

Established as the Cape Ann Scientific and Literary Association in 1876, the **Cape Ann Historical Association** (3) maintains a repository of Gloucester art and artifacts including fine furniture, ship models, china, silver, and portraits. *Open Tues.–Sat. Mar.–Jan.*

The eclectic Gloucester **City Hall** (4) was constructed over two years (1869–71) to replace a town hall burned beyond repair in 1869. The tower is 148 feet above the street and 1,194 feet above sea level.

The **Colonel Joseph Foster House** (5) was the home of the military leader of Gloucester's home defenses during the Revolution. He led the town's successful resistance when the British sloop of war *Falcon* attacked the harbor on August 8, 1775. The British lost three men and twenty-four were captured; the Americans recovered ten men impressed into service by the British.

In the eighteenth century, when Middle Street was called Cornhill, the town's whipping post stood on the site of the present-day **YMCA** (6). As late as 1770 the lash was still used, to punish a woman for stealing.

The group of literary-minded townsfolk whose club would become the **Sawyer Free Library** (7) was organized in 1830. Emerson, Thoreau, Dana, and Holmes are among the luminaries who appeared here prior to 1869. A modest book collection was added in 1854, and moved to this mansion when merchant Samuel Sawyer deeded it to trustees.

When Middle Street was first laid out in 1738, the First Parish Church was built on the site of **Temple Ahavath Achim** (8). A cannonball was shot into the spire of the church when the British bombarded the town from the *Falcon*. The present building was raised by the Unitarians in 1828 after fire destroyed the old church.

A terraced lawn with a series of stone steps leads up to the gambrel-roofed Georgian **Sargent-Murray-Gilman-Hough House** (9), built by Winthrop Sargent in 1768. The frame structure, with much interior carving and paneling, was the home during the late 1780s of the founder of American Universalism, Rev. John Murray, who was married to Sargent's daughter. John Singer Sargent, noted nineteenth-century portrait painter, is among the artists whose works hang here. The house also contains antiques and early glassware.

The **Rogers-Babson House** (10) stands upon land that was purchased in 1663 by Isabel Babson. It is now the headquarters of the Open Church Foundation, established by Roger W. Babson to encourage Bible study, meditation, and prayer.

Sailing regatta off Gloucester

Rev. John Murray, who arrived in Gloucester in 1774, preached salvation for all souls, baptized or not—a doctrine that refuted the concept of eternal punishment and shocked conservative Gloucester elders. He quickly made friends, however, married Judith Sargent, and made 49 Middle Street the center of Universalism. The **mother church (11)** was erected in 1804; it has a Paul Revere bell in its Christopher Wren-style steeple, and a Sandwich glass chandelier in the auditorium. The steeple has four stories: porch, clock, peristyle, and lantern, and is lighted at night.

The neoclassic **American Legion Hall (12)**, with its massive columns, originally served as the town hall during 1844–67. An arch was erected in the adjacent square in 1892 to commemorate the 250th anniversary of the town's incorporation. The arch soared a dizzying forty feet above street level, proclaiming "The road to fortune is paved with Cape Ann granite."

Alfred Mansfield Brooks was (until his death at age ninety-three) the standard-bearer of the upper class in Gloucester. His uncle, George Rogers, brought Boston architecture to town when, in 1850, he transported two separate interiors from across Massachusetts Bay. He placed one atop the other, and created the Brick House, which in time came to be known as the **Brooks House (13).**

Nearby is the **Captain John Somes House (14).** Somes was a ship's commander in America's civilian Navy during the Revolution. Aboard the privateer *Wasp* he roamed the Atlantic in search of prize ships and aided the Patriot cause by harassing enemy commerce. His 1770 home is surrounded by hawthorn trees which burst into bloom every May.

The **Addison Gilbert House (15),** once surrounded by meadows, is the last of the dignified residences that graced the West End. Now the old Puritan Hotel, sporting a Warhol-like soft drink ad, dominates this section of Gloucester. Built in 1810, it was the scene of most of the important social functions of the community during the nineteenth century. Farther up Main Street, the West End is characterized by brick business blocks built after the Great Fire of 1830. Common party walls separate these Federal-style buildings.

The three-bench **Hidden Park (16)** is often used by artists painting scenes of fishing boats tied up along the wharves of Gloucester's inner harbor. Lobster boats and those smaller draggers which participate in the box fishery set a scene that is the Gloucester known to much of America.

A Clam Lover's Guide to Longnecks, Cherrystones, and Quahogs

The pilgrims might never have survived their first years in America without the sea's bounty. Most abundant were clams, crowded shell to shell in mud flats along the shore. Despite two hundred years of feasts and clambakes, these delectable mollusks are still plentiful on New England's coast.

Two main types are eaten: soft-shelled and hard-shelled. The Indian name for hard clam is quahog. This variety tastes best when small—the two-inch size, called littlenecks, are often served raw on the half shell. Slightly larger ones, from two to three inches, are called

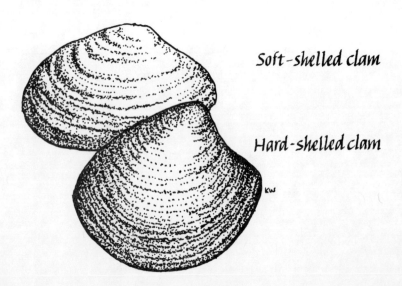

Soft-shelled clam

Hard-shelled clam

cherrystones. Some use the term quahog only for four-to-five-inch hard-shelled clams. These are often so tough they are only eaten chopped or ground in chowders.

Soft-shelled, or longneck, clams are mostly found north of Cape Cod. The best are steamers—those less than two inches long. Only clams which are tightly closed when dug should be eaten.

To prepare steamers for cooking, the clams must be thoroughly scrubbed, then soaked in salt water to rid them of sand. Melt some butter in a large pot, and sauté finely chopped onion and parsley. Pour in several cups of water, bring to a boil, and add the clams. Cover the pot tightly and steam for five to eight minutes—just until the shells open. Discard any clams that remain shut, and serve the rest immediately with melted butter. A healthy appetite can demolish two dozen steamers in minutes.

Concord

Literary Haven, Flashpoint of War

A farming town simmering with unrest, Concord burst into glory on April 19, 1775, when its ragtag militia engaged a sizable force of British regulars in the first battle of what would become the American Revolution. A year earlier the focus of revolutionary activity had been brought here as the First Provincial Congress met in the Concord Meeting House and authorized the collection of supplies in readiness for war. It was those stores that the British sought when General Gage ordered eight hundred light infantry into Concord. The secret mission was uncovered, however, and the alarm was spread over the countryside by William Dawes and Paul Revere. When the British captured Revere in Lincoln, Dr. Samuel Prescott, returning home from courting a Miss Mulliken, jumped his horse over a stone wall and carried the alarm to Concord.

When the long, scarlet column appeared, the Concord men realized they were badly outnumbered. They retreated across the North Bridge (with fifes and drums playing "We had grand music," one later recalled), where men from surrounding towns swelled their ranks to about four hundred. In town, the British found wooden gun carriages and set them ablaze. Smoke rose over Concord. The militiamen had no way of knowing what was happening but feared the worst. They advanced to the bridge, where the British opened fire. The Provincials fired back, killing two soldiers and forcing the rest to withdraw. Exhausted by their long march from Boston and the unexpected resistance, the expedition became a rout. Under constant fire and low on ammunition, the British column limped back to Boston. By dusk, militia companies from as far away as New Hampshire and Connecticut

CONCORD

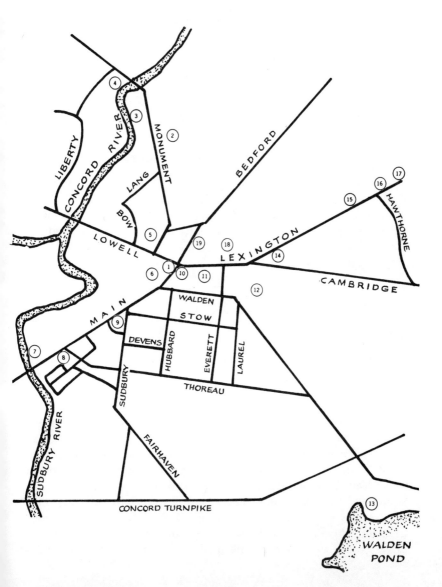

Minuteman Statue

were still arriving—the nucleus of the Continental Army of which General Washington took command on July 3, 1775.

When the Revolutionary smoke had cleared, Concord became associated with a remarkable era of American thought and literature which Van Wyck Brooks called the "Flowering of New England." The beauty and tranquillity of the area (and its proximity to Boston publishers) played a significant role in the lives and works of Emerson, Thoreau, Hawthorne, and Alcott. Emerson found Concord a "fit" place for a poet, where a walk in the woods had a "breath of immortality in it." Thoreau, a native literary son, wrote, "I have never got over my surprise that I should have been born into the most estimable place in all the world, and in the nick of time, too."

A sense of history lingers in the buildings and battlefields, museums and monuments of Concord. A few steps from **Monument Square** (1) will evoke pages, even whole chapters, of America's past. Retreating from the North Bridge toward Concord and stopping to drink at the well of the **Elisha Jones House** (2), British soldiers were just a horse's length away from a shed containing hidden stores. Thinking the troops were gone, Jones poked his head out of the door in time to hear a bullet whistle past his ear and lodge in the wall. The building is still known in Concord as "The Bullet Hole House." Although it has undergone several additions and alterations, the house has title to being the oldest in Concord, dating from 1644. It is privately owned and not open to the public.

At the **North Bridge** (3) the "first spark was struck" that altered the balance of an empire. The entire area of the bridge was acquired by the National Park Service, which operates a **Visitor Center** (4) near the west end. The area, from which cars are banned, looks much the same as it did when it was filled with stinging smoke and echoed to the crack of musketfire. Down the path—past a field in which a band of Algonquin Indians once lived—is the tall obelisk where eighty British grenadiers stood to fire and where two fell dead. Their graves are a few feet away. Across the bridge (a replica of the original) is the Minuteman Statue where the Americans stood to return fire in a battle that lasted only a few minutes but was "the shot heard 'round the world." Two patriots died here. The statue was sculpted in 1875 by Daniel Chester French, whose masterwork is the seated Lincoln in Washington's Lincoln Memorial. The plow on which the patriot figure's left hand rests is symbolic of the minuteman's readiness for battle (although none of the Concord minutemen left their plowing on April 19—the alarm came just after midnight).

Rev. William Emerson, who built the **Old Manse** (5) in 1770, gathered many of his flock around him that day as they watched the battle unfold. Hawthorne said, "It came, and there needed but a gentle wind to sweep the battle smoke around this quiet house." Like most of the pastors of Boston and the surrounding countryside, Emerson—grandfather of Ralph Waldo Emerson—was a fiery patriot and briefly took part in the skirmish. Nathaniel Hawthorne brought his bride, Sophia, to spend the first three blissful years of their marriage here.

North Bridge

Until then, Hawthorne wrote, the house "had never been profaned by a lay-occupant." Despite Sophia's cheerfulness, Hawthorne was haunted by melancholy, out of which would spring the themes for many of his works. *Mosses from an Old Manse* was written here, and gave the house its name. The Concord River, which flows to the rear of the manse, was also a source of inspiration for Concord authors. Emerson said, "The good river god has taken the form of my valiant Henry Thoreau here and introduced me to the riches of his shadowy, starlit, moonlit stream."

A marker indicates the location of the **Old Jail** (6). Thoreau was jailed here for one night in 1846 for refusal to pay his poll tax. Afterward he wrote *Civil Disobedience*. "If the alternative is to keep all

Old Manse

men in prison, or give up war and slavery, the State will not hesitate which to choose," he wrote. "That government is best, which governs not at all."

From the **South Bridge** (7) Captain Munday Pole was dispatched by the British on a gentlemanly search of nearby homes. Nearby is the Major Joseph Hosmer House (572 Main), one of those searched. The British did not find the ammunition which lay hidden under Granny while she rested on her feather bed.

The **Thoreau Lyceum** (8) is dedicated to the preservation of the author's ideals. To the rear of the Lyceum stands a replica of Thoreau's cabin at nearby Walden Pond. "I had three chairs in my house: one for solitude, two for friendship, three for society," he wrote. He was, in his own words, "self-appointed inspector of snow storms and rain storms," and friend of Channing, Emerson, Alcott, and Hawthorne. Several original manuscripts of the Concord authors are housed in the nearby **Concord Library** (9). *Open Mon.–Sat.*

Built in 1747, **Wright Tavern** (10) was the mustering point for Concord's militia, and later temporary headquarters for the British force. According to legend, British Major Pitcairn ordered a glass of brandy "and stirred it with his bloody finger, remarking, 'He hoped he could stir the Yankee blood so before night.' " Hours later, the retreating British deserted the tavern not suspecting that the town's communion silver had been hidden in the inn's soap barrel. The next day it was recovered, blackened by lye but safe. Beside the tavern is the site of the **Meetinghouse** (11), where Rev. Emerson preached on Sundays. In October 1774 the First Provincial Congress, presided over by John Hancock, met here and resolved not to pay the King's taxes. The delegates also decided to collect military stores and muster a militia force.

Along Lexington Road is a sense of grace in the old houses and the great trees that shade them, many of which were standing when the British marched past in 1775. There were no grand houses in Concord, for there were no great fortunes here; the dwellings, to use a New England word, were "comfortable." The 1828 frame **Emerson House** (12) was the home of the great philosopher from 1835 to his death in 1882. Still owned by his descendants, it remains intact except for his library and study, which have been moved to the Antiquarian Museum across the street. Emerson was born in Boston but knew Concord well and had spent some time at the Old Manse which his grandfather built as pastor of the Concord church. After he moved into this house he became very much the citizen of Concord, walking the fields and streets, attending town meetings, and devoting himself to civic activities. The town, in turn, deeply loved and respected him. Emerson House contains a fine collection of many of his books, personal effects, and furniture.

A side trip down Walden Street leads to **Walden Pond** (13). It was into these woods in 1845 that Thoreau went. No recluse, Thoreau journeyed several times a week to see family and friends in Concord during his two years at Walden. Today this pleasant sheet of water is not cluttered with summer cottages as are so many New England lakes, and its wooded shores are little changed from those Thoreau knew a century ago. A cairn marks the site of Thoreau's cabin.

One of America's best small museums is the Concord **Antiquarian Museum** (14). In fifteen period rooms (from Colonial to Victorian) are displayed authentic furniture, Ralph Waldo Emerson's study, and items from Thoreau's Walden Pond cabin. Among the most interesting displays are relics from the 1775 battle and one of two lanterns that hung in Boston's Old North Church on the night of Paul Revere's famous ride. A diorama depicts the fight at the North Bridge. *Open daily.*

A half mile down Lexington Road is **Orchard House** (15), home of the Alcotts from 1858 to 1877. It enshrines many of the girlhood pleasures that Louisa May Alcott brought to life in *Little Women*. The book was an instant success, and Louisa rescued the family from debt. The home is an old farmhouse, so run-down when the Alcotts bought it that many felt it was "only good for firewood." But Bronson Alcott supervised its restoration and soon friends who had called the house hopeless came to admire it. Under a canopy of pines on the grounds of Orchard House is the School of Philosophy, a small chapel founded by Bronson Alcott in 1879, when he was eighty. The final session in 1888 was a memorial service for Alcott.

Alcott House

The Wayside (16), home of Samuel Whitney, was another storage place for supplies at Concord. When Paul Revere's alarm reached town, citizens worked through the night to carry the stores farther west before the British arrived. At various times the house was owned by Margaret Sidney (creator of *Five Little Peppers*), the Alcotts, and Nathaniel Hawthorne. Although Hawthorne was no longer the recluse he had been in Salem, he was still shy, lonely, and brooding in Concord. He spent long hours meditating on a path behind the Wayside and confided in Emerson: "This path is the only remembrance of me that will remain."

Ephraim Wales Bull was neither a patriot hero nor a literary figure, but he contributed to Concord's fame in another field: He originated and perfected the Concord grape. Bull, whose hobby was horticulture, planted thousands of seedlings and in 1849 succeeded in developing a variety of grape that matured before the early frosts. The grape's success was enormous but others profited instead of an embittered Bull. He died in poverty and his inscription in Sleepy Hollow Cemetery reads, "He sowed, others reaped." His home, **Grapevine Cottage** (17), is a fine white clapboard residence, now private, on Lexington Road. Note the grape arbor east of the house.

Back in the village proper and housed in a 1753 residence is the Concord **Art Association** (18). Inside is a recently discovered secret room which was used for storage of munitions during the Revolution and as a stop on the underground railroad for runaway slaves before the Civil War.

West of the museum is the **Old Hill Burying Ground** (19), with graves dating from 1677. John Jack, a black slave who had bought his freedom, was the last person buried here, in 1773. Across Bedford Street is Sleepy Hollow Cemetery, the burial place of Hawthorne, Bull, Thoreau, Emerson, and the Alcotts. Their graves are situated on a lovely knoll called "Author's Ridge." Of the long, low ridge, Emerson wrote, "The blazing evidence of immortality is our dissatisfaction with any other solution."

Boston—the Freedom Trail

Echoes of Sam Adams and Mother Goose

Boston's past hangs upon it like a fine but faded coat, and here and there about the city are scattered reminders of influence and importance in stone and bronze. That Boston appreciates its heritage more than most cities is evident during a walk along the Freedom Trail, a collection of sites central to the life of the city and the nation. They are within easy walking distance of each other, down slits of streets weaving incongruously through the skyscrapers.

The tour of the oldest part of Boston begins at the new **Government Center complex (1)**, built on the site of old Scollay Square, a colorful

City Hall

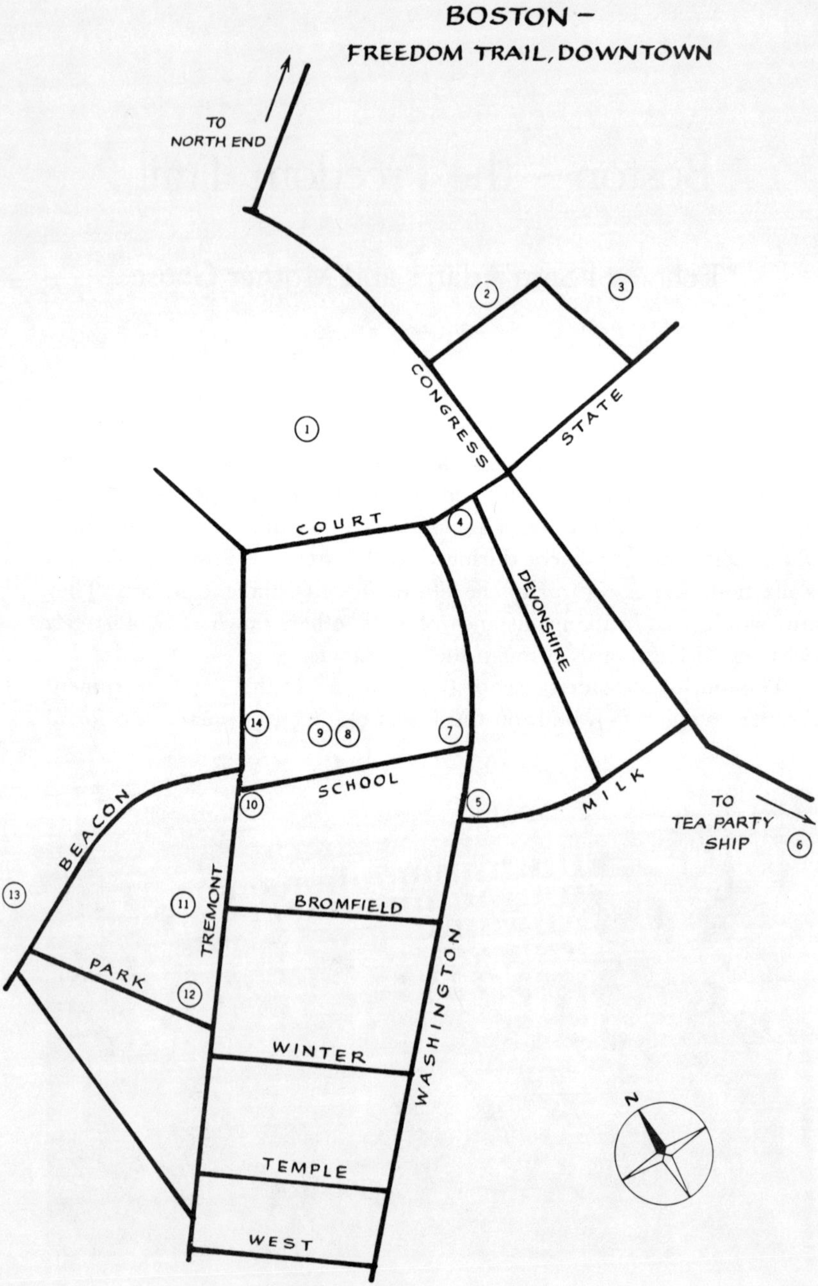

BOSTON –
FREEDOM TRAIL, DOWNTOWN

TO
NORTH END

① ② ③ ④ ⑤ ⑥ ⑦ ⑧ ⑨ ⑩ ⑪ ⑫ ⑬ ⑭

CONGRESS

STATE

COURT

DEVONSHIRE

SCHOOL

MILK

TO
TEA PARTY
SHIP

BEACON

TREMONT

BROMFIELD

WASHINGTON

PARK

WINTER

TEMPLE

WEST

N

but dilapidated section of Boston where the famous Old Howard burlesque theater once stood. Today cheesecake has given way to businessmen and bureaucrats. The heart of Government Center is City Hall, whose design by Kallmann, McKinnell and Knowles won a four-year competition for a new city hall. Both the building and surrounding plaza symbolize the ideals of openness and accessibility in government. In clement weather the plaza serves as a stage for political rallies, plays, and concerts. Tours of the building leave from the information booth every half hour between 10 and 4 on weekdays.

The first official site along the Freedom Trail is **Faneuil Hall** (2), historic marketplace and the political forum for Revolutionary leaders. Merchant Peter Faneuil built the hall and gave it to the city in 1742, as a replacement for an earlier structure. The first market, built of wood, was torn down by an angry mob who were unconvinced that a fixed market was better than house-to-house peddling. The present hall is made of brick. Town meetings here were so active that John Adams named it "The Cradle of Liberty." Reflecting Faneuil Hall's dual role as meeting hall and market, Francis Hatch wrote:

> *Here orators*
> *In ages past*
> *Have mounted their attack*
> *Undaunted by proximity*
> *Of sausage on the rack.*

In front of the hall is a statue of Sam Adams, in a placid pose uncharacteristic of the fiery patriot. Beginning with the Sugar Act of 1764, Adams chaired the town meetings at Faneuil Hall, and preached resistance to British attempts at taxation. *Open daily.*

Quincy Market (3), true to its beginning as a grocery market, is a cornucopia of French crêpes, Italian sausages, Danish cheeses, Greek pastries, Irish coffee, German beer, American hot dogs, Syrian bread, Chinese noodles, Irish stew, candies, chowders, and burgers. The variety seems endless. Merchants and craftsmen display pewter, wood, leather, and textiles, and the market is an arena for people-watching and socializing. *Open daily.*

As early as 1634 the Puritans used the site of the **Old State House** (4) to set up their pillory and stocks. Offenders were locked up, shouted at, and pelted with rotten vegetables. Later the square became a meeting place for political protest before the Revolution. One of the oldest public buildings in the country, the Georgian structure was built

Faneuil Hall

in 1713. In the Council Chamber, in 1761, James Otis fought against
the Writs of Assistance, resulting in the law that no one can search a
house without a warrant. The Declaration of Independence was first
read to the people of Boston from the balcony on July 18, 1776 (it's
still read from there every July 4). The lion and unicorn statues higher
up are symbols of the British crown. These are copies—patriots destroyed the originals. *Open daily.*

Nearby is Devonshire Street, formerly known as "Pudding Lane,"
"Crooked Lane," and "Wilson's Lane." A former resident of the street
was Elizabeth Vergoose, or Mother Goose, who came to live here with
her daughter upon the death of her husband. Her son-in-law was the
first to gather and publish the songs she sang to her grandchildren.

On Milk Street is a bust of Benjamin Franklin and the words

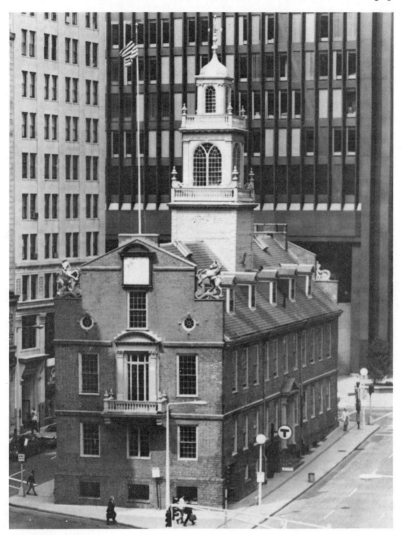

Old State House

"Birthplace of Franklin" carved in relief. Nearby is the **Old South Meeting House** (5). On December 16, 1773, some 5,000 outraged citizens gathered in and around this building to decide what they would do with the three tea ships at Griffin's Wharf. At a word from Sam Adams, men disguised as Indians, followed by those inside the build-

Old South Meeting House

ing, boarded the ships and dumped the tea into Boston Harbor. Then, with commendable military precision, the "Indians" arranged themselves in rank and file, shouldered their tomahawks, and marched up the wharf to the music of a fife. At the end of the wharf was a house where the British admiral was staying. As the procession passed by, he raised a window and called, "Well, boys, you've had a fine pleasant evening for your Indian caper, haven't you? But mind you have got to pay the fiddler yet!" Boston did pay the fiddler when the British retaliated by closing the harbor—an act which further united the colonies and brought them one step closer to war. *Open daily.*

The Tea Party Path, a fifteen-minute side trip down Milk and Congress streets, leads to the **Boston Tea Party Ship and Museum** (6); displays include one of the 240 chests thrown overboard that night. *Open daily.*

Across from the Old South Meeting House is the **Old Corner Bookstore** (7) at School and Washington streets. The present building was erected in 1711 as the home of apothecary Thomas Crease and was converted from residence to bookstore in 1828. In the mid-nineteenth century the Old Corner became famous as a gathering place for Longfellow, Emerson, Hawthorne, Holmes, Whittier, Julia Ward Howe, and Harriet Beecher Stowe. Inside are several rare first editions and Oliver Wendell Holmes's desk. *Open Mon.–Sat.*

Old City Hall (8) is a Victorian building which has been recycled to house private offices and a chic French restaurant. One of the few remaining examples of French Second Empire architecture in Boston, the building was based on one of the pavilions of the Louvre. The artist who sculpted the Franklin statue in front of the hall said that Franklin's left profile wears the serious face of a statesman, while his right profile bears the whimsical expression of the author of *Poor Richard's Almanac*. Passersby can judge for themselves.

Franklin attended the Boston **Latin School** (9), whose original site near here makes this spot part of the Freedom Trail. In 1634 the town decided that "Philemon Pormont be intreated to become a schoolmaster for the teaching and nourtering of the children with us," "children" referring exclusively to boys. The Latin School was the first public school in the United States, and its alumni include John Hancock, Robert Treat Paine, and Sam Adams.

At the end of School Street is the famous **Parker House** (10) at 60 School, where Parker House rolls originated. Both Ho Chi Minh and Malcolm X worked here as waiters (though not at the same time).

The **Granary Burying Ground** (11) takes its name from a barnlike structure which used to stand here and which was supposed to store grain for poor people in time of need. In the words of old records, though, "the weevils have taken the wheet, and mice annoy the corn." Dating back to 1600, the burying ground is filled with the bones of patriots. Near the entrance is the grave of the Boston Massacre victims, and next to it, the grave of Sam Adams. John Hancock's marker is the white pillar near the church wall. Adams and Hancock rose together as leaders of the Revolution; people used to say that Hancock paid the postage while Adams did the writing. They both signed the Declaration of Independence and they shared the distinction of being the only two patriots outlawed by King George III. Along the brick wall near Adams's grave is the tomb of Robert Treat Paine, the third signer of the Declaration buried in the Granary. One of the most handsome stones is that of Jabez Smith, Jr., "Lieutenant of Marines on board the Continental Ship Trumball," who has a beautiful three-masted ship carved on the top of his stone in place of the traditional skull and wings. Back on the main path is the grave of Paul Revere. The fancy white monument was erected by the city; Revere's original and unpretentious stone is in front of it. When not on a horse Revere worked in metals, edited a newspaper, pulled teeth, made gunpowder, and engraved the plates for and printed the first U.S. paper currency.

From the Granary continue on Tremont Street to Park. For years Park Street was the dividing line between business and residential Boston, or as the saying went, "No gentleman takes a drink before three o'clock or east of Park Street." At the **Park Street Church (12)**, William Lloyd Garrison gave his first antislavery speech in 1829. The site of the church was once called Brimstone Corner, because brimstone for gunpowder was stored in a cellar here during the War of 1812. Built in 1809 on a knoll overlooking Boston Common, the 217-foot spire of this church still dominates the landscape.

North of the church along Park Street is the **Massachusetts State House (13)**, whose Archives Museum displays documents dating back to the Pilgrims (see Beacon Hill).

Past the Chester Harding House (1808) and the private Boston Athenaeum library (1807) is **King's Chapel and burying grounds (14)**, built during 1749–54 on the site of the first Anglican church in New England. The chapel later became the first Unitarian church in America. Puritan Isaac Johnson was the first to be buried here, in 1631. Over the years other members of the colony asked to be buried next to him, and the plot began to fill up. Before the Revolution, King's Chapel was the seat of the Church of England and of royalism. Inside the chapel are high enclosed pews designed to keep their occupants warm during lengthy winter services. To the right of the main entrance is a special pew where condemned prisoners heard their last sermon before being hanged on the Common. In the burying ground is a fine collection of slate stones from the seventeenth and eighteenth centuries, marking the graves of a long list of governors of Massachusetts, among them John Winthrop (1588–1649). Near the end of the path by the chapel is the stone of Elizabeth Paine, a young Puritan branded with an "A" for adultery because she bore a child by her minister. Two hundred years later Nathaniel Hawthorne retold her story in *The Scarlet Letter*. His stone is nowhere to be found, but legend says that Captain Kidd is also buried in the cemetery. In the 1690s Kidd was sent by the royal governor of Boston to capture pirates off the coast, but rather than pursue pirates he became one. Convicted and sentenced to death in England, Kidd pleaded with his judges, "For my part, I am the most innocent person of them all." A right turn on Tremont Street leads back to the cosmopolitan bustle of Government Center.

Boston—the North End

Crucible of Conflict

Boston's ethnic pot has never really melted—witness the North End, the city's tribute to Europe. This part of Boston is old, crowded, and in many places, dilapidated. But it has great vitality and charm, and its architecture and foreign flavor make it unique in the city. The North End has been the port of entry for every major ethnic group that lives in Boston. The Yankees and blacks lived here first, in the original Puritan settlements. Next it was the Irish. Eastern European Jews migrated to this section of town and claimed it for a time; now the area is a very close-knit Italian-American community.

From the statue of Sam Adams in front of Faneuil Hall, the tour leads to Union Street. The stretch from Union to the Expressway is the **Blackstone Block** (1), Boston's oldest commercial area—a district that retains original seventeenth-century street patterns and alleyways.

At 41 Union Street is the **Capen House** (2), built between 1713 and 1717. Louis Phillipe, later to become King of France, gave French lessons to wealthy Boston merchants when hard pressed for money and awaiting relief from Europe. Since 1826 the building has housed the Union Oyster House, the oldest restaurant in Boston.

The **Ebenezer Hancock House** (3), at 10 Marshall Street, dates from 1760. John Hancock owned it from 1764 to 1785, during which time it was occupied by his brother Ebenezer, paymaster of the Continental Army.

Across from the Hancock House is the **Boston Stone** (4), embedded in a building housing a gift shop. All distances to and from Boston are measured from this point, the official centerpoint of the city.

Around the corner is Blackstone Street, the home of Boston butchers

BOSTON –
NORTH END

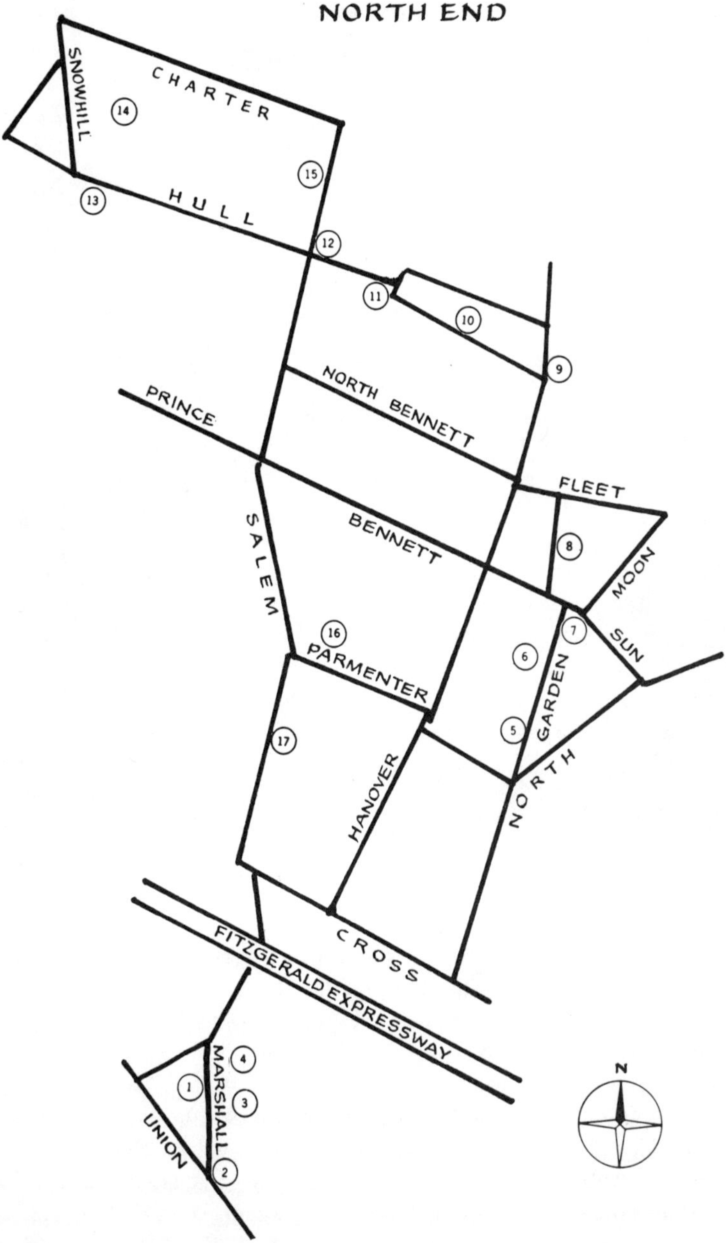

SNOWHILL

CHARTER

⑭

HULL

⑬

⑮

⑫

⑪

⑩

NORTH BENNETT

⑨

PRINCE

FLEET

BENNETT

⑧

MOON

SALEM

⑯

PARMENTER

⑦

SUN

⑥

GARDEN

⑰

⑤

HANOVER

NORTH

CROSS

FITZGERALD EXPRESSWAY

④

MARSHALL

①

③

UNION

②

N

Paul Revere statue

for three centuries (originally, a nearby creek was the only place in town where animal entrails could be disposed of legally). A detour up Blackstone Street leads to Haymarket, where on Fridays and Saturdays fresh produce is sold from carts and stands of street vendors.

Beyond the pedestrian tunnel is the North End proper. Turn right on Cross Street and walk one block over to Hanover Street. Before the Revolution, the street was lined with the mansions of Boston's Tory aristocrats. With the defeat of the British, the Loyalists fled to Canada, and their houses were appropriated by merchants.

In colonial Boston, North Street was named Ann Street and was the site of several taverns where patriots gathered to foment unrest. By the nineteenth century it had degenerated into a rowdy waterfront area of brothels, saloons, and gambling houses. The "nymphs of Ann Street" were notorious until 1854 when the neighborhood was cleaned up.

At 29 North Square is the **Moses Pierce-Hichborn House** (5). Hichborn was Paul Revere's cousin and a prosperous shipbuilder. This three-story home is one of the two eighteenth-century residences still standing in this part of the city. The huge wooden beams are held together with "trunnels," or wooden pegs, instead of nails.

Next door is the **Paul Revere House** (6), the oldest wooden building in Boston. A previous house on the site belonged to a Captain Kemble, who posterity records as having to suffer two hours in the stocks for "lewd and vicious behaviour." He had kissed his wife in public after a three-year absence at sea. Ownership of the home then passed to the Mathers, whose members included eminent preachers Cotton and Increase. Paul Revere purchased a newer house in 1770 and moved in

Paul Revere House

with his wife, mother, and five children. Paul's second wife bore seven more children. The unusual size of the Revere family made this house the only one in North Square that did not have to quarter British soldiers during the Revolution. The interior furnishings have been restored to the style of the period. *Open daily.*

At 11 North Square is the **Mariner's Home** (7), built in 1838. The home served as an all-purpose lodging house and refuge for seamen and a reminder of Boston's importance as a port city.

Rose Fitzgerald Kennedy was born in the brick tenement building at **4 Garden Court** (8) in 1890. After the wealthy fled Boston following the Revolution, buildings like these began to fill the old gardens and open spaces of the North End. Successive famines, especially the potato-crop failures of 1824 and 1847, brought thousands of Irish immigrants to the area. John "Honey Fitz" Fitzgerald, Rose's father and a mayor of Boston, was the son of one such family and was born in the vicinity of North Square.

St. Stephen's Roman Catholic Church (9), at the corner of Hanover and Clark, was originally the "New Old Meeting House," and included Paul Revere among its members. The Italian Renaissance building was designed in 1802 by Charles Bulfinch. Twice gutted by fires, it was completely restored in 1865 to its original design. The simple, white interior includes two handsome pewter chandeliers, each eight feet in diameter. *Open daily.*

The **Paul Revere Mall** (10) connects the church with Christ Church nearby. Like its European counterparts, the open space is a natural gathering place and neighborhood park. The walls of the mall are lined with bronze plaques sketching the city's history. One is dedicated to the Salutation Tavern, a patriot's drinking house of whom many patrons were ship's caulkers. To summon them to meetings messengers would run through the narrow streets of the North End shouting "Caulkers! Caulkers!" The word degenerated into "caucus," adding a new political term to the American lexicon.

The **Clough House** (11) is the second of the North End's eighteenth-century homes. Built in 1715, it was one of six identical houses. Ebenezer Clough was a member of the Sons of Liberty and one of the war-painted participants in the Boston Tea Party. The building, not open to the public, has been restored and is used by Christ Church.

The oldest church in Boston, **Christ Church** (12), popularly known as "Old North," was built in 1723 as the second Anglican church in the city. Two lanterns shone from the steeple on the fateful night of

Old North Church

April 18, 1775, to warn the people across the Charles River that the British were marching to Lexington and Concord. The graceful interior contains the original high pew boxes, brass chandeliers, and wineglass pulpit. A chalice designed by Paul Revere is used at communion services. Every year on April 18, at an evening memorial service, a descendant of one of the three who spread the alarm in 1775—Paul Revere, William Dawes, and Robert Newman—hangs two lanterns from the highest window. The most interesting of the many plaques in the church gardens is one commemorating the flight of John Child from the steeple of the church in 1757 in a birdlike contraption. *Open daily.*

Leave the Old North Church by way of Hull Street. At **Number 44 (13)** is the narrowest house in Boston. Across the street is **Copp's Hill Burying Ground (14).** The Snowhill side of the cemetery was originally reserved for slaves and freedmen, of whom more than 1,000 are buried here. The Mathers—Cotton, Increase, and Samuel— share a large tomb surrounded by an iron railing near Charter Street. One of Cotton Mather's most famous sermons at the Old North Church concerned "divine delights" and was delivered in 1686, two weeks after he had married Abigail Phillips. His most "divine delight," he confessed, was reading the Bible.

Leaving the burying ground, a right turn at the top of the hill leads to Charter Street. To the south is a view of Government Center, the Hancock Tower, and the Prudential Center. It was here that the original charter for the Massachusetts Bay Colony was hidden after the British attempted to revoke it. Here, too, is the summit of Copp's Hill, the North End's highest point. The homes along Charter Street were excellent vantage points for spectators during the Battle of Bunker Hill. Afterward, the street was converted into a makeshift hospital for the wounded on both sides. Across the river is Charlestown, Chelsea, and East Boston. The gray obelisk to the left is the Bunker Hill Monument.

At 190 Salem Street is **Dodd House (15)**, built in 1805. The Dodds were the last of the North End's old families, and were so entrenched in the past that they continued to use a fireplace for cooking long after stoves had come into common use.

Salem Street today is distinctly Italian-American, and provides a sense of the area as a living community. Aromas of freshly baked bread and pastry waft through the air; at Eastertime whole lambs and goats hang in butcher shop windows. Around the corner of

Parmenter Street is the **North End Branch Library** (16), designed after a Roman villa with an open-air atrium. In the summer there are Italian-style puppet shows here. Behind the library is the home of DeFerrari, the street peddler who invested in the stock market and became a millionaire.

On Salem Street, **Number 99** (17) is the site of the oldest bakery in America, where bread was prepared for the Continental Army. Today the foot of the street is a shopping mall and open-air market similar to Haymarket. The mall leads to the pedestrian tunnel and back to Faneuil Hall.

Shades of Our Ancestors

In the decades before the camera, the itinerant silhouette maker was the photographer of his day. The simplest technique was to mount a profile snipped from black paper on a white card. Other methods included outlining on silk, glass, ivory, and metal, and filling in with black paint (often a combination of pine soot and beer). Accomplished artists advertised their ability in "skiagraphy"; others called themselves "scissor-graphists," and the inimitable "Master" Hubbard announced himself as a "papyrotamist." Oliver Wendell Holmes poked fun at an unknown lady whose silhouette he had seen in Boston's Athenaeum:

Pray did you ever hear, my love,
Of boys that go about
Who, for a very trifling sum
Will snip one's portrait out?
I'm not averse to red and white,
But all things have their place;
I think a profile cut in black
Would suit your style of face!

Boston—Beacon Hill

Brahmins and "Others"

"Hub of the universe," Bostonians call their city, magnifying Oliver Wendell Holmes's more modest assessment that its State House was "the hub of the solar system." But Beacon Hill, that bastion of proper Boston, was founded by a less than proper Anglican clergyman named William Blackstone. Accompanying a shipload of London laborers and petty criminals under grant to colonize Shawmut Peninsula, Blackstone arrived in Massachusetts in 1622. The ill-prepared settlers gave up and returned to England several years later, but Blackstone stayed, built a house, planted an orchard, and led an uneventful life until the Puritans arrived. With his taste for strong drink and friendly manner with local Indians, Blackstone annoyed his strait-laced neighbors. He outraged them further by taking moonlight rides along the beach astride his tame white bull. But when the Puritans began to suffer from their foul water supply, Blackstone offered them his spring and surrounding land. Governor Winthrop moved his settlement to Blackstone's side of the river and Blackstone left Massachusetts for Rhode Island and some peace and quiet.

In 1634 the burgeoning colony ordered that "There shalbe forthwith a beacon sett on the sentry hill att Boston, to give notice to the country of any danger." The area eventually took its name from this landmark. The original beacon, set up to warn the settlers of Indians and hostile ships, was torn down once the settlement was fortified. The Sons of Liberty erected a new beacon in 1768 primarily to irritate the British, but it was blown down by the wind after the Revolution. Finally, the city commissioned Charles Bulfinch, Boston's foremost architect, to design a lasting monument for the site. But the new beacon,

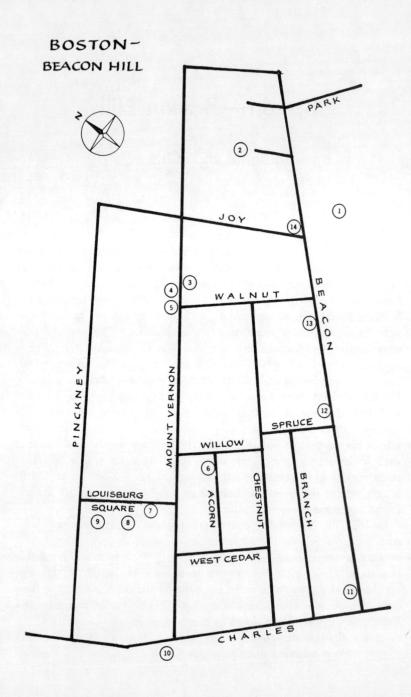

too, was short-lived. Gravel was quarried from the hill beneath the monument by John Hancock's heirs, and the structure had to be pulled down in the early 1800s. The plaques and eagle were stored in the State House for decades, and are now incorporated into the present monument, a copy of the Bulfinch design, which stands in the State House parking lot.

Beacon Hill is the oldest residential area of a large American city, and its residents take fierce pride in its architectural integrity. Gas streetlights burn day and night, and the brick sidewalks were saved from destruction in 1947 by the ladies of West Cedar Street, who sat upon them to prevent their removal. The Beacon Hill Architectural Commission prevents any outward change, even a flashily painted door, if it offends the Hill's good taste. Another emotion that unites Hill residents is love of privacy. Streets are narrow and one-way to discourage traffic, and tree-shaded backyard courts provide oases of calm a few steps from bustling Beacon Street.

Boston Common (1), which borders Beacon Hill to the south, has served as a cow pasture, martialing ground, and public park since it was set aside by the Puritans in 1634. It was soon discovered, however, that all three were not compatible. Cows were occasionally shot by errant musket fire, and the cows in their turn "were not polite to the ladies." The cows and soldiers left, and the people who wanted to sit or stroll remained.

The **Massachusetts State House** (2) sprawls over two blocks of Beacon Hill near the Common. The original colonnaded structure with the golden dome was completed in 1798, and is considered one of Charles Bulfinch's architectural masterpieces. The front yard was terraced and outlined with a brick wall, and legislators tethered their horses in a lot behind the building. During the 1800s the wall was changed to iron and stone and two fountains were installed, but the noise of running water scared passing horses, and they were removed. The Archives Museum contains a number of historic documents, including the Mayflower Compact. Also in the building are two guns, *both* of which are said to have fired the first shot of the American Revolution at Concord. In the House Chamber hangs the celebrated wooden codfish, "a memorial to the importance of the Cod Fishery to the welfare of this Commonwealth." *Open daily.*

Henry James called Mount Vernon "the only respectable street in America." (He wrote the dramatization for *Daisy Miller* at Number 102.) Julia Ward Howe, author of "The Battle Hymn of the Repub-

State House and Archives

lic," lived at **Number 32** (3), and gave some of the best parties in Boston. To her Beacon Hill was "the frozen ocean of Boston life." **Fifty-five Mt. Vernon** (4) was once the home of Rose Nichols, writer and landscape architect, and is open to the public.

Daniel Webster lived for a time at **Number 57** (5), later the boyhood home of writer Henry Adams. Adams once turned down a teaching post at Harvard because, he said, he knew "nothing about history, less about teaching, and too much about Harvard." As for the Hill, it "lowered the pulsations of the heart."

Down Willow Street is a stone-lined trench—**Acorn Street** (6)—one of the few old cobblestone streets left in Beacon Hill. Coachmen who serviced nearby mansions used to live there; now members of a wealthier class fight for a chance to occupy these charming houses.

Louisburg Square (7) is one of the most popular sights in the city, although the park itself is private. **Number 10** (8) is the former home of Louisa May Alcott; Jenny Lind married accompanist Otto Goldschmidt at **Number 20** (9).

Back in the days when the waterfront was closer (and the Charles River was cleaner), baptisms took place near the **Meeting House (10)** at 70 Charles. But the Meeting House is best known as the forum for antislavery activists such as William Lloyd Garrison, Wendell Phillips, Frederick Douglass, Harriet Tubman, and Sojourner Truth. Political activists still use the building, as evidenced by the posters in the basement snack bar.

Beacon Street, "the sunny street for the sifted few," is warmed by the patina of old brick. **Number 63–64 (11)** contains a few panes of the famous Beacon Hill purple glass. Between 1818 and 1824 several residents installed ordinary glass from England in their windows, only to see it gradually turn a translucent lavender. The windows drew so much attention that the manufacturers tried to duplicate the error. When they succeeded, however, residents of the Hill turned their noses up at the new glass because it lacked tradition.

Another Bulfinch design, **45 Beacon Street** (12), was the residence of Harrison Gray Otis, a rich landholder-merchant whose lavish parties and gold-trimmed clothes were the talk of early nineteenth-century Boston. Apparently this high style of living did nothing to shorten his life—Otis lived to be eighty—but he spent his last forty years suffering from gout.

Down the street are the 1818 **Appleton-Parker houses** (13), now the Women's City Club. Inside is the room where Longfellow married Fanny Appleton. Plaques near the State House mark the site of **John Hancock's house** (14). During the Revolution, when British troops occupied Boston, Mrs. Hancock wrote to British authorities complaining that soldiers training on the Common were disturbing her with all their noise. History does not record the reply.

Fannie Farmer's Boston Baked Beans

Boston baked beans—a dish that's cheap, hearty, and dates back to colonial times—has come to epitomize Yankee fare. The tradition of beans for Sunday dinner recalls the days when no work was done on the Puritan Sabbath, and the brick oven, where the beans were started on Saturday morning, kept the pot warm until Sunday night.

There are almost as many recipes for baked beans as there are New England cooks. The following first appeared in print in 1896, when Fannie Merritt Farmer published the recipes from her famous Boston Cooking School. The first cookbook to standardize measurements for recipes, it was the bible of American cooking for a generation.

Soak 1 quart of pea (navy) beans overnight. Drain, cover with fresh water, heat slowly, and cook until tender. Scald the rind of ½-pound piece of fat salt pork, scrape it, and cut off a ¼-inch slice to put in the bottom of the bean pot. Score the rind of the remaining pork. Put the beans in the pot and push in the pork, leaving the rind exposed. Mix 1 tablespoon salt, 1 tablespoon molasses, and 3 tablespoons sugar; add 1 cup boiling water and pour the mixture over the beans. Add more boiling water to cover the beans. Cover the pot and bake slowly (at 250° F.) for 6–8 hours, removing the cover for the last hour to brown the rind. Add water if necessary. Miss Farmer adds that ½ tablespoon mustard may make the beans more easily digested.

Boston—the Waterfront

Privateersmen and Wharf Rats

The Waterfront was Boston's commercial heart for more than two centuries. A 1663 visitor described the city's houses as "for the most part raised on the Sea-bank and wharfed out with great industry and cost." "Wharfing out" has gone on ever since, including four major landfills which turned sea into city each time her ships outgrew their berths. Captains praised the depth of her harbor, the natural breakwater, and the beauty and protection of her surrounding landscape.

Revolutionary guns had barely cooled before Yankee ships were scouring the world for trade; earnings helped to stabilize the young Republic's chaotic economy. Boston prospered, despite the mid-nineteenth-century changeover from sail to steam, but its maritime wealth was seriously undercut by the rise of the railroads and the growth of New York City. With the Depression many of the once-great wharves were in use only as fish piers and refuges for Bohemian "wharf rats." Waterfront buildings decayed gradually until the 1950s, when an ambitious urban-renewal program began to reverse the trend.

A good starting point for a walking tour of the waterfront is **Quincy Market** (1), the product of the first of many landfills. By 1820 the old Puritan Town Dock had degenerated into a squalid area littered with oyster shells and dead cats. Mayor Josiah Quincy had part of the adjacent cove filled in as an early attempt at urban renewal. On the new land Alexander Parris designed a spectacular granite market building, flanked by granite warehouses. *Open daily.*

North of the expressway, Mercantile Street leads past the granite **Mercantile Wharf** (2), the last of such stone waterfront buildings. The building, erected in 1857, borrows heavily from Renaissance

BOSTON—WATERFRONT

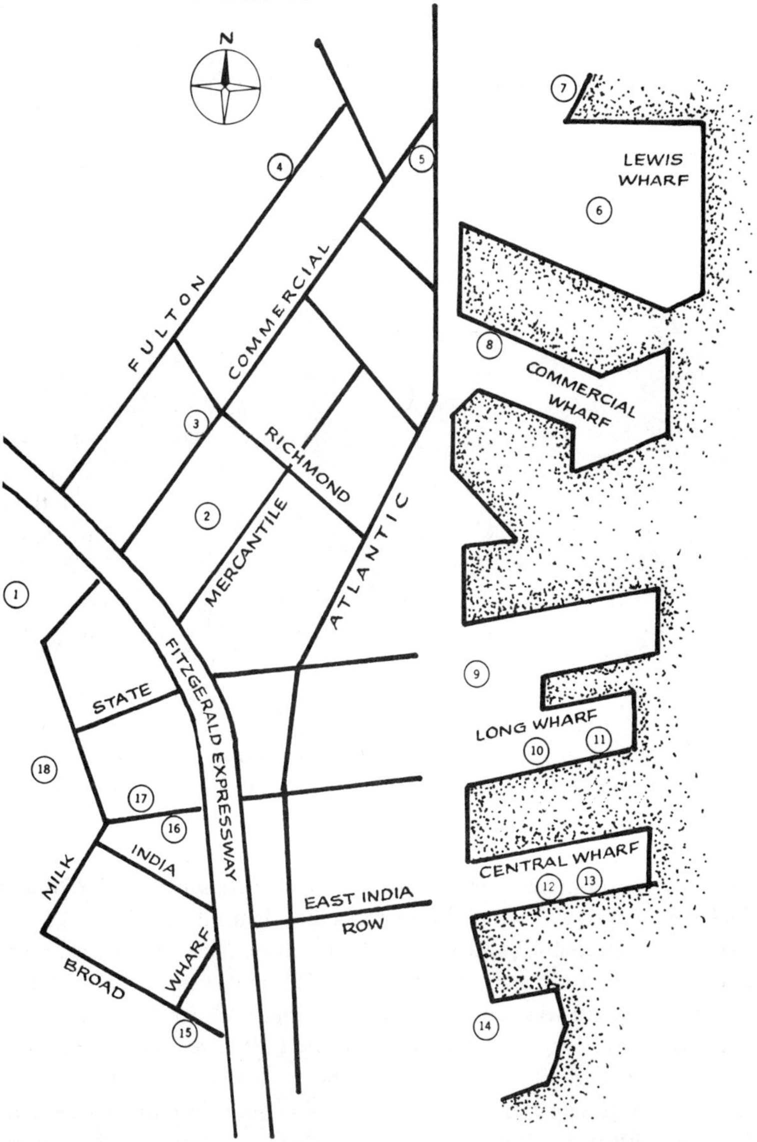

N
LEWIS WHARF
FULTON
COMMERCIAL
COMMERCIAL WHARF
RICHMOND
MERCANTILE
ATLANTIC
STATE
FITZGERALD EXPRESSWAY
LONG WHARF
INDIA
MILK
CENTRAL WHARF
EAST INDIA ROW
BROAD
WHARF
1
2
3
4
5
6
7
8
9
10
11
12
13
14
15
16
17
18

Faneuil Hall

palazzos, but at street level is uses heavy posts and lintels to create
large doorways where shopkeepers could easily display their wares.
The host of dockside trades that flourished with the shipping industry
—sailmakers, chandlers, ropemakers, and riggers—provided the market's original tenants. (Ropemakers stored their lines in the damp
basement so as to increase the rope's weight—and thus the price.)

In the 1830s and '40s **Commercial Street** (3) skirted the very edge
of Town Cove, and has been preserved relatively intact as an example
of nineteenth-century commercial planning and architecture. The
oldest buildings here, and those on nearby Fulton Street, are of brick
and combine earlier Federal upper stories with post-and-beam shop
fronts on the ground level. The **McLauthlin Building** (4), at 120 Fulton, is a proto-skyscraper built in 1863, the oldest building in Boston
with a complete cast-iron facade. It still houses the elevator company
that originally owned it.

Atlantic Avenue (5) represents a drastic change in the waterfront area. The street was built in the 1860s as a roadbed for a railway between North and South stations. In the process, it sliced through many of the great wharf buildings, cutting them off from the sea. The railway was a sign that the city was beginning to face inland with the rest of the country.

The first full view of the harbor is at the end of **Lewis Wharf** (6), one of the first wharves to be built and used for foreign trade. Ships ran slaves from Africa to West Indies plantations in exchange for molasses, which was turned into rum in New England distilleries, then used to barter for more slaves. Boston merchants traded other goods, usually in barefaced defiance of British law, which sought to limit New England's export market. The conflict began unofficially with the Navigation Acts in 1660, and continued unabated for another century.

Smuggling was an honorable trade in Boston port, and no one was more honorable than John Hancock, who owned Lewis Wharf in the 1760s. In 1768 one of Hancock's ships arrived from Madeira with a full hold of wine. When a customs officer boarded the ship for inspection, he was imprisoned until the wine had been unloaded. The next morning the captain appeared at the customs house with a few barrels, claiming that they were his entire cargo. When officials tried to seize the ship, they were badly beaten by a mob of waterfront thugs. A British detachment had to be dispatched to settle the fray.

The present wharf was built in the 1830s, during the heyday of the China trade. Lean, fast clipper ships crowded Boston Harbor, boasting forests of sails and crews who "worked like horses at sea and behaved like asses ashore." Trade lured many Yankee skippers to Canton, the only port where "foreign devils" were admitted. There they bartered ginseng root, furs, trade goods, and "singsongs"—cuckoo clocks—for teas, silks, and porcelains. One enterprising Bostonian, Frederic Tudor, hit on the idea of shipping New England's abundant ice to tropical ports. Townsfolk called it a "slippery speculation," and sailors feared the melting ice would swamp Tudor's brig. But ice packed in sawdust carried well, and Tudor became the "Ice King."

The attractive small building on Sargent's Wharf is the **Pilot House** (7), built around 1860 and used as a transfer station for cargo traveling by rail. In 1972 renovators discovered a false floor, leading to the speculation that the building might also have been used by opium smugglers.

Commercial Wharf (8) is the next wharf along Atlantic Avenue.

Replica of the brig *Beaver*—the Boston Tea Party ship

Built in Greek Revival style in 1834, the building's north side is of "the best Charlestown brick" while the south side is Quincy granite. Today the portion of the dock that fronts the water houses offices and apartments. Between Commercial and Long wharves was T Wharf, which paralleled the shoreline. T Wharf did a thriving business in fish and packet cargoes until the early twentieth century; at one time it was possible to walk between the three wharves on the decks of the vessels moored there.

In colonial times, **Long Wharf** (9) was part of a road from the State House to the harbor and was lined with elegant brick warehouses in the same style as the **Gardiner Building** (10), the only eighteenth-century building that survives. At the head of the wharf stood the Bunch of Grapes Tavern, in John Adams's words, "a breeding ground for bastards and legislators." John Hancock directed the Long Wharf Company, and may have had an office in the Gardiner Building. John Singleton Copley, the famous portraitist, grew up on the wharf, where his mother kept a tobacco shop.

The granite **Customs House Block** (11), now used for shops and apartments, was built in 1845 by Isaiah Rogers. Nathaniel Hawthorne served there as an apprentice, and by all reports was a miserable failure as a customs agent. Other footnotes in Long Wharf's history include the departure in 1819 of the first missionaries to Hawaii, the arrival in 1871 of the first bananas in New England, and the start of Joshua Slocum's one-man around-the-world voyage in 1895. The wharf also witnessed the California gold rush of the 1850s, when cowboy-hatted New Englanders, drunk on whiskey and high hopes, departed for San Francisco.

Many of the harbor islands, visible from Commercial Wharf, have stories of their own. George's Island was used as a fort and prison, and during the Civil War, a woman was executed there for trying to free her husband. Her black-clad ghost is said to haunt the island still. A smaller island, Nix's Mate, was named in honor of the pirate who was hanged there. He predicted that the island would disappear as proof of his innocence. Today the island is submerged at high tide.

Central Wharf is the site of the **New England Aquarium** (12). The focal point is the 200,000-gallon ocean tank, the largest enclosed salt-water tank in the world. The ship *Discovery* is home to bottle-nosed dolphins and sea lions, and is berthed next to the aquarium.

A film called *Boston and the Sea* is shown at the adjacent **Museum of American China Trade** (13), the former home of Captain Robert Bennett Forbes. Central Wharf, which saw its peak during the nineteenth-century cotton and fruit trade, was part of an elaborate development designed by Charles Bulfinch, whose India Wharf was destroyed in the 1960s to make way for the **Harbor Towers** (14).

Present-day Broad Street once led to India Wharf, and is notable for its early nineteenth-century brick and stone buildings. On Half Moon Lane is a **lead shot tower** (15) once used by the Chadwick Lead Works. Molten lead, poured from the top of the tower, formed small, uniform balls of solid shot by the time it reached the ground.

The High Victorian fruitcake of a building up Milk Street is the **Grain Exchange** (16). Across the street is the old brick **Jenny Building** (17). Beyond is Boston's **Custom House** (18), built in 1847 and for years the tallest building in Boston. An observation floor provides a last view of Boston Harbor.

Charlestown

Birthplace of Boston

Charlestown is older than Boston. Its founders were a small group of Puritan settlers sent by the Massachusetts Bay Company in 1629 to inhabit the company's holdings in the wilds of New England. A shipload of additional settlers, led by John Winthrop, joined the original ten families a year later, and the outpost flourished despite epidemics, fear of Indians, and a water supply so foul that most of the colony packed up and moved across the Charles River to a new site—Boston. But a handful remained loyal to the old town, and by the end of the seventeenth century, it had a church, a school, and a mill, and the dubious distinction of having hanged Massachusetts' first witch.

Patriot sympathies ran deep in Charlestown, and when the Revolution finally erupted, its first major battle was fought here. Following the Battle of Bunker Hill, Charlestown residents watched as their city was burned to the ground in reprisal. Rebuilding began in earnest in the 1780s and 1790s, and many of the fine buildings still standing are products of the brash enthusiasm of the new Republic.

In 1786 a bridge between Charlestown and Boston opened amid shouts of "You Charlestown Pigs, Put on your wigs, And come over to Boston town." By the time of the Civil War, a public transit system of sorts made commuting possible—most of the present buildings on Main Street are a result. Waves of Irish immigration swelled Charlestown's population and brought about the introduction of row houses.

Charlestown's Navy Yard was built in the early 1800s and was for more than a century the town's chief employer. Thirty-five warships were launched here between 1825 and 1868. Shipbuilding flagged following the Civil War, but flourished anew during World War II: 141

CHARLESTOWN

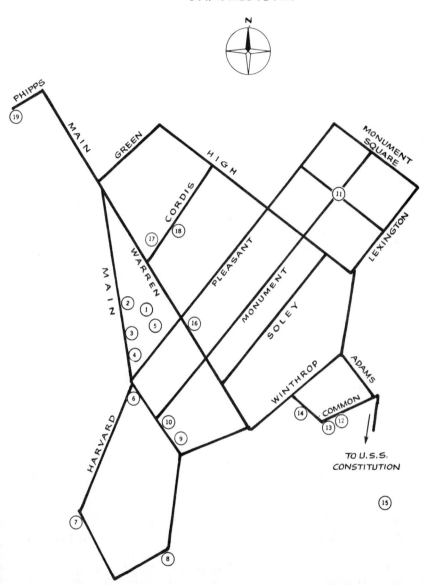

ships were built and more than 5,000 were serviced between Pearl Harbor and 1945.

But most of the twentieth century was a dark time for Charlestown. The Depression struck the working-class town with cruel severity. Businesses failed, employment plummeted, and fine old houses were left to decay. Since the 1960s an active urban-renewal program has brought new life to the graying stone and brick of the community. Homeowners have restored most of the eighteenth-century houses, and the old, sprawling Navy Yard has been recycled as a park dedicated to U.S.S. *Constitution*—"Old Ironsides."

The heart of Charlestown is **Thompson Square Triangle (1)**, a slice of land between Warren and Main that was once known as Craft's Corner, after an apothecary that occupied the site until 1869. The square was renamed after a prominent Charlestown family.

The first notable building along Main is **Armstrong House (2)**, once a printing company. Among its customers were the Universalists, forerunners of the Unitarians, who met upstairs while the rest of Charlestown looked on in disapproval at their sinful doings.

Timothy Thompson, a carpenter by trade and a veteran of Bunker Hill, set up shop at **119 Main Street (3)** in 1794. Next door is the old **Warren Tavern (4)**, restored to resemble a 1790s tavern, a good spot for lunch or a beer. Built soon after the burning of the town, it belonged in 1780 to Eliphalet Newell, a baker. At one time the tavern was headquarters for King Solomon's Lodge, which numbered Paul Revere among its charter members. Around the corner on Pleasant Street is another of Timothy's homes, the **Thompson-Sawyer House (5)**.

The odd-looking stone house at the corner of **Harvard and Main (6)** was built in 1822 by General Nathaniel Austin, a sheriff of Middlesex County who carried out the execution of Michael Martin. Martin, alias "Captain Lightfoot," was the last of a dying breed—the highwaymen. Bad luck also befell Edward Everett, owner of the magnificent Federal-style **Everett House (7)** at 16 Harvard Street. A famous orator during the Civil War, he gave the two-hour speech that preceded Lincoln's Gettysburg Address. Built by merchant Matthew Bridge for his daughter in 1812, the house was purchased by Everett in 1830.

Harvard Street leads to **City Square (8)**, which was the heart of colonial Charlestown. It began as the Market Place, an open area in front of the governor's mansion. Site of the first permanent Charles-

Bunker Hill Monument

town settlement, the area is still known as Town Hill. Colonists raided a fort in 1629 on the site of present-day Harvard Mall to protect themselves from Indians. Later, deciding that such protection was unnecessary, they replaced the fort with a frame house for Govenor Winthrop. The governor, however, carted the house with him when he moved across the river to found Boston. Undaunted, the remaining settlers built another mansion, the Great House, which became the administrative center of the foundling colony. By the Revolution, City Square was a bustling commercial center. Paul Revere began his midnight ride here. He recalled in his journal: "When I got into [Charlestown], I met Colonel Conant and several others; they said they had seen our signals. . . . I got a horse of Deacon Larkin." Harvard Mall itself was the gift of a Harvard alumnus to commemorate John Harvard, a minister who settled in Charlestown in 1637 and died of consumption a year later. Rev. Harvard gained immortality by bequeathing his library (320 books) and half of his estate to the struggling college in Cambridge.

The section of Main Street near the bridge was a leather district in the last century. Most of the buildings here are nineteenth-century, built to house shops on the street level and families on the upper floors. At 55-61 Main is the 1795 **Deacon Larkin House** (9), home of the man who loaned Paul Revere a horse. (Larkin never did get his horse back—a British officer at a roadblock forced Revere to trade his fresh mount for a tired one.) The **John Hurd House** (10) next door is of the same period, but both have lost some architectural detail with restoration.

Within musket range of Monument Avenue is **Breed's Hill** (11) and the Bunker Hill Monument, where a ragtag army of patriots first engaged the British in a major battle. On the morning of June 17, 1775, sailors on board the man-of-war *Lively* awoke to see a group of citizens busily fortifying the nearer of two hills above Charlestown. The Americans had learned of British plans to attack nearby Dorchester Heights the following day, and deliberately sought to draw British fire. The ploy worked. With scant ammunition, the colonists were given the famous order not to fire "until you see the whites of their eyes." Three thousand Redcoats advanced and met a volley from farmers who prided themselves on their marksmanship. One third of the advancing formation is said to have been mowed down. A second attack met the same fate. Charlestown was set aflame in retaliation, and the Revolution began in earnest. The obelisk that now stands on

Assault on Bunker (Breed's) Hill

the site was designed by Solomon Willard; visitors can climb to the top for a view of Boston. *Open daily.*

Now peaceful, Winthrop Square was a training ground for soldiers bound for the Revolution, the War of 1812, and the Civil War. The old **Salem Turnpike Hotel (12)** and the yellow **Arnold House (13)** are handsome Federal buildings dating from the early nineteenth century. The **Old Training Field School** (14) was built in 1827 and has been restored as a private home.

East of Winthrop Square is the Charlestown **Navy Yard** (15), and its most conspicuous attraction, the U.S.S. *Constitution*. Founded in 1800, the yard covers forty-three acres by the confluence of the Charles and Mystic rivers—the spot where the British launched their attack on Bunker Hill. The facility has built, launched, and refitted ships for

U.S.S. *Constitution*

every war since 1812. Part of it is now an official National Historic Site. "Old Ironsides," the most famous ship in American history, was built here in 1797. Intended as the showpiece of the Revolution, the frigate did not see action until the unofficial war with the Barbary pirates at Tripoli in 1803, and was condemned as unseaworthy in 1830. The public outcry was so great that she was rebuilt and made a National Historic Landmark. To keep rigging and spars weathered equally on both sides, the historic ship makes an annual turnaround cruise in the harbor. A Navy Yard building houses the Constitution Museum, devoted to the ship's colorful history. Other sights in the yard include a quarter-mile-long rope walk building, where all the rope for the U. S. Navy was made until 1971, the restored Commandant's House, and the Alexander Parris Building. The Bunker Hill Pavilion nearby stages a multimedia presentation called "Whites of Their Eyes." *Open daily.*

West of the Navy Yard, a number of striking Federal houses grace Warren Street. **Number 81 Warren** (16) was built in 1790; the house at the back of the court was completed seventy-five years later. Cordis Street, surveyed in the 1790s, reflects the post-Revolutionary building fever that raised Charlestown from the ashes. **Number 16 Cordis** (17) is a small, dark residence built in 1799—the oldest on the street. Fine brickwork characterizes **21 Cordis** (18), a Federal house dating from 1802.

At Phipps Street is a neatly trimmed **Burying Ground** (19), surrounded by a sprawl of urban-renewal projects and elevated highways. This important cemetery is kept locked, but can be opened by arrangement with the Boston Parks Department. More than one hundred seventeenth-century stones survive, most of them graced in simple Puritan style with only the names and dates of death. Early eighteenth-century stones favored skulls and angels, while the Federalists were partial to classical urns and willow designs. The layout is unique: Families were buried in rectangular plots corresponding to the location of each family's house on Town Hill. The cemetery thus provides the only surviving house-by-house record of pre-Revolutionary Charlestown, as well as a touchstone of seventeenth-century America.

"Old Ironsides'" Greatest Battle

U.S.S. Constitution's *nickname of "Old Ironsides" came from a gunner who witnessed solid shot bounce off her thick oaken hull during her famous battle with the frigate* Guerrière *on August 19, 1812. Isaac Hull and British Captain James Dacres, old friends, are said to have bet their hats on the outcome of a duel between their ships. It was decided in thirty minutes of cannonading off Halifax, Nova Scotia, with the War of 1812 but two months old. Expert American gun crews methodically holed* Guerrière *with deadly accuracy, and finally dismasted her. Cried a gunner, "We've made a brig of her! Next time we'll make her a sloop!" Dacres had no choice but to surrender his crippled ship, which was burned after the crew had been taken prisoner. Captain Hull, who had split his breeches during the battle, helped his wounded adversary aboard and—legend says—refused Dacres' sword but remarked, "I'll trouble you for that hat!"*

Cambridge

Preachers, Patriots, and "God's Acre"

Cambridge's future was sealed in 1638, when the Massachusetts Great and General Court decided to locate their recently founded college there, within the parish of "the holy, heavenly, sweet-affecting, soul-ravishing preacher," Rev. Thomas Shepard. The town's name was changed from Newtowne to Cambridge, in honor of the university where many of the Puritan fathers had been educated, and the college was named Harvard, after the man who bequeathed his library and half his property to the fledgling school. Though it is an industrial and commercial town as well, Cambridge's past and present are closely linked to the universities in its midst. The city is a walker's haven, where jaywalking has been perfected to a fine art, and where twisting roads, a bane to motorists, bring delight to those on foot.

Harvard Square (1) is probably the most eclectic block in all of New England. It is the domain of Cambridge natives, local craftsmen, street hawkers, canvassers, and evangelists, and has the largest number of bookstores per square foot in the country.

In sharp contrast is nearby "God's Acre," the **Old Burying Ground** (2), which dates to 1635. The first eight Harvard presidents are buried here alongside Revolutionary War veterans and early Cambridge settlers. The variety of stones is impressive, ranging from the matter-of-fact to the sweetly sentimental and chronicling America's changing attitudes toward death. A mileage marker by the fence dates from 1794.

Completed in 1761, **Christ Church** (3) is the oldest existing church in Cambridge. During the Revolution, Tory Anglicans were chased from town by patriots, who used the church as a barracks and melted down the organ pipes for ammunition. *Open daily.*

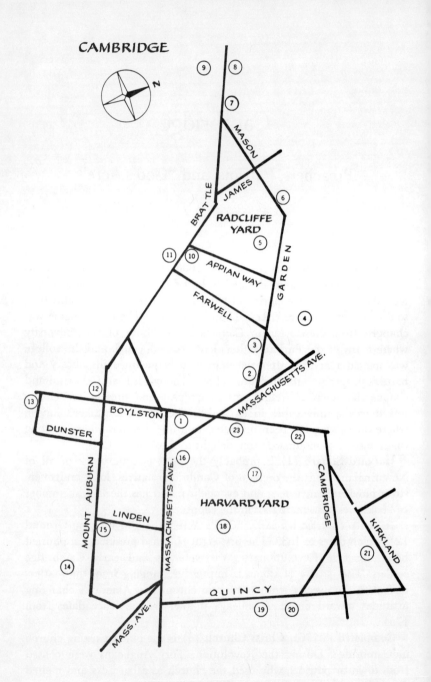

CAMBRIDGE

N

9   8

7

MASON

BRATTLE

JAMES

6

RADCLIFFE
YARD

5

GARDEN

11   10

APPIAN WAY

FARWELL

4

3

2

MASSACHUSETTS AVE.

12

13

BOYLSTON

1

DUNSTER

23

22

16

17

CAMBRIDGE

MOUNT AUBURN

MASSACHUSETTS AVE.

HARVARD YARD

KIRKLAND

LINDEN

18

15

21

14

QUINCY

19   20

MASS. AVE.

Cambridge Common (4) has been the focal point of the city's religious, social, and political life for three centuries. It also served as Washington's main camp in 1775–76. According to legend, Washington reluctantly took command of the 9,000 men who had gathered there to form the Continental Army. An eighteenth-century elm planted to commemorate the event died in 1923, but a replacement cutting nurtured at the Arnold Arboretum has taken its place.

Across Garden Street is **Radcliffe Yard** (5). The surrounding buildings include Fay House, an 1806 mansion; the Radcliffe Gymnasium, built in 1898; and Agassiz House, named after Radcliffe's first president. Founded in 1879 as the "Society for College Instruction of Women," Radcliffe provided instruction from those Harvard professors who could be coaxed into presenting lectures. Today the schools are essentially coeducational. However, Radcliffe maintains several institutions of its own, including the Schlesinger Library, the most extensive library of women's studies in the world.

The **First Church, Congregational** (6), shares with First Parish, Unitarian, the distinction of being the first congregation established in Cambridge. Both date from the 1630s. Crowning the church spire is a weather vane depicting Shem Drowne, a devout church deacon who cast weather vanes as a hobby. Drowne also made the grasshopper on Faneuil Hall and an Indian, once atop the colonial governor's mansion, now in the Massachusetts Historical Society. *Open daily.*

The sweeping white limestone library of the **Episcopal Theological Seminary** (7) is juxtaposed with the rest of the seminary buildings, all ivy-covered and medieval in character. The Greek Revival Hastings House next door houses divinity students.

During the eighteenth century, Brattle Street was nicknamed Tory Row, after the English sympathizers who lived here in Georgian country estates that stretched down to the river. Remarkably, all of these mansions still stand, sharing the street with more recent additions. The **Longfellow National Historical Site** (8), at 105 Brattle, is a fine example. Built in 1759, the two-story frame house has a hip roof and Ionic pilasters. George and Martha Washington lived here during the siege of Boston, and Longfellow made it his home from 1837 to 1882. Throughout the rooms are scenes familiar to readers of Longfellow's poetry. In the front parlor, one of many rooms with black carved woodwork, is the famous portrait of the Longfellow daughters as they appeared coming down the front stairway in his poem "The Children's Hour." Nearby is the upright desk at which he stood to write *Evangeline. Open daily.*

ENTER
TO GROW IN WISDOM

Harvard Gate

Longfellow Park (9), once part of the Longfellow estate, indicates Brattle's former expansive, pastoral setting. On the corner of Brattle and Appian Way is the Harvard **Graduate School of Education (10)**, founded in 1820 and dominated by the modern Gutman Library with its splash of bright interior colors. At **54 Brattle (11)** is the former home of Dexter Pratt, Longfellow's "village blacksmith." The site of the "spreading chestnut tree" is marked with a granite tablet.

Winthrop Square (12), on the corner of Mount Auburn and Boylston, was the original market square of old Cambridge. Farther down, the **Hicks House (13)** is a gambrel-roofed, wooden-frame dwelling built around 1760. Its original owner was shot in a skirmish with British soldiers returning from Lexington and Concord in 1775. **Lowell House (14)** is one of the handsomest of the Harvard houses. The bells inside its blue-domed tower came from the Danilov Monastery in Russia. The whimsical parody of a Flemish castle across the street is, appropriately, headquarters of the Harvard **Lampoon (15)**.

Harvard Yard, that venerable symbol of academic tradition, is entered through the gate opposite Holyoke Center. **Wadsworth House (16)**, built in 1726, was the official residence of Harvard's presidents until 1849. Washington used it as one of his many headquarters, and supposedly finalized plans to oust the British from Boston in the Wadsworth parlor.

Elegant **University Hall** (17) was designed by Bulfinch and built of Chelmsford granite in 1815. The statue of John Harvard out front is known as the "Statue of Three Lies." The inscription reads "John Harvard, Founder, 1638." In fact, the college was founded in 1636, Harvard was the benefactor, not the founder, and the model for the 1885 statue was a Harvard student.

Behind University Hall, the **Harry Elkins Widener Library** (18), Memorial Church, and Sever Hall form a quadrangle. Widener, one of the largest libraries in the country, contains some fifty miles of shelves and ten floors of stacks. The building is a memorial to Harry Widener, a young book collector who drowned in the sinking of *Titanic. Open daily.*

The glass and concrete **Carpenter Center for the Visual Arts** (19), completed in 1963, is the only U.S. building designed by French architect Le Corbusier. A few Bostonians have described it as "two great pianos wrestling," but most agree that it has a striking, sculptural effect. The ground floor, open to the public, exhibits the work of students and local artists. Next door is the **Fogg Art Museum** (20), built in Harvard's familiar neo-Georgian style, and also open to the public. **Memorial Hall** (21), which Henry James called "the great bristling brick Valhalla," is a Victorian building designed as a monument to the Civil War dead and finally completed in 1878.

In the farthest corner of the Yard, the freshmen dormitories Hollis, Lionel, Stoughton, and Mower form a square to the north of **Harvard Hall** (22). In 1810, when John Kirkland became president, he found this part of the campus an "unkempt sheep-commons," cluttered with a brewery and various privies. He is responsible for the present-day trees, footpaths, and plantings. The original Harvard Hall burned to the ground in 1764; the present hall contains classrooms. **Massachusetts Hall** (23), built facing Harvard Hall in 1720, is Harvard's oldest existing building. The upper two floors are used as a dormitory; the president's office is also here.

Fitting Epitaphs

Notoriously economical of speech, New Englanders nonetheless have a disarming capacity for wit and wisdom. Nowhere is this more evident than in their epitaphs. The descendants of a man buried at Searsport, Maine, are said to have had so much fun poked at them because of this epitaph that they had it effaced:

> Under the sod and under the trees
> Here lies the body of Solomon Pease.
> The Pease are not here there's only the pod
> The Pease shelled out and went to God.

A tombstone in Putnam, Connecticut, depicts Phineas G. Wright wearing a beard, a watch, and a worried expression. Beneath it a legend reads "Going, but know not where." In Glastonbury, another bit of final verse:

> Here lies one wh
> ose life thrads
> cut asunder she
> was strucke dead
> by a clap of thunder.

Finally, the bittersweet reality of pioneer life is reflected in this epitaph credited to Burlington, Massachusetts:

> Here lies our infant son
> and now he never hollers.
> He graced our home for 14 days
> and cost us forty dollars.

Plymouth

More than a Rock

Fighting the elements, sickness, and their own ignorance of wilderness survival, the Pilgrims who landed at Plymouth Rock in 1620 are the subject of one of the most romantic and inspiring stories in American history.

Disenchanted with Anglican England Dutch culture in Holland, a group of religious dissenters—the Separatists—looked to America. Arrangements were made for the pilgrimage, financed by London businessmen anxious to develop trade with the New World. There were to be two ships. The Dutch *Speedwell* was to take one group to England, where a second group of Separatist Pilgrims would be waiting with the British wine ship, *Mayflower*. *Speedwell*, an old ship beset by leaks, was abandoned, several travelers quit the expedition, and the remaining Pilgrims crowded aboard the *Mayflower* for the crossing.

Two months later, anchored off Provincetown, the Pilgrims bowed down and thanked God for the sight they beheld—land—their "proper element." Here, too, the Mayflower Compact was drawn and signed, and the Pilgrims held what is regarded as the first New England town meeting. An expedition led by Myles Standish (a non-Separatist) set out in a shallop (a large dory) to find a suitable site for a settlement. It was the second such journey that landed in Plymouth, an area named by Charles I some years earlier.

That first winter, half the population died of scurvy and other diseases. Their graves were planted with the corn so that the Indians would not know of the reduced number of able-bodied men. Later, the colonists struck a peace accord with Massasoit which lasted for the lifetime of the Indian leader. It was Massasoit who brought twenty In-

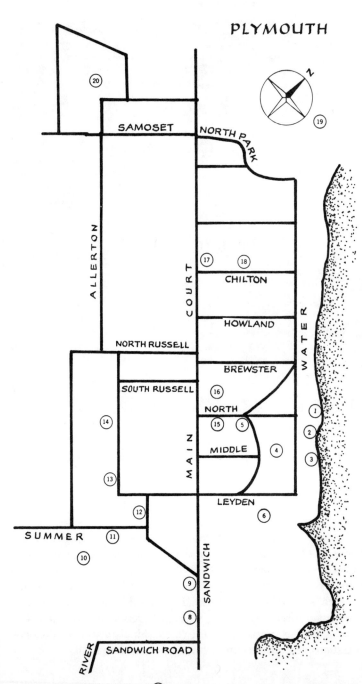

Governor Bradford statue

dians to the fall harvest feast of 1621—the first Thanksgiving. Renewed that year by the arrival of a second group of settlers, the colony continued to grow in the spirit proclaimed on the plaque on Burial Hill: "What your fathers attained with such difficulty, do not basely relinquish."

Begin a walking tour of Plymouth at the State Pier and the **Mayflower II** (1), a full-scale reproduction of the vessel that carried the settlers from England in 1620. Built in England and only slightly longer than a tennis court, *Mayflower II* sailed across the Atlantic in 1957 with a crew of thirty-three. Exhibits depict life aboard ship during the sixty-six-day voyage in which the vessel was crowded with 102 passengers and twenty-five crewmen. Shipboard and dockside demonstrations describe seventeenth-century maritime skills.

On Water Street are the stocky wooden **First** and **1627 houses** (2). Surrounded by a stake fence stockade, the First House has a steeply pitched roof thatched with reeds. The simple architecture reflects the Pilgrims' way of life. Poor, honest, and unworldly, they wanted only to live unencumbered by burdens of power and wealth.

The visitor's first contact with **Plymouth Rock** (3) is apt to be disappointing. It is smaller than most imagine, with a crack running through it and the date 1620 carved into the top. The bars around it, the overshadowing monument, and the historical doubt that this is where the Pilgrims actually came ashore take something away from it. But like the Pilgrims, the rock remained—a symbol of those who proved that, with faith and endurance, the colonization of New England was possible.

Across Water Street from Plymouth Rock is **Cole's Hill** (4). At the top of the thirty-seven steps is a sweeping view of Plymouth Beach,

First House

Myles Standish Monument, and Clark's Island. Dominating the hill is the statue of Massasoit, chief of the Wampanoag Indians, who befriended the Pilgrims and helped them survive the first winter. Several of the original settlers are entombed in the Sarcophagus. The Plymouth **National Wax Museum** (5) portrays, with 150 figures and twenty-seven scenes, the Pilgrims' years in England, their escape to Holland, the *Mayflower* voyage, and the settlement's beginnings. *Open Mon.–Sat.*

At the foot of Leyden Street lies one of the loveliest spots in Plymouth, **Brewster Gardens** (6). Here, in Town Brook, the Indians caught herring which they taught the Pilgrims to place on each hill of corn for fertilizer, a technique that produced the abundant crop that resulted in the first Thanksgiving. The reeds used for thatching early buildings came from the banks of the stream. The Pilgrim Maiden Statue is dedicated to the "intrepid English women whose courage and fortitude brought a new nation into being." Thirsts can be quenched at the cool, clear Pilgrim Spring nearby.

A long but worthwhile side trip south of downtown Plymouth leads to **Plimouth Plantation** (7), a living, full-scale re-creation of the village as it was in 1627. At different seasons "villagers" can be found shearing sheep, harvesting crops, or preserving foodstuffs. As they go about their work there is always time to stop and talk with a neighbor —to hear the latest news from England or the local herbal remedy for a cold. Not far from the village is Wampanoag Summer Settlement, where a wigwam, firepit, and cornfields occupy the site of a similar Indian encampment four centuries ago. Researched, developed, and staffed by Native Americans, the settlement re-creates the summer camp and activities of a Wampanoag band of the early 1600s. After spending the winter in permanent inland villages, individual families migrated to the coast to fish, hunt, and farm during the warmer months. It was on such a site that the Pilgrims settled in 1620. *Open daily.*

Visitors can participate in many of the traditional crafts demonstrated at the 1677 **Harlow House** (8). The massive beams of this early residence came from the original Pilgrim fort. When the fort was dismantled after King Philip's War, the beams were given to Sergeant William Harlow by the town. Costumed hostesses are skilled spinners and weavers of wool and flax, and demonstrate these and other household arts of the seventeenth century.

Over one wooden bridge and under a second is the **Jabez Howland House** (9), built in 1667. Of this residence, historian William T. Davis wrote, "Owned and occupied by Jabez Howland before the death of his father and mother, it is fair to presume that its floor has been trodden by those two passengers of the *Mayflower,* and that its walls have listened to their voices." Now owned by the Pilgrim John Howland Society, it displays original furnishings and artifacts.

A working replica of the 1636 Jenny Grist Mill is operated at the **Grist Mill Village** (10). Saltwater herring or alewives "climb" a fish ladder adjacent to the mill during April and May spawning runs. On Summer Street, the **Richard Sparrow House** (11) is the town's oldest (1640). In the rear rooms are the shop and workrooms of the Plymouth Pottery Guild.

On the corner of the Town Square is the newly renovated 1749 **Court House** (12). The heavy timbers and boards are believed to have come from the earlier 1686 County House which stood on the site. The building and its predecessor served as colonial capitol, county courthouse, probate court, registry of deeds, town house, and, for a few years, as a Sunday school. Furnishings and exhibits reconstruct a public building of the eighteenth century.

The **First Church** (13) is actually the fourth church to occupy the site. The first, built in 1648, was located just across the corner of the Square. Before 1648, services were held in the fort and the Meeting House.

Behind the church is **Burial Hill** (14), where the first fort was

Jenny Grist Mill

located. The cemetery's setting is one of the loveliest in New England. Graves of important persons are carefully marked, and include a monument to Governor William Bradford (1590–1657) and other graves of the eight "undertakers" of the Plymouth Colony. One particularly striking stone is that of Patience Watson (d. 1767), whose carved portrait is unusually lifelike and attractive.

The Spooner family occupied the **Spooner House (15)** for almost two centuries. Upon his death in 1954, James Spooner left the house, and its rich collection of heirlooms, as a museum. Across North Street,

Burial Hill

the **Mayflower Society House** (16) was built in 1754 by Edward Winslow, great-grandson of Governor Edward Winslow. Its nine rooms are furnished in seventeenth-, eighteenth-, and nineteenth-century style.

Built in Greek Revival style in 1824, the **Pilgrim Hall Museum** (17) is the oldest historical museum in the country, and contains the finest collection of Pilgrim artifacts.

The **Antiquarian House** (18) was erected in 1809 and is furnished with priceless period antiques. The china closets, filled with Lowestoft, Canton, and Staffordshire, are of particular interest.

What's in a bog? Cranberries, an important New England crop with its own museum—**Cranberry World** (19). Operated by Ocean Spray Cranberries, Inc., the visitor center tells the story of the not-so-humble cranberry and its people, and features a working cranberry bog and daily cooking demonstrations. *Open Mon.–Fri.*

To the west is the eighty-one-foot **Pilgrim Monument** (20), a figure of Faith surrounded by symbolic images. The park is a welcome place to rest and drink in the scenery before the long but pleasant walk back to town.

Oak Bluffs

Vineyard Sampler

Martha's Vineyard is the relic of the terminal moraine of a glacier which swept down from Labrador some 60,000 years ago and melted, leaving this curve of sand and rock to fend for itself against the sea. Martha's Vineyard is an island, and there the magic starts. There is no place on the Vineyard where you can't smell the sea, and the weather is so notoriously fair that if it rains for three days' running, locals have a fit. Yet they wonder why the grass is not as green as England. Or even Plymouth.

OAK BLUFFS

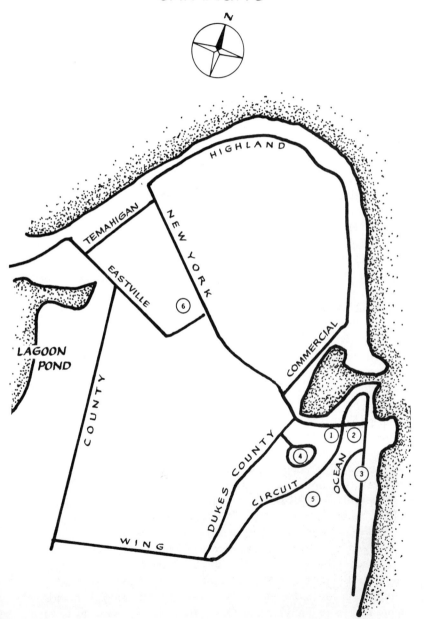

By the late nineteenth century the great whaleships, whose cargoes of oil and bone paid for many of the island's homes, had disappeared or lay rotting in dry dock. During that same period, Oak Bluffs, which was called "Cottage City" until 1907, emerged as the Vineyard's first summer resort. Vineyarders whose fathers and grandfathers were fishermen, whalers, or shipbuilders are today merchants, real estate dealers, hotel owners, artists, and writers.

Oak Bluffs burgeoned with the rise of the Baptist and Methodist religious meetings that swept the country in the early part of the last century. By the late 1800s, a horse railway ran from the Baptists' East Chop to the Methodists' "Promised Land" at Oak Bluffs. The faithful took salvation seriously, and even referred to passing over the Oak Bluffs causeway as crossing "over Jordan." Today's main road into Oak Bluffs follows the same route.

Art galleries, antique shops, and boutiques line Circuit Avenue, Oak Bluffs' main street. Centerpiece of the town is the famous **Flying Horses** (1). The beloved carousel, one of the oldest in the country, has delighted riders and onlookers alike for more than one hundred years. Children (and adults) can still thrill to the whirling horses, the carousel music, and the chance of catching the brass ring for a free ride.

Facing Ocean Park is one of New England's most unusual monuments. Built shortly after the Civil War, it depicts a **Confederate soldier** (2) and is dedicated to the South. The benefactor was a Southerner and, the story goes, not a Yankee voice was raised in protest.

Bright gingerbread Victorian houses of eclectic architectural design fringe **Ocean Park** (3), south of the monument between Ocean Avenue and the Edgartown Road. Of special interest are the houses' patterned shingles. The octagonal bandstand in the center of the park is used for concerts on Sunday evenings during the summer. Below a high retaining wall across the street is a beach restricted to Oak Bluffs residents in season.

"Reformation" John Adams, a lion-maned itinerant preacher from New Hampshire, founded the **Wesleyan Grove Camp Meeting** (4) in 1835. What Adams lacked in formal education he more than made up for in zeal, preaching, praying, and weeping his way from one end of the island to the other. He was especially adept at gathering converts from the Congregationalists, who sat on rough-hewn oak benches listening with rapt attention to the preacher's impassioned rhetoric. As more and more church groups came from the mainland to be saved,

The Tabernacle, Wesleyan Grove Camp Meeting

they pitched tents nearby. In the 1850s a circus tent was erected in the center of the campground for the meetings. In 1870 this was replaced by the present tabernacle, an open building with a stage that was the most impressive building on the island for many years. Camp Meeting members who wanted to stay on the island after the meetings closed began to build permanent cottages, each attempting to outdo the other in ingenuity and design, until every cottage was draped with verandas, steeply pitched roofs, gables, turrets, spires, and fancy scrollwork. Today the effect of these houses, many not more than four feet apart, is that of a fairy-tale village.

Soon the area drew the secular, who built houses, stores, and hotels between the campground and the steamboat wharf. Disgruntled Camp Meeting members erected a seven-foot fence against such temptations of the flesh, but the religious fervor that fueled the camp had waned, and their cottages eventually fell into the hands of residents and vacationers. Illumination Night, held near the end of August, remembers those years when the campground was used solely for religious gatherings. The closings of such meetings were celebrated by decorating the cottages with lighted lanterns. Today each cottage is festooned with Japanese lanterns.

In 1871 the townsfolk outside the seven-foot fence decided to build a **nondenominational church** (5) to serve the growing community. The chapel, reported the local paper, "when complete with the spire reaching an altitude of 96 feet will overtop anything." The unusual, octagonal-shaped building has a wraparound balcony and domed ceiling. All in all, 1871 was a big year on the island, what with the building of a new drawbridge, the purchase of a new paddle steamer, and the celebration of the founding of Tisbury with the Vineyard Haven Concert Band playing their newest composition, "The Bartholomew Gosnold Quickstep." Today Oak Bluffs has, within a six-block area, five churches.

Near the turn of the century, Oak Bluffs boasted a large number of impressive buildings, including several great hotels which were tragically destroyed by fire. The stately Sea View Hotel, which hung over the waterfront above the town wharf, turned into an inferno on the night of September 24, 1892. With it burned the turning track for the island's only railroad. Undeterred, the railroad operators simply ran

backward to Edgartown and forward to Oak Bluffs. Uneconomical and fickle in stormy weather, the train ceased operation in 1896.

Inland from the harbor, a side trip out New York Avenue leads to the **Hansel and Gretel Doll Museum** (6), next to the 4-H building. Dolls and doll furniture from the early nineteenth century are displayed in this private museum, along with such rare toys as a complete wooden jointed circus set, its corners rounded by several generations of loving hands.

"*I do not know of any spot with such a fascinating air of dreams and idleness about it as the old wharf. . . . What a slumberous, delightful, lazy place it is! The sunshine seems to lie a foot deep on the planks of the dusty wharf which yield up to the warmth a vague perfume of the cargoes of rum, molasses, and spice that used to be piled upon it. . . ."*

Thomas Aldrich, 1874

Edgartown

Roses, Chickens, and a "Bridge of Sighs"

Edgartown, most picturesque of the Vineyard villages, is noted for the large white clapboard houses built by its nineteenth-century whaling masters. Fortunately, neither fire nor the War of 1812 affected Edgartown the way they did other island towns. Its rise as a summer resort came after whaling had declined near the turn of the century; today it remains a strikingly graceful New England community.

Edgartown's maritime heritage is traced in displays at the **Dukes County Historical Society** (1) on School Street. The house was constructed for Thomas Cooke by shipbuilders in 1765, as evidenced by the slanted beams, wide floors, and marine-type bracing. The crown-glass Fresnel lens from the Gay Head Lighthouse is exhibited in a small brick tower on the grounds. A carriage shed houses a Button hand-pumped fire wagon, a whale boat, and a peddler's cart. Not far away are the remarkable gravestones of Nancy Luce's chickens. Eccentric Nancy lived alone in West Tisbury with her flock of chickens and one cow. When a hen died, Nancy composed a poem to it and had the verse inscribed on a marble headstone which she placed on its grave. She wasn't so strange, however, not to capitalize on her notoriety. She sold curious audiences photographs of herself holding a chicken, as well as bound copies of her poetry. Another building here contains an excellent collection of books on whaling lore and genealogy, as well as ship's logs, whaler's journals, and other island documents. *Open daily May–Sept*.

The **First Federated Church** (2), built in 1828, once served as the town's Congregational Church, but in 1925 the original parish agreed to merge with local Baptists. Inside are the original pew boxes as well

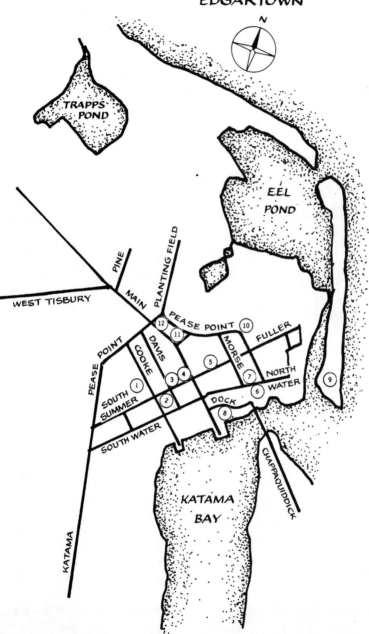

EDGARTOWN

N

TRAPPS POND

EEL POND

PINE

WEST TISBURY

MAIN

PLANTING FIELD

PEASE POINT

PEASE POINT

COOKE

DAVIS

MORSE

FULLER

NORTH WATER

SOUTH SUMMER

SOUTH WATER

DOCK

CHAPPAQUIDDICK

KATAMA

KATAMA BAY

Edgartown Light

as a rare Hook and Hastings organ installed in 1895. Whale-oil lamps hang from a chandelier.

Despite cramped quarters and ancient equipment, the staff of the **Vineyard Gazette (3)** manages to produce one of the finest and most famous small newspapers in the country. The old and weathered shingle house has never been remodeled, and a number of old architectural touches are noticeable. Edgar Merchant founded the paper in 1846. His son, George, followed in his footsteps and under the pseudonym "Abigail Spookendike" even brought out a second paper. The four-page broadsheet, called *The Hornet,* was short-lived, but the *Gazette* is still published twice a week in summer and weekly during the rest of the year.

One of the *Gazette*'s responsibilities is covering the doings across the

street in the Dukes County Courthouse and the **Town Hall** (4). The
edifice was built in 1858; the Town Hall, just beyond, was completed in
1828 and originally served as the Methodist Church. On North Summer Street is the ivy-covered **Saint Andrews Episcopal Church** (5),
with a pulpit made from the bow of a fishing dory.

The brown-shingled building across the street from the library is the
Daggett House Inn (6). Breakfast is served in the 1750 Public Room,
once a waterfront tavern. In two centuries the inn has been a store, a
sailor's boarding house, and, during the whaling era, the Counting
House. Several of the stately old captains' houses nearby were built at
a slight angle to the street to permit a direct view of homebound ships
rounding Cape Pogue. Their white picket fences are splashed in summer with the roses for which Edgartown is famous. Several of the
houses are of almost identical construction and design. The **Bliss
House** (7), one of the finest of these, was built in 1832 for one of the
Vineyard's famous whalemen, Captain Jared Fisher. The present
owners have placed a mannequin of a woman in a bonnet holding
a spyglass and gazing out to sea on the widow's walk. She looks so natural that many who see her for the first time believe she is real.

The Edgartown **Town Dock** (8) originally served whaleships,
coastal schooners, and the paddle steamer from New Bedford. During

an annual Memorial Day parade, schoolchildren toss flowers into the harbor in memory of island men who have died at sea. The ferry to Chappaquiddick, known as the *On Time* because she has no set schedule, also docks here. The fare for the short ride is 25¢ per person, 25¢ per bike, and 75¢ per car. The original ferry owner was blind, but managed to make the run without incident, despite the apprehension of off-island passengers.

The long wooden walkway that once led to the Edgartown **Lighthouse** (9) was known as the "Bridge of Sighs" after all the swooning lovers who strolled this way on romantic evenings. In 1935 the Coast Guard proposed replacing the old lighthouse with a large steel structure, and islanders, led by Mrs. Henry Beetle House, moved quickly to obtain the present, traditional light from Ipswich.

On the road back to town is the **Emily Post House** (10). The renowned social arbiter of her day preferred the simplicity and charm of Edgartown to the elegant digs of her avid followers in Newport and Bar Harbor.

Enormous Gothic columns grace the imposing Methodist or **Old Whaling Church** (11). Built in 1843 with whaling money, it was attended by as many as eight hundred people on any Sunday a century ago. The congregation today is small, but the church remains the most handsome on the island.

Just beyond the church is the large, square **Dr. Daniel Fisher House** (12), completed in 1840. Dr. Fisher was the Vineyard's local tycoon; he made his fortune by cornering the market on whale oil for all the government-operated lighthouses in the country and also owned a large spermaceti factory on the waterfront. Dr. Fisher personally directed construction of the house, and insisted on only the finest materials throughout, including copper nails. He also found time, occasionally, to practice medicine.

Masterpieces of the Ship Carver's Art

Figurehead carving dates back to the ancient custom of decorating bows to invoke guiding spirits to dwell within. St. Paul journeyed on an Alexandrian vessel that bore a figurehead of Castor and Pollux, deities worshiped by mariners. Centuries later, dragons and lions found favor among Elizabethan seamen. From England, where families such as the Hellyers of London passed the trade down seven generations, the skill of figurehead carving came to America.

The carver usually kept shop in a vacant sail loft near the wharf. Shipbuilders drew on the floor the lines of the bow to indicate where the figure would go. The carver then set to work on a block of pine with hammer, chisel, and gouge. He often carved classical heads; Hercules once adorned Constitution. *Sometimes he used live models: captains' wives and daughters, even a stand-in for General Washington. Indians, too, were popular subjects: The bust of Tecumseh decorated the warship* Delaware. *Today a bronze copy stands at the U. S. Naval Academy, whose midshipmen toss pennies at it for luck. Such deference is nothing new. When the wooden hat was shot off the figurehead of H.M.S.* Brunswick *during a 1794 battle, sailors ran aft and demanded the captain replace it with his own. He did.*

Nantucket

Architectural Treasures Built by Whale Oil

In *Moby Dick,* Herman Melville wrote: "And thus have these naked Nantucketers, these sea-hermits, issuing from their anthill in the sea, overrun and conquered the watery world like so many Alexanders."

Whale oil built Nantucket. As the demand for it grew in the eighteenth century, those dependent on the whaling trade began to cluster around Nantucket's huge, protected harbor with its ample space for wharves, warehouses, and homes. For a century and a half whaling dominated the island's industry, and Quaker religion its way of life. Even the islanders' language became a curious mix of nautical and Quaker phrases. Nantucketers invented deep-sea whaling, perfected the art of harpooning, and coined the phrase "Nantucket sleigh ride" for the perilous chase of a harpooned whale. They endured mutiny, cannibalism, privation, and loneliness during voyages which lasted up to five years and carried them around the globe. But a "greasy" trip could mean $50,000 dollars or more in profits—to most, well worth the trip.

After the discovery of the lucrative Japanese whaling grounds following the War of 1812, Nantucket entered its golden era as the whaling capital of the world. It was during this period that most of the captains' mansions, many of which still stand, were built. The interiors were furnished in precious silks, Indian rugs, porcelains, Chinese furniture, and other articles brought back on the whaleships. Culture flourished and Quaker traditions of simplicity waned.

A series of devastating setbacks diminished Nantucket's whaling trade, beginning with a tragic fire in 1846 which gutted 360 wooden buildings. As the town struggled to recover, word of the gold rush

NANTUCKET

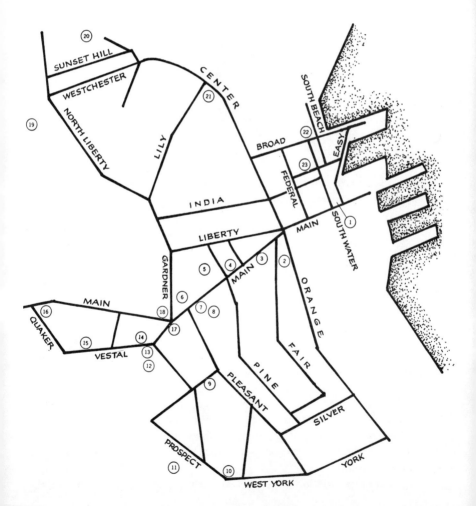

Old Mill

spread and many seamen deserted their trade to seek easy wealth in California. In 1859 the first petroleum well was drilled in Pennsylvania, followed by the outbreak of the Civil War. Within a few years Nantucket's economy was dead.

But in losing its economy, Nantucket preserved its heritage. While most of New England busily tore down its old buildings in the name of progress, Nantucket slept, to be rediscovered by newcomers—tourist and resident alike—interested in its priceless architectural heritage and aura of history.

With a population of 10,000 and some one hundred ships in the fleet, Nantucket was one of the busiest, richest ports in America, whose warehouses brimmed with exotic cargoes. One such warehouse was the **Pacific Club building** (1), built in 1772 by William Rotch, a wealthy shipowner whose brigs *Beaver* and *Dartmouth* were involved in the Boston Tea Party. Even during the Revolution, Nantucket merchants carried on direct trade with London in oil and candles. In 1859 a group of former whaling-ship masters who had sailed the Pacific formed a club and bought the building. Here they spun yarns and played cribbage.

Over a hundred-year period, Orange Street, with its fine view of the harbor, was the home of 126 whaling captains. The **Old South Tower** (2), built in 1809, was originally a Congregational Church, but the parishioners gradually grew more liberal and embraced Unitarianism. The church bell has rung continuously for more than 150 years, three times a day—at 7 A.M., noon, and 9 P.M. (at one time the curfew hour). From the belfry town criers announced the arrival of ships and the latest news from the mainland.

Meetings are still held in the 1838 **Friends Meeting House** (3) during the summer months. The stark, gray building is the only remaining Quaker church on the island.

The 1723 Christian or **Nathaniel Macy House** (4) was built by the grandson of the first white settler on Nantucket. The house's exterior, starkly simple yet graceful, exemplifies the style of many eighteenth-century Quaker homes. Its furniture, primitive utensils, and huge fireplace are typical of the period.

In the early days, Nantucket had no public schools, only "Cent Schools," where parents paid a penny a day to have their children attend class. Following the Revolution, Sir Isaac Coffin founded a **school** (5) to be attended by Coffin children (and there were many). The original school was located at Fair Street; the present building, with its Doric columns, was erected in 1852.

The **Three Bricks** (6) are perhaps the most famous of Nantucket's houses. The three identical Georgian brick mansions were built in 1838 by Joseph Starbuck for his sons William, Matthew, and George. All have identical porticoes with black wrought-iron fences, and are known simply as "East Brick," "Middle Brick," and "West Brick." One of Starbuck's whalers, *Three Brothers,* returned in 1859 with 6,000 barrels of oil—a record. At one time, Starbuck's three daughters lived across the street in Greek Revival mansions built by **William Hadwen** (7). They are nearly identical, although the columns on 94

Hadwen House

Main Street are reputed to be copied from the portico of the "Tower of the Winds" in Athens. Number 96, owned by the Nantucket Historical Society, is open to the public.

The handsome **Baptist Church** (8), built in 1840, is evidence of the decline of the Quaker religion at that time. Down Mill Street, the **1800 House** (9) is a typical Nantucket residence of the early whaling days. Inside are a central chimney with six flues, beehive oven, huge beams, borning room, and spinning room.

Four windmills once stood in the vicinity of the **Old Mill** (10). The one mill that remains, with its original wooden machinery and millstone, still grinds corn as it has for more than a century. During time of war, the mill was used for signaling ships approaching Nantucket Harbor. Bordering nearby Prospect Street is **St. Mary's Cemetery** (11), with its old and interesting gravestones.

Hinchman House (12) is a natural science museum run by the Maria Mitchell Foundation and housing an interesting display of the island's plant and animal life. Next door is the island's only remaining **cooperage** (13), or barrel-making shop, the sole remnant of dozens of such establishments. Across Vestal Street are the **Library and Observatory of Maria Mitchell (14)**, professor of astronomy at Vassar College and the first woman Fellow of the American Academy of Arts and Sciences.

Constructed of oak logs bolted with iron, the **Old Gaol (15)** has four cells with iron bars on the small windows. Two cells have fireplaces, and one is sheathed in iron for more dangerous prisoners. According to accounts, the cells were empty most of the time. Another interesting graveyard, the old **Friends Cemetery (16)** is nearby. Main Street leads to the **Civil War Monument (17)** and the **Old Fire Hose Cart House (18)**, a small museum housing some of the earliest fire-fighting equipment.

The Old Gaol

In the **Old North Burying Ground (19)** are records in stone of the colorful lives of Nantucket seamen. Near the road is a stone describing the exploits of Robert Ratliff, whose first adventure was to take part in the British raid on Washington in 1814. In 1818 he was a member of the escort taking Napoleon to St. Helena; in 1820 he was shipwrecked on Nantucket, where he remained until his death in 1882. Farther away two identical stones mark the graves of Amos Otis and Thomas Delap, both of Barnstable, both "Cast a shore on Nantucket December

the 6th 1771 & perish't in the Snowstorm there." Also buried here is
Robert Inot, commander of *Savannah,* the first steamship to cross
the Atlantic, in 1819.

Built in 1686 and the oldest in Nantucket, the **Jethro Coffin House
(20)** was a gift for Jethro and his bride from their fathers. Outstanding architectural features of the residence include massive beams,
diamond-shaped windows, an "Indian closet," and a huge center
chimney with a horseshoe design believed to be an antiwitch device
(the house was built during the Salem witch hunts).

The huge, Gothic **Congregational Church (21)** was built with
whaling money in 1834. Inside are a *trompe l'oeil* painting and a huge
brass chandelier that measures seven feet across and weighs six hundred pounds. The old vestry behind the church was built about 1725.

On Broad Street stand the **Peter Foulger and Whaling museums
(22)**, both managed by the Historical Association. Originally a candle
factory built in 1847, the Whaling Museum has a replica of a brick
tryworks (for rendering whale fat into oil), bailers, skimmers, harpoons, lances, scrimshaw, ship models, and a forty-four-foot whale

Whaling Museum

Sanderson Hall, Whaling Museum

skeleton. The Peter Foulger Museum is a diary of the island's past and contains objects from the China trade, antique tools, silver, and a maritime library. *Open daily.*

At the corner of Federal and Pearl streets is the **Atheneum (23),** a handsome Greek Revival building. The original library was gutted by the fire of 1846 which destroyed the center of town, but it was rebuilt within six months. Today it is one of the oldest libraries in continuous use in the country.

Crystal Luxury

Glass was a distinct luxury in early America—rare and costly and found only in the houses of the wealthy. Except for windows, glass was not considered a necessity. Yet the high prices demanded for it by English exporters prompted ambitious colonists to make their own, beginning with a short-lived bottle works in Salem in 1641. But for more than a century, attempts to establish glassmaking in New England met with failure. Glassmaking was not only an ancient, highly technical skill shrouded in secrecy; it was also a business requiring considerable equipment, construction, raw materials, and capital.

To Deming Jarves, a man of great talent and imagination, this was a challenge. From sketchy written accounts and experimentation he uncovered the methods of glass production, and founded his Sandwich Glass Company on Cape Cod in 1825. Local farmers supplied fuel wood at fifty cents a cord; silica sand was shipped all the way from Demerara in British Guiana. Spurred by Jarves' success, other glassworks sprang up, and soon a vast assortment of tableware, punch bowls and decanters, tumblers, candlesticks, and lamps in various colors brought a new luxury to the land.

One Yankee innovation was pressed glass, a technique by which molten glass was pressed into molds instead of being blown into them. The revolutionary technique was speedier and cheaper and dealt a severe blow to the glassmakers of Europe, who could not compete with this new, mass-produced glass.

Lacy Compote

Glass bank with chicken finial

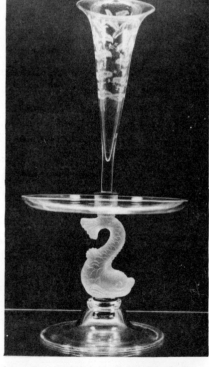

Epergne with frosted dolphin base

Vermont Travel Division 34, 38, 39, 41, 45, 46, 57, 71, 90, 94, 96
Dennis Waters 154, 164

Additional photographs and drawings by the authors.